TEACHING AND LEARNING MATHEMATICS

PETER G. DEAN

University of London Institute of Education

Drawings of school pupils and teachers
by

JOANNA WHITING

Shene School, Richmond upon Thames

WOBURN PRESS

First published 1982 in Great Britain by
THE WOBURN PRESS
Gainsborough House, Gainsborough Road,
London, E11 1RS, England

and in the United States of America by
THE WOBURN PRESS
c/o Biblio Distribution Centre
81 Adams Drive, P.O. Box 327, Totowa, N.J. 07511

British Library Cataloguing in Publication Data

Dean, Peter G.
  Teaching and learning mathematics.
  1. Mathematics—Study and teaching
  (Secondary)—Great Britain
  2. Mathematics—Study and teaching
  (Elementary)—Great Britain
  I. Title
  510′. 7′1041   QA14.G7

ISBN 0 7130 0168 2 (Cased)
ISBN 0 7130 4007 6 (Paper)

Phototypesetting by Bookform, Formby, Merseyside
Produced by Book Production Management Services

**Printed and bound in Great Britain by
Robert Hartnoll Limited Bodmin Cornwall**

TEACHING AND LEARNING MATHEMATICS

The Woburn Education Series

General Editor:
Peter Gordon, Institute of Education, University of London

Games and Simulations in Action
Alec Davison & Peter Gordon

The Education of Gifted Children
David Hopkinson

Slow Learners: A Break in the Circle
A Practical Guide for Teachers in Secondary Schools
Diane Griffin

The Middle School: High Road or Dead End?
John Burrows

Teaching and Learning Mathematics
Peter G. Dean

Music in Education
Malcolm Carlton

CONTENTS

ACKNOWLEDGEMENTS

The author acknowledges the contributions made by Patricia Dean, who read the manuscript and discussed amendments, Joanna Whiting, who illustrated parts of the text and Peter Gordon, who provided both detailed and general advice. With their help, this book has become a more useful educational text.

Permission to reprint selected passages has been granted by these authors, publishers or copyright holders: The Association of Teachers of Mathematics to quote from *ATM Supplement,* number 22, 1979; International Computers Limited to quote from *ICL Computer Education in Schools project newsletter,* number 34, January 1980; George C. Harrap and Company Limited to quote from *Exercises in elementary mathematics,* Book I, by K. B. Swaine, 1950; National Society for the Study of Education to quote from *Mathematics education: yearbook 69.1,* 1970; Macmillan Education to quote from P. H. Taylor *et al's Purpose, power and constraint in the primary school curriculum* (Schools Council Research Studies), 1974; The Mathematical Association to quote from *Mathematics in School,* volume 3, number 4, 1974 and volume 2, number 5, 1973 and from *Mathematics in middle schools,* 1976; Open Books Publishing Limited to quote from M. Rutter *et al's Fifteen Thousand Hours,* 1979; Schools Council to quote from *Mixed-ability teaching in mathematics* (Evans/Methuen Educational), 1977; Science Research Associates Inc. to quote from *Learning and the nature of mathematics* by William E. Lamon, 1972; University of London Press to quote from D. Lawton's *Social change, educational theory and curriculum planning,* 1973; Woburn Press to quote from D. Griffin's *Slow learners,* 1978 and D. Hopkinson's *The education of gifted children,* 1978.

PREFACE

This book is about mathematics teaching and learning in primary, middle and secondary schools. In some places, the book is definitive (eg. 'a full understanding of a limited amount of mathematics always provides the foundation for successful progress') or provides practical advice (eg. 'marking pupils' work with just ticks or crosses is rarely sufficient'). However, as all schools are different and as each school is continually changing, another aim is for this book to be informative. Present day mathematics education does not stand alone; it is related both to previous mathematics education and to other parts of the national education system. These two are therefore also included in the book because a reader who considers them is then more likely to understand today's mathematics teaching and learning. This understanding is the basis from which teachers can make informed professional decisions.

GLOSSARY

This glossary contains special British educational terms. In the text of this book, many other educational terms are explained and the explanations can be found by referring to the index.

Adviser – A *Local Education Authority* officer who can advise teachers in the *L.E.A.*'s schools. An adviser usually has previous experience as a teacher and will often provide advice about both general education and particular subject teaching. In some *L.E.A.*'s, advisers are termed inspectors.

Comprehensive school – A school for pupils of a wide spread of abilities, aptitudes and interests. The term often implies a *secondary* comprehensive school, as all British *primary* schools are comprehensive.

Department of Education and Science (D.E.S.) – The government department which deals with educational policy in England and Wales.

Headteacher – A teacher appointed by the *Local Education Authority* to be in charge of a school's pupils, staff and curriculum.

Her Majesty's Inspector (H.M.I.) – A *Department of Education and Science* officer who links education at *D.E.S.*, *Local Education Authority* and individual school levels.

Infant class – See *primary* school.

Junior class – See *primary* school.

Local Education Authority (L.E.A.) – An organization whose members are responsible for implementing national policy in a local group of schools. Each L.E.A. controls education in a distinct geographical area, which often contains between fifty and two hundred schools.

Middle school – A school for pupils who are usually aged from 8 to 12, or from 9 to 13 years. See *tier*.

Primary school – A school which may have three parts: reception classes, infant classes and junior classes. Pupils often start primary school at age 5 years. See *tier*.

Reception class – See *primary* school.

Scottish Education Department (S.E.D.) – The government department which deals with educational policy in Scotland. The *S.E.D.* and the *Department of Education and Science* have somewhat different responsibilities.

Secondary school – A school for pupils aged from 11 to 16 or 18 years. See *Sixth form and Tier*.

Sixth form – The lower and upper sixth forms are for pupils aged from 16 to 18 years. These sixth forms may be part of a *secondary* school or *upper* school; alternatively, they may be in separate premises, perhaps as part of a *tertiary* college. See *tier*.

Tertiary college – A college for pupils (students) aged 16 years and over. These colleges can often offer a wide choice of academic and vocational courses.

Tier – A distinct phase of education characterized by schools of one type, eg. *primary* schools. Most *Local Education Authorities* have:

    1. a two-tier system (*primary* and *secondary*)

or 2. a three-tier system (*primary, secondary* and *sixth form*)

or 3. a three-tier system (*primary, middle* and *upper*).

Upper school – A school for pupils aged from 12 or 13 to 16 or 18 years. See *middle* school and *tier*.

ASSOCIATIONS AND JOURNALS

The following associations and journals are linked with mathematics education. Addresses are included where applicable and permanent.

International associations

I.B.O.	International Baccalaureate Office, Palais Wilson, PO Box 36, 1211 Geneva 14, Switzerland
I.C.M.I.	International Commision for Mathematical Instruction
I.F.I.P.	International Federation of Information Processing Societies, 3, rue de Marché, 1211 Geneva 11, Switzerland

British associations

A.P.T.	Applied Probability Trust, Hicks Building, The University, Sheffield S3 7RU
A.T.M.	Association of Teachers of Mathematics, Market Street Chambers, Nelson, Lancashire BB9 7LN
B.C.S.	British Computer Society, 13 Mansfield Street, London W1M 0BP
C.E.G.	Computer Education Group, North Staffordshire Polytechnic Computer Centre, Blackheath Lane, Stafford ST18 0AD
I.B.M.	International Business Machines, Schools and Colleges Computer Information Service, c/o

	I.B.M. United Kingdom Ltd., 101 Wigmore Street, London W1H 0AB
I.C.L.—C.E.S.	International Computers Limited – Computer Education in Schools, 60 Portman Road, Reading, Berkshire RG3 1NR
I.M.A.	Institute of Mathematics and its Applications, Maitland House, Warrior Square, Southend on Sea, Essex SS1 2JY
J.M.C.	Joint Mathematical Council
M.A.	Mathematical Association, 259 London Road, Leicester LE2 3BE
M.U.S.E.	Minicomputer Users in Secondary Education, Freepost, Bromsgrove, Worcestershire, B61 7DR
N.A.M.A.	National Association of Mathematics Advisers
N.A.T.F.H.E.	National Association of Teachers in Further and Higher Education (Mathematics Education Section), Hamilton House, Mabledon Place, London WC1H 9BH
N.C.A.V.A.E.	National Committee for Audio-Visual Aids in Education, 33 Queen Anne Street, London W1M 0AL
N.C.C.	National Computing Centre, Oxford Road, Manchester M1 7ED
N.D.P.C.A.L.	National Development Programme in Computer Assisted Learning (1973–77). Linked with the Council for Educational Technology, 3 Devonshire Street, London W1N 2BA
S.C.E.G.	Scottish Computer Education Group, Moray House, Holyrood Road, Edinburgh EH8 8AQ
U.D.E.M.S.G.	University Departments of Education Mathematics Study Group

North American associations

A.F.I.P.S.	American Federation of Information Processing Societies, 210 Summit Avenue, Montvale NJ 07645
C.B.M.S.	Conference Board of the Mathematical Sciences
M.A.A.	Mathematical Association of America, 1225 Connecticut Avenue NW, Washington DC 20036
N.A.C.O.M.E.	National Advisory Committee on Mathematical Education
N.C.T.M.	National Council of Teachers of Mathematics, 1906 Association Drive, Reston Va 22091

S.S.M.A. School Science and Mathematics Association, PO Box 1614, Indiana University of Pennsylvania, Indiana Penn 15701

Journals and publishers

American Mathematical Monthly	M.A.A.
Bulletin of the I.M.A.	I.M.A.
Computer Education	C.E.G.
Computers in Schools	M.U.S.E.
Mathematical Education for Teachers	N.A.T.F.H.E.
Mathematical Gazette	M.A.
Mathematical Pie	West View, Fiveways, Nr. Warwick
Mathematical Spectrum	A.P.T.
Mathematics in School	M.A.
Mathematics Teaching	A.T.M.
School Science and Mathematics	S.S.M.A.
Teaching Statistics	A.P.T.
The Arithmetic Teacher	N.C.T.M.
The Mathematics Teacher	N.C.T.M. ·

For research journals see chapter 4 in Dorling A.R. (1977) *Use of mathematical literature*. Butterworths: London, Boston

CHAPTER 1

LOOKING BACKWARDS AND LOOKING FORWARDS

Figure 1.1 Mathematics is a special subject

Introduction

Mathematics is probably the second most important subject in school, as first priority must be given to English. Before school, and during the years at school, a child learns an appreciable amount about English by listening, talking and reading. The child learns this from his or her teacher and also from parents, friends, books, films

1

and television. Mathematics never has the same everyday opportunities to influence a child and can generally only be learnt from the school curriculum. Therefore the strength of the mathematics in a school directly affects the achievements of the pupils, whose successful learning depends on good teaching. In this first chapter it will be shown that mathematics teaching and learning should be considered as a continuous process.

Looking at a pupil

A good way to start discovering how pupils learn mathematics is to think about an individual pupil. This pupil serves as an example which can help a teacher to understand how all pupils learn, in a rather similar way to that in which pupils are given mathematical examples which can help them to understand mathematics. Learning can be explained as a change from not understanding something to understanding it. Therefore the evidence that learning has taken place is only obtained by looking back to a time when this pupil was unable to do some mathematics which he or she can now do. If this piece of mathematics has really been learned well, it can be recalled for use in the future and we will therefore have to also look for retention of that learning. Perhaps the example which has just been given begins to clarify the title of this chapter, 'Looking backwards and looking forwards'. Whenever we use a theory to explain why this pupil is learning mathematics, we must realize that the theory considers the pupil's development over a period of time. A useful theory cannot just look at the present time, it must look back over the stages of development through which the pupil has already passed and look ahead to the stages through which he or she may pass in the future.

Looking at a mathematics lesson

Pupils learn most of their mathematics during lessons and in a typical lesson they are guided by the teacher through a part of the curriculum. The mathematics curriculum is itself structured so that the lesson is based on some earlier mathematics which the pupils have understood, and a successful lesson will lead on to more mathematics. A clear example of this curriculum structure is provided by almost any text book, or set of work cards, which may be used by the pupils. The teacher is able to combine various methods of teaching to give different styles of teaching. In each lesson, his or her choice of a certain style depends on earlier experiences with pupils and may even be greatly influenced by the teacher's own time as a pupil. It is fortunate that the changes in education which have occurred since the Second World War have encouraged some teachers to adapt their older teaching style to suit new patterns within the curriculum and within school organization. In any lesson, therefore, the events which occur depend on both the past and the future. Here again, we find the theme of 'looking backwards and looking forwards'.

Looking at educational aims

This chapter has already looked at pupils, teachers and curriculum, which are the three elements in every classroom, but it is also necessary to look at the aims of education. In the school where I started my teaching career, the educational aims were well defined. As these aims were accepted and approved by the members of staff (and by nearly all the pupils) there was a clear rôle to be played by a young mathematics teacher. Young teachers, nowadays, often have a much more difficult task because there is less agreement in a school about its educational aims. To help these teachers to do their job well, the support and guidance of a good senior mathematics teacher is very important. He or she can develop and lead a team of teachers who will make mathematics a lively subject in the school. Then most pupils, parents and teachers will be pleased with the outcomes. It is important that these mathematics teachers agree on the balance between academic, practical and social aims, and this balance cannot be decided without looking both backwards and forwards in time. The teachers may decide, for example, that an existing mathematics course is unsatisfactory for the next group of pupils. Therefore, the course will be modified to meet the mathematical aims which are suitable for those pupils.

Illustrations of teaching and learning mathematics

The previous sections have given hints about the content of this book but have not said why the book uses different verbal and pictorial illustrations of mathematics education. While teaching pupils and training teachers, I have discovered that any situation is more likely to be understood if the learner gains an overall view of it. A first example of this is the young pupil, handling triangles and other polygons of various shapes, sizes and colours, who is more likely to understand the properties of triangles than the pupil who has been given only red triangular shapes. A second example is the school teacher, considering the mathematics curriculum in his or her school, who is more likely to understand the details when they are seen in the context of the whole curriculum and its historic development. This book is an attempt to help more primary and secondary school teachers to gain an overall view of teaching and learning mathematics. Where possible, it provides various verbal and pictorial illustrations in the belief that these allow an individual to select those which stimulate his or her effective learning.

CHAPTER 2

HISTORICAL ASPECTS OF MATHEMATICS IN SCHOOLS

Introduction

We cannot escape the effects of change because today's mathematics lessons form a stage in an evolutionary development. Therefore, to put the present state of mathematics education in the right perspective, we need to know something of the historical stages through which it has passed. These stages, which have taken place within the national education system, are tabulated in figure 2.1.

In this chapter I will deal factually with these historical aspects, referring mainly to the education systems in England and Wales. It must be emphasized that I am in no way implying that these systems are superior to other systems, such as those in other parts of the British Isles which are not controlled by the Department of Education and Science (D.E.S.). In fact, especially since the end of the Second World War, there have been rather similar developments in most countries. The corresponding development of systems in North America has already been described in two books[1,2] published in 1970 by the 'National Council of Teachers of Mathematics' (N.C.T.M.).

The beginnings of mathematics education

From the thirteenth century, grammar schools associated with collegiate churches in Britain were founded. Their main aim was to teach Latin and Greek grammar but they also taught a small amount of whole number arithmetic. Arithmetic played a similar minor role in the public (ie. independent) schools from the foundation of the first, Winchester, in 1373.[3] In the next centuries there were advances in university mathematics but these had no effect on elementary education. Schools served those parts of society which needed to encourage a strong classical tradition and the teachers maintained this by using Euclid's geometry books when any mathematics beyond simple arithmetic was considered suitable or necessary.[4]

The beginning of the nineteenth century heralded the start of widespread British systems of voluntary and then compulsory education,[5] in which mathematics slowly took a broader and more central role. Education for some poorer children was begun in schools set up by beneficent groups such as the 'Church of England National Society' founded in 1811 and the 1808 Nonconformist 'British and Foreign School Society', which were both helped by government grants from 1833 onwards. These schools typically provided instruction in basic arithmetic (for its utilitarian value) with perhaps a little geometry. Meanwhile the public schools and endowed grammar schools were expanding their syllabuses to include arithmetic and algebra with their study of Euclid's geometry and assistant masters were then employed to teach these branches of mathematics.

The selection of mathematical topics to be taught in schools was limited by the teachers' knowledge but it also began to be governed by university entrance requirements. Pupils who were going up to university needed to pass an examination such as the London Matriculation, set up in 1838. These university entrance examinations became coincidentally used as school leaving examinations, even when specific school leaving qualifications such as the 'Oxford and Cambridge Local Examinations' (1858) were established. Few secondary school pupils were entered for these examinations before the turn of the century, because many schools were not sufficiently academic and also because the secondary school teachers did not wish to be controlled by examinations in the way that elementary school teachers were already controlled.

Payment by results

Elementary education, at this time, was almost wholly confined to reading, writing and arithmetic. This was brought about, mainly, by the insidious system whereby Government inspectors annually examined pupils at the six standards which they had to attain if grants were to be paid to their teachers. Not only did this encourage a narrow syllabus but it also encouraged 'cramming' knowledge into the pupils instead of teaching them by more enlightened methods. People realized that this system of 'payment by results' was educationally unsatisfactory and it was ended in 1897.

NATIONAL EVENTS	MATHEMATICS IN SCHOOL
1833 Education grant act	
1837 Queen Victoria's accession	
	1840 Grammar schools' act entitled governors to introduce mathematics
	1862 Elementary teachers paid by results on six standards of achievement which all included arithmetic
	1864–68 Reports recommend more and better teaching of mathematics
1870 First English elementary education act	
1880 Compulsory school age 5–10	1871 Mathematical Association began
1891 English elementary education free on demand	1889 Technical instruction act allowed support of technical instruction
1893 Compulsory school age 5–12	
1895 Report on secondary education	
1899 Compulsory school age 5–13	1897 End of teachers payment by results
1901 Edward VII's accession	
1902 Secondary education authorized and financed	
	1904 Regulations require mathematics for a four year secondary course
1906 First school meals provided	1905 Binet-Simon intelligence tests
	1907 Free places in secondary schools bring selection examination at age 11
1910 George V's accession	
1914–18 First World War	1911 Central schools started with practical general education
	1917 School and Higher School Certificate examinations
1918 Compulsory school age 5–14	
1921 Education act restricts work for children under 14	1921 Burt's standardized attainment test
1926 First Hadow report recommends general adolescent education from age 11 in senior schools	1923–53 Mathematical Association reports on teaching content and methods
1931 Second Hadow report encourages separate primary education up to age 11	
1936 Edward VIII's accession	
1936 George VI's accession	
1939–45 Second World War	1938 Spens report proposes mathematics which 'faces and has content with the world'
1941 Norwood report	
1944 Butler education act requires separate primary and secondary schools	1944 Separate mathematics courses in secondary grammar, modern, technical and multilateral schools
1947 Compulsory school age 5–15	
	1951 General Certificate of Education examinations at ordinary, advanced and scholarship levels
	(continued)

Figure 2.1 Educational events in England and Wales since 1833

Figure 2.1 *(continued)*

NATIONAL EVENTS		MATHEMATICS IN SCHOOL	
1952	Elizabeth II's accession	1952	Association of Teachers of Mathematics began
1954	First purpose built London comprehensive, Kidbrooke		
		1955	Mathematical Association report on teaching mathematics in primary school
		1957	School computer education began
		1958	Ministry of Education report on teaching mathematics in secondary schools
		1960	Mixed ability mathematics teaching starting
		1961	Modern mathematics secondary school projects began
1963	Newsom report		
1964	Schools Council started	1964	Publication of *Some lessons in mathematics* (Fletcher)
1965	Planned national change to comprehensive secondary education	1965	Certificate of Secondary Education examinations
1967	Plowden report	1969	Decimal coinage began
1972	Compulsory school age 5–16		
1975	Assessment of Performance Unit started		
		1977	HMI's appraisal of school mathematics
1978	DES survey of primary schools	1978	Cockcroft committee established
1979	DES survey of secondary schools		

Compulsory education, 1870

Education in England and Wales was made compulsory for all children from 1870. It was therefore essential, after that date, for the State to control standards of education. This was done by a combination of training for people who wished to qualify as teachers, approved examinations and Government inspectors. Around that time, the secondary school curriculum almost always included 'indispensable' arithmetic, supported by algebra and Euclid's geometry. There had already been criticism of mathematics education and the 1868 Schools' Inquiry Commission had reported that the teaching of all mathematics was rarely satisfactory while the unsuitability of Euclid's books was evident. Major discussions about the contents and aims of mathematics education began after the publication of this report and similar discussions have periodically recurred.

Teachers begin to influence the syllabus

The discussions which took place from 1870 to 1939 produced syllabus revision but not syllabus revolution, and maybe our realization of the problems brought about by the modern mathematics revolution of the 1960s shows the wisdom of the Victorians and Edwardians. Their desire for syllabus revision led to the foundation in 1871 of the 'Association for the Improvement of Geometry Teaching' which was later to widen its sphere of influence and be re-named the 'Mathematical Association' (M.A.).[6] Changes slowly occured[7] in geometry syllabuses and teaching;[8] one instance was the examiners' acceptance from 1903 of any sound geometrical proof instead of their insistence upon the standard Euclidean proofs. The educational aims of mathematics teaching also caused concern. Some people considered school mathematics as a utilitarian subject while others wished it to be almost as rigorous and logical a subject as university pure mathematics. It is interesting to compare that concern with the present day concern. Now, there are discussions about mathematics education in primary and secondary schools. These discussions consider it in various rôles: as a subject in its own right, as a support for other subjects, as a preparation for adult life and as a reflection of the nature of mathematics itself with its axiomatic structure, proofs, generalization, etc.

Psychology begins to have an effect

The 1930s brought the first general interest in the influence which psychological data (then considered to be 'at present very imperfect') should bring to bear on the education of primary school pupils. Many teachers had expected impossible achievements from some of these children, yet had not allowed them adequate scope to achieve possible things. One reason was that 'this stage had commonly been regarded as preparatory to some other stage rather than as constituting a definite stage of mental development'.[9]

These psychological ideas (see figure 2.2), together with data on physical growth, suggested the need for children up to the age of 11 years to receive a separate education in primary schools. These children were to be taught mathematics which included pattern designing and model making to realize spatial properties, arithmetic, the mensuration of plane and solid figures, and the development of skills in measurement and drawing. These requirements supported the

CHAPTER III. THE MENTAL DEVELOPMENT OF CHILDREN BETWEEN THE
AGES OF 7 AND 11

34. The available psychological data: The mental characteristics of young children: The Stratification Theory: The Recapitulation Theory

35. The intellectual characteristics of young children

36. Sensory capacities; vision; hearing; muscle sense; touch; movement

37. The Higher Mental Capacities: attention, fatigue, weariness, memory

38. Imagery and Ideas: reproductive imagination; constructive imagination

39. The working contents of the young child's mind

40. The child's definitions of his own ideas

41. Reasoning; perception of relations; deductive reasoning; inductive reasoning; logical criticism; suggestibility

42. The development of aesthetic appreciation in the widest sense in children between the ages of seven and eleven

43. Emotional Qualities of Young Children: Their normal interests

44. The child's interests as revealed by play

45. The child's interests as shown by spontaneous drawing

46. The child's interests as revealed in spontaneous reading

47. Sex differences on the intellectual and emotional sides

48. The Influence of Environment on children: The physical, mental and emotional effects of poverty and its concomitants

Figure 2.2 Psychological ideas about primary school education in 1931. (See reference no. 9)

general opinion that the curriculum be thought of in terms of activity and experience as well as of knowledge and facts, an opinion which is practised in today's primary schools.

The English school system in the late 1930s

Education in England and Wales has always been prescribed nationally but put into operation with a great deal of local autonomy, so the school system illustrated in figure 2.3 only represents the general pattern.

Part of a local system might change one year if a new school were built, or the name of an old school might be retained for new buildings in deference to strong local opinion. For instance, in 1939 the historic word 'National' still appeared in the names of some schools in Wales and it is desirable to have such reminders of the roots of a community, even if a variety of such names may occasionally cause confusion.

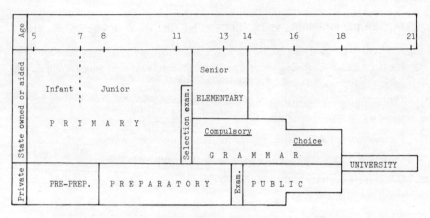

Figure 2.3 The general pattern of English education in the late 1930s

Selection for grammar school and university education

Although some of the wealthier boys and a few girls went to preparatory and then public schools, most children went to the state system primary schools. These schools entered some 11 year old pupils for the grammar school selection examination which established an order of merit among the candidates. In this examination the candidates had to answer mathematics questions of varying complexity selected from direct numerical calculations, problems and simple mensuration. There was not much concern for the candidates' mathematical experiences as 'the subjects introduced into the questions seem on the whole far more closely related to the interests of the examiners than of the children'.[11] The examination syllabuses, in both mathematics and English, were usually designed to ensure that pupils had an adequate grounding for grammar school studies rather than to assess the learning achieved in the primary school. The status of a primary school, in the eyes of the local community, often depended on the number of pupils who were selected for grammar school by 'passing the scholarship examination'. Therefore, whether intentionally or not, the requirements for grammar school entrance often dictated part of the curriculum in the last two years at primary school. Pupils who entered grammar or public schools, most of which were single sex, studied compulsory mathematics until the School Certificate examination taken at the age of 16. Those who wished to go on to university continued at school for two more years and could choose to study more advanced mathematics for their final Higher School Certificate examination. The 11 year old pupils who did not pass, or did not enter, the selection examination continued to study mathematics, often with a practical or utilitarian bias in elementary schools, until they left at the age of fourteen.

Some early reports on mathematics education

So far, this chapter has been about changes mainly in the content of school mathematics but it would be wrong to ignore the interest in the different styles of teaching and their comparative effectiveness. Although inspectors had commented on these styles before 1920, growing interest in their effectiveness was shown by the development of training courses and by the content of reports. Initial training was available at the training colleges throughout Britain and some teachers already in schools began to take part in discussions to improve the quality of their teaching. These people, and others, were also helped by reports which linked the mathematical content and method; for example, one important series with the general title 'The teaching of (e.g. algebra) in schools' was published for the Mathematical Association.

Mathematics education had come a long way [12] since the early days when only whole number arithmetic was taught and the position reached by the start of the Second World War in 1939 can be judged by two reports, one about younger pupils and the other about older pupils. The first, *Arithmetic in Primary Schools,*[11] was prepared by a committee of the Metropolitan Branch of the 'Training College Association' and published in 1940. Few copies were distributed before an incendiary bomb raid on London destroyed all the remaining stock so it was republished in 1947, with only minor changes to the introduction, as a report of the renamed 'Association of Teachers in Colleges and Departments of Education' (A.T.C.D.E.). This report recommends suitable methods and sequences for teaching number and spatial knowledge in infant and junior schools, indicating the level to be expected within each two-year age group. Information about measurement units such as a furlong (the furrow-long in ploughed land) and numerical operations required in trade and commerce emphasizes social changes which have occurred since then but it is salutary to realize that many of the report's criticisms are still with us. For example, 'mechanical skills...are of still less significance...and...calculating machines can be used'; 'A new generation of teachers knows nothing of the old "standards" and finds nothing definite to put in their place'; and 'It is frequently said that the standards of accuracy in calculation have deteriorated in recent years'. (These quotations are from the introduction of the A.T.C.D.E. report.) In the second of these reports, which deals with older pupils, mathematics was still seen as a compulsory subject for all boys and most girls to take to School Certificate examination standard. This 1943 Norwood report says that 'Amid the changes in curriculum which have taken place in the last forty years Mathematics perhaps more than any other subject has retained the position assigned to it by tradition.'[13] However, within this position the curriculum itself had changed and some laborious formal proofs and rigid logical sequences were replaced by shorter methods in which the emphasis was on principles and applications, which sometimes required the introduction of more advanced mathematical ideas. Having approved a curriculum which still contained 'parts of Arithmetic, Algebra, Graphs, Geometry and Trigonometry' the report suggested that they should be taught as interdependent, rather than independent, topics. For example, numerical and graphical methods were to be used to illustrate and develop other work. The report was concerned about those pupils, often girls, 'whose disability in Mathematics is established beyond reasonable doubt'. There was no suitable alternative mathematics course for those pupils and this led to the development of 'Special Arithmetic' papers. At the other end of the 'ability' scale the report suggested that more pupils should enter for the difficult 'Additional Mathematics' examination and here we see a concern about the underachievement of gifted pupils which reappeared in 1977.[14]

Separate branches of mathematics: arithmetic, algebra, etc.

Just before the Second World War, the 1938 Spens report[15] highlighted the unsuitability of examining older pupils in three separate branches of mathematics, namely arithmetic, algebra and geometry. This invariably led to the branches being separately taught, even though mathematics was not really a piecemeal subject. The School Certificate examination papers for 16 year old grammar school pupils made the subject even more piecemeal by regularly providing a question on each topic, such as logarithms, linear simultaneous equations and Pythagoras' theorem. Therefore a move began to promote a new style of unified examination which would encourage a unified style of teaching. Again, as with the scholarship examination at age 11, this demonstrates the power of the examinations to determine the teaching done in many classes, although some teachers have always managed to 'do their own thing' and their pupils still passed examinations.

AFTER THE SECOND WORLD WAR

Unified mathematics – the Jeffery syllabus

During the Second World War resources such as manpower and new textbooks were not available to promote the change in mathematics teaching and learning in schools. Therefore it was 1945 before any secondary schools began to use the new unified mathematics course which was offered as an alternative syllabus by examination boards.

The traditional examination set three papers in arithmetic, algebra and geometry while the alternative but equal standard examination set only two papers. These two papers included differential calculus as an extra topic and, in general, encouraged the use of a broader approach in answering examination questions (see figure 2.4).

There are two reasons why this new syllabus did not have a greater effect on mathematics education. Firstly the new text books and examinations were for use in grammar schools which educated only a minority of the children. Secondly there was, and still is, the independence of teachers to retain or change a school mathematics curriculum, and some teachers can justify the retention of an established curriculum which they know they can teach successfully and which the pupils can learn. In this context, by continuing to examine for syllabuses where there is a reasonable teacher demand, the examination boards have acted as loyal servants rather than as controllers and it was not until 1978 that the Cambridge Local Examinations Syndicate withdrew the traditional three paper mathematics examination.

Post war reorganization of secondary schools

The 1944 Education Act, which followed the 1943 recommendations of the Norwood committee,[13] led to a restructured school system with three types of secondary school: grammar, modern and technical. These types existed either individually on separate sites or in some form of combination when they were known as multilateral schools. The secondary grammar schools were mainly the previous grammar schools and they continued to cater for approximately that quarter of the pupil population which was most academically able. The secondary modern schools catered for most of the other children who, from 1947, did not leave school until 15 years of age. These schools grew from central and higher elementary schools. Finally there were a few secondary technical schools which catered for the pupils whose ability and interest were in the field of craftsmanship and mechanics. In these technical schools, the mathematical knowledge and skills of the artisan could have real and prime relevance.

The provision of these three types of secondary school throughout England and Wales was unequal and was often determined by the types of schools previously in existence. In an area where there were two or three secondary grammar schools it was possible for them to select as much as 35% of the pupils (whose ability would be deemed suitable to study academic mathematics), while in a contrasting area with one grammar school only 20% might be selected. This unbalanced intake between the grammar schools in two areas left an

EXERCISES IN
ELEMENTARY MATHEMATICS

BOOK I

BY

K. B. SWAINE M.A.

formerly Scholar of St John's College Cambridge
Senior Mathematics Master Yeovil School

GEORGE G. HARRAP & CO. LTD
LONDON   SYDNEY   TORONTO   BOMBAY

Figure 2.4 The title page and preface from an unified mathematics textbook

PREFACE

THE set of books of which this is the first is planned to meet a need felt by those teachers who are following the recommendations of the 1944 Conference of Representatives of Examining Bodies and Teachers' Associations, and who are working to the Alternative Syllabus in Elementary Mathematics in the School Certificate Examination.

The main suggestion of the 1944 Conference was the importance of treating Elementary Mathematics as a single unified subject. An attempt has therefore been made to weld together the parts of Arithmetic, Algebra, Geometry, and Trigonometry that belong to the elementary stage. This has been done partly by planning the order of the work as far as possible as a continuous course rather than as a succession of separate sections. The unity of the subject, however, lies not so much in the stage when the pupil is mastering new ideas and methods as in the stage when he or she is acquiring the ability to decide which method or process is the appropriate one for dealing with a particular problem. The ability to apply knowledge gained only comes with practice. For this purpose a set of Revision Tests is supplied in each book. Though placed, for convenience, at the end of the book, these tests are designed to be taken at intervals regularly throughout the course, except in the first term, when there is little to revise. For the end-of-year revision, a set of short Revision Exercises, topic by topic, appears at the end of each book.

An important feature of the Alternative Syllabus in Elementary Mathematics is the latitude allowed to the teacher to indulge in his or her own pet ideas. To allow for this, the scope of these books is fairly wide, details being included here and there merely to awaken interest and suggest new ideas. Each of the first three books of the set contains one year's work, and the fourth book includes the last two of a five-year course. In order to allow a little more freedom, successive books are made to overlap, the end of each of the first three books being reprinted at the beginning of the next book. To facilitate revision, each book begins with a summary of previous years' work.

These books are intended solely as class books and not as a treatise. Hardly any bookwork is included, the author's purpose being only to provide a set of examples from which the pupil can learn by doing. The worked examples, which form the bulk of the text, are not exhaustive, and are only included as a help with revision or after absence from school. As many examples as possible have been taken from the pupil's everyday life, so that there shall appear to him or her to be some purpose in Mathematics.

The author wishes to acknowledge his indebtedness to Messrs Harrap's mathematical readers for advice and helpful criticisms, and to his colleagues at Yeovil School and the mathematics mistress at Yeovil High School for many valuable suggestions.

YEOVIL, 1947   K. B. S.

unbalanced remainder of pupils to go to the other secondary schools, so that nationally there was a variable spread of abilities between similarly designated schools. One way to get rid of these inequalities was to provide larger schools which would educate pupils of all abilities. These were called secondary comprehensive schools and they were introduced with the aim of giving equal opportunities to all pupils. The first immense purpose-built comprehensives of the middle 1950s were heralded by some people as the idols of a glorious new post war era of education and during the next twenty years comprehensive schools were introduced into almost every town and county.

One cumulative effect of these two reorganizations is that mathematics teaching in Britain has been within an unsettled school system at some place or other for at least thirty years. This was the period during which the 'Association of Teachers of Mathematics' (A.T.M.) beneficially influenced mathematics education in both secondary and primary schools. The A.T.M. was founded in 1952 as the 'Association for Teaching Aids in Mathematics' by teachers who saw problems, often associated with academic-style teaching being given to non-academic pupils, and wanted to form a group which would help to solve these problems.

Primary and middle schools in the post war years

During the post war years primary school buildings were renovated, extended or replaced so that most pupils and teachers now work under more pleasant conditions in rooms which are much lighter and more open. Classes are also smaller because the maximum number of children in a class was first reduced to around 40 and then later to 35. Another improvement is that the training of all new teachers has enabled them to make good use of the apparatus and other resources which have been introduced[16] so that each pupil can receive a variety of learning experiences rather than a body of knowledge taught with the aid of blackboard and textbooks. Fortunately these educational changes have come about with the general agreement of teachers and parents, and without the many disruptions which have come with secondary school reorganization.

Pupils do not always leave primary school at age 11+ to go to secondary school; an alternative became possible in 1965 when the newly elected Labour government authorized the establishment of middle schools.[17] These schools educate children aged from 8 to 12 or from 9 to 13 in a three-stage primary, middle and high school system which has been adopted within some fifty Local Education Authorities (L.E.A.s). As usual with educational change, this three-stage system was adopted for various practical and theoretical reasons. The practical ones included the generally smaller number of pupils per school; this enabled existing buildings to be used and acknowledged parental preference for smaller schools, at a time when there was no longer either the money or the desire to continue constructing very large schools. By this three-stage system L.E.A.s could meet their aim to introduce comprehensive schooling, while also accepting the Plowden committee's educational rationale[18] for transfer at a later age than 11+.

Mixed ability teaching for pupils of middle school age

It was not easy to find a successful way of teaching mathematics to the pupils who came to the new secondary comprehensive schools. These pupils were usually grouped into classes of about 35. These classes covered a wide spread of abilities and were the usual groups for many lessons. Because most mathematics teachers felt that their lessons would be more successful if given to pupils of similar ability, classes were regrouped into ability sets for their mathematics lessons. Then, as the benefits of mixed ability classes were realized (see chapter 5), teachers discussed their adoption for all subjects. From choice or compulsion in the 1960s and 1970s, most mathematicians agreed to accept mixed ability teaching[19,20,21] for at least the first one or two years of secondary school.

If it was to be well done, mixed ability teaching required a different class organization using new books, workcards and other resources (see following chapters). In many schools the need for such reorganization was not initially realized and sufficient money was not made available, but the teachers persevered. At least they managed to make mixed ability teaching acceptable to the pupils until better resources were available. Groups of teachers often wrote and tested resources until they were sufficiently developed to be implemented in other schools. Information about these mixed ability schemes might then be disseminated through meetings held at *Teachers' Centres* which L.E.A.s had established to improve primary and secondary school teaching.

The history of the *Kent Mathematics Project* (K.M.P.) provides an example of the development of a successful scheme for mixed ability teaching. It originated in 1962 at Ridgeway School, Tunbridge Wells[22,23,24] and then, from 1967, the scheme began to be used with pupils aged from 9 to 16 years in other schools. This led to its formal adoption as the K.M.P., with its own staff and finance, enabling the scheme to be implemented in over seventy Kent schools during the 1970s. About this time the K.M.P. was used as a model for the Inner London *Secondary Mathematics Individualized Learning Experiment* (S.M.I.L.E.),[25] which is now used in many of their schools. Other schools used commercially produced resources which had again been prepared with the help of practising teachers. Examples of these mixed ability schemes are *Mathematics for Schools*[26] which started around 1968 and the latest *School Mathematics Project* scheme[27] started in 1972. Both these schemes aim to provide structured and sequential mathematics for pupils during the years when they are, or might be, at middle school.

Figure 2.5 A mixed ability class using worksheets and apparatus

In the early 1970s it was realized that pupils, in schools which were then suffering from a high turn-over and serious shortage of specialist mathematics teachers, could be greatly helped by the mathematical structure and sequence imposed by some mixed ability schemes. This realization led to a new *Structured Mathematics Scheme* being introduced in the City of Birmingham[28] specifically to enable the non-specialist teacher to contribute to mathematics teaching in schools.

G.C.E., C.S.E., Schools Council and R.O.S.L.A.

Four more national developments have affected the work in post war schools. The first was to replace the old examinations for grammar school pupils. In 1951 the *School Certificate* and *Higher School Certificate* were replaced by the *General Certificate of Education (G.C.E.)* at Ordinary-level and Advanced-level respectively, for which pupils were no longer forced to study defined combinations of subjects as in the School Certificate. During the next few years parents, teachers and employers of secondary modern school pupils began to feel the need for a similar externally assessed examination. This need was fulfilled by the newly developed *Certificate of Secondary Education* (C.S.E.) examinations which began in 1965.[29,30,31] They were enthusiastically adopted as a target for the end of a four or five year course by many modern and comprehensive schools. The examinations' popularity eleven years later can be judged from figure 2.6 which shows that the entries for C.S.E. mathematics were the largest groups for both boys and girls. The sexual inbalance in G.C.E. entries shows the continuation of that historical link between boys and academic mathematics. (More recent examination developments such as the C.E.E. and G.C.S.E. are included in chapter 10.)

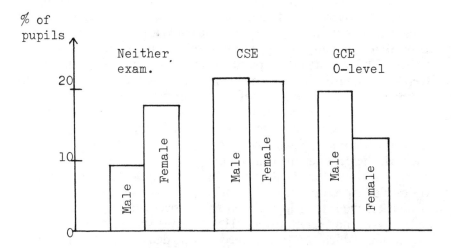

Figure 2.6 1976 mathematics examination entries (Data from DES Statistics in Education)

The third development occurred in 1964 with the introduction of the *Schools Council for the Curriculum and Examinations*. This Schools Council has sponsored, or is still sponsoring, a large number of significant projects, investigations and developments about mathematics education.[32,33] It is a cooperative partnership between the government and the L.E.A.s; it includes teachers among its members and its formation was an important milestone in curriculum development. Until then changes in mathematics education had been instigated and controlled by mathematics specialists in almost complete isolation from other subject teachers. This isolation allowed no way of considering the effect of new mathematical content or teaching methods[34] on the pupils' other school work.

The fourth and last development occurred in 1972–73 and was the

Raising of the School Leaving Age (R.O.S.L.A.) to 16 years. This was disturbing at the time, as some teachers had to quickly devise new courses [35] for their average and low ability pupils who resented staying at school an 'extra' year. Similar pupils now expect to stay at school until the age of 16 and teachers have now gained more experience with this non-academic group but it was not until 1976 that specially designed curriculum materials began to be generally available. [36]

Mathematics in post war primary schools

The new or renovated primary school buildings have allowed a major change from mainly class teaching, where knowledge is transmitted, to a focus on individual learning where knowledge is assimilated. This change has necessitated a further move away from the yearly syllabuses and standards which had existed in some form since 1862. In the new approach individual pupils have been encouraged to develop at their different natural rates, so that the yearly syllabuses have had to become guidelines for progress throughout the years at primary school. Thus, instead of pupils being expected to reach certain average standards because of their ages, their achievements were related to their individual stages of development. Teachers, who were usually not specialist mathematicians, wanted to know how to use this new approach and several authoritative reports gave guidance based on successful classroom teaching. [37,38,39,40] Teachers also needed practical help, and the outstanding example was the in-service training enthusiastically provided by Miss Edith Biggs, one of Her Majesty's Inspectors for mathematics. Her clearly explained goal was to help teachers to help children to discover and represent mathematical facts and relationships. Her example should make us realize the amount which can be achieved by one dedicated mathematician.

With the introduction of comprehensive secondary schools fewer and fewer primary school pupils had to be prepared for a competitive examination at the age of 11. This created a new situation in which pupils did not have an externally determined end-point to reach so that teachers had more freedom to introduce new topics and to try out the discovery methods which were currently being recommended. Understandably, teachers could not know how to balance individualized discovery learning and traditional teaching. The discovery method seemed to provide short-term achievement and a good future attitude to mathematics while traditional teaching could provide end-point satisfaction from a good structured knowledge of mathematics. Probably, in many primary schools the balance initially swung too far towards meeting short-term goals, which are also often more satisfying for the teacher, and then started to swing towards a central position in the late 1970s.

The Nuffield mathematics project

The post war years brought a renewal of help to schools by societies, firms and business companies. The original help of this sort had been vital in earlier centuries for the foundation of public, grammar and elementary schools and in the twentieth century the active and financial support by these groups and their educational trusts encouraged many local and national projects, both small and large. A major national mathematics project, for 5 to 13 year old pupils, was set up in 1964 with the support of the Nuffield Foundation and included in the project was this difficult task of helping primary school teachers to introduce new mathematical ideas to their pupils. These ideas were expected to be developed continuously until the pupils were in the lower classes of secondary schools.

This Nuffield mathematics project[41] was founded on ideas which included discovery learning and the theories of Jean Piaget (see chapters 3 and 7), and it involved practising teachers in the development of its teachers' guides[42] and films. These resources were specifically for teachers and suggested ways by which pupils could discover facts for themselves. The project has had a beneficial influence on classroom teaching which is not as obvious as the influence of projects whose textbooks are regularly seen by visitors to a school.

Electronics influence education

The immense advances in electronics have had an effect both outside and inside the schools. Just after the last war there were very few television sets, so that most children had no opportunity of watching programmes. During the next thirty years a television set became a prominent feature of most households and most schools now own one or more colour television sets and videotape recorders. These are used by the pupils to watch special schools programmes. There are mathematics programmes at various levels which cater for different age ranges and abilities and the powerful influence of television is used beneficially in schools. Another electronic advance has been the development of computers until they now directly or indirectly affect all adults. Their impact has been so great that many secondary schools have included computer education (see chapter 9) in the curriculum. This computer education invariably became the responsibility of mathematics departments in secondary schools, where the extra work made staffing shortages even more intense.

The latest advance, made possible by the development of the cheap 'electronic chip' during the 1970s, is that pocket calculators are in common use. These are changing the need for pupils and adults to learn traditional arithmetic skills. This change is deplored by some teachers but, as it is impossible to eliminate pocket calculators, the only intelligent response is to turn this electronic development to our advantage. Investigations are already showing that these pocket calculators can be used to enhance mathematics at many stages from the primary school[43] through to the sixth form.[44]

The changing sixth form

The grammar schools had strong academic sixth forms in which pupils stayed for two years to study three subjects from a rather limited set of combinations. Mathematics, which could count as either one or two subjects, was generally studied with physics or chemistry and generally could not be studied with languages, geography, history or even biology because of the way the school timetable was constructed. From the early 1960s such limitations slowly disappeared, partly because university entrance requirements changed when university subjects like biology and geography became more dependent on mathematical techniques. The schools were also introducing new sixth form subjects like economics and computer science which did not belong to any historic combination of school subjects.

These broadened academic sixth forms were one basis for planning suitable courses for the secondary modern and comprehensive school pupils who were then choosing to remain at school after the age of 16. These so-called 'new sixth formers' needed courses at a lower academic level as they were unlikely to have passed many G.C.E. Ordinary-level examinations. Some also needed shorter courses as they only intended to stay at school for one extra year.

Mathematics in the new sixth form

The new sixth form had (and still has) pupils whose ability ranged from the brilliant to the average but who were all full-time pupils. The most able of these still took three G.C.E. Advanced-level courses, while others took perhaps only one A-level course and also lower level courses. These might include O-level mathematics which some pupils feel they must attempt, even against all advice to the contrary. Other lower level courses use the knowledge from parts of A-level courses (see for example the Mathematical Association booklets of 1965 and 1967)[45] with the aim of the pupil developing a feeling for mathematics as well as learning that factual knowledge.

Some groups of teachers felt that this balance (see figure 2.7) of feelings and facts could be achieved by emphasizing the application of mathematics to solve practical and theoretical problems. This emphasis led to the foundation, in 1969, of the *Sixth Form Mathematics Project*.[46] Although many teachers have been reluctant

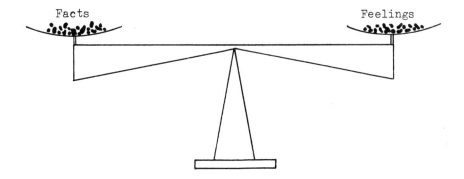

Figure 2.7 The double-F balance: aims of a mathematics course

to use this unfamiliar emphasis on applications, the project has developed to provide a supporting series of *Mathematics Applicable* books[47] and associated examinations are administered by the University of London School Examinations Board. Another approach at sixth form level has related the mathematics teaching to a pupil's interest, or need, in another subject. This was done in the 1971 *Continuing Mathematics Project* whose work units are now published by Longmans and in the Mathematical Association suggestions for linking numerical mathematics with computing.[48] Such work could lead to a qualification in the General Certificate of Education, the Certificate of Extended Education or the International Baccalaureate which are all discussed in chapter 10. None of the above approaches catered for the least mathematical pupils in the sixth form. Courses for them have not received much national attention; they might need fairly basic mathematics courses linked with simple everyday needs[49] or, realizing their memories of previous failure at school mathematics, they might benefit from a new approach such as successfully investigating the mathematical properties of a suitably chosen simple situation.[50]

Modern and traditional mathematics

Before the unified syllabus became really established it was overtaken in the early 1960s by the introduction of modern mathematics into secondary and primary schools. The new mathematics was intended to be modern in two senses: in its content and in its method of learning. The new content had its roots in earlier syllabuses. Geometry courses which once demanded the original formal Euclidean proofs now emphasized a practical treatment of shapes using transformation geometry as in figure 2.8.

Also the unified structure of mathematics was illustrated in such ways as applying matrix algebra to this transformation geometry. The new method expected a more precise use of mathematical language and a more empirical individual approach to mathematical theories.

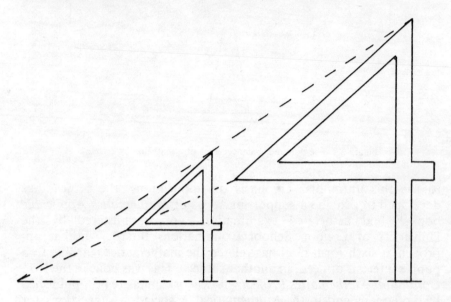

Figure 2.8 The enlargement of a Figure to twice its original size; an example of transformation geometry

Modern mathematics courses in schools created interest and strong feeling among parents and teachers. This emotional response brought continual discussion and exposition and ranged from early explanations about its aims and content[51] through an account of its dissemination in education[34] to a speech for its defence at an international congress[53] in 1972 and sets of case studies of individual projects.[54,41] Because so much has already been written on this topic, it is sufficient to point out that some projects are now appearing in a revised form while others have faded away.[55]

The contrast between traditional and modern mathematics has diminished so that school and examination syllabuses are stabilizing in some middle area. It is now unnecessary to use either of the adjectives traditional or modern when referring to mathematics as a school subject.[56,57]

Conclusion

This chapter about the historical aspects of mathematics in schools has contained three major themes. The first was the growth of a state system, to provide all children with education before they started work. The second theme was the mathematical content of that education, from an early limitation to simple arithmetic and the books of Euclid through to the present day content which reflects a major involvement of mathematics in economics, science and technology. The third theme was the growing realization that, for any mathematical content, there can be different styles of teaching.

Annotated References for Chapter 2

1. N.C.T.M. (1970) Bidwell J.K. & Clason R.G. eds. *Readings in the history of mathematics education*. National Council of Teachers of Mathematics: Washington.

   A consideration of the significant books and reports from 1828 to 1959 which have influenced the evolution of American mathematics education.

2. N.C.T.M. (1970) Jones P.S. et al. eds. *A history of mathematics education in the United States and Canada:* yearbook 32. National Council of Teachers of Mathematics: Washington.

   A discussion of the sequence of factors which have led to today's curriculum.

3. Curtis S.J. (1948) *History of education in Great Britain*. University Tutorial Press: London.

   Mathematics is mentioned sixteen times in this book.

4. Howson A.G. (1974) Mathematics – the fight for recognition. *Mathematics in School,* vol. 3, no. 6, pp. 7-9.

   Information about independent schools in the nineteenth century.

5. Hyndman M. (1978) *Schools and schooling in England and Wales (1800-1977)*. Harper & Row: London.

   A documentary approach to explaining the development of national education.

6. Combridge J.T. (1971, 1972) 'The rise of the Mathematical Association'. *Mathematics in School*, vol. 1, no. 1, pp. 3-5 & vol. 1, no. 2, pp. 6-8.

   These two articles cover the periods 1871-1897 & 1897-1971.

7. Howson A.G. (1973) Charles Godfrey (1873-1924) and the reform of mathematical education. *Educational Studies in Mathematics,* vol. 5, no. 2, pp. 157-80.

   A paper about educational change which offers an insight into English mathematics teaching

8. Archer R.L. (1921) *Secondary education in the nineteenth century*. Cambridge University Press: London. Reprinted (1966) Frank Cass: London (See chapter 13).

   A book which includes sections on notable pupils, events, schools, universities and institutions.

9. H.M.S.O. (1931) *Report of the consultative committee on the primary school*. His Majesty's Stationery Office: London (See p. 33).

   This report covers almost every aspect of primary school education.

10. Gordon P. (1980) *Selection for secondary education*. Woburn Press: London.

A historical survey which describes the 1907 Free Place Regulations, and refers to arithmetic and mathematics.

11. A.T.C.D.E. (1940/47) *Arithmetic in primary schools*. Longmans: London; New York.

Probably the first publication of the Association of Teachers in Colleges and Departments of Education.

12. H.M.S.O. (1958) *Teaching mathematics in secondary schools*: pamphlet no. 36. Her Majesty's Stationery Office: London.

This comprehensive report was the first since 1934 which concentrated on mathematics.

13. H.M.S.O. (1943) *Secondary Schools Examination Council: Curriculum and examinations in secondary schools*. His Majesty's Stationery Office: London (See p. 104 & others).

This Norwood committee report recommended an all-round education examination at 16+ and a particular-study examination at 18+.

14. H.M.S.O. (1977) *Gifted children in middle and comprehensive secondary schools*: Matters for discussion 4. Her Majesty's Stationery Office: London.

Giftedness is defined and its place in school and subject is considered.

15. H.M.S.O. (1938) *Secondary education, with special reference to grammar schools and technical high schools*. His Majesty's Stationery Office: London.

This report contains eight critical and constructive pages about school mathematics.

16. Vaughan B.W (1974–75) The only thing we can be sure of is change ; a series of five articles. *Mathematics in School*, vol. 3, no. 5, – vol. 4, no. 4, various pages.

A thorough consideration of the process of change, referring mainly to primary school.

17. Burrows J. (1978) *The middle school – high road or dead end?* Woburn Press: London.

A useful book with its three parts; the framework, the schools and the tools.

18. H.M.S.O. (1967) *Central Advisory Council for Education (England): Children and their primary schools*, vols. 1 & 2. Her Majesty's Stationery Office: London.

This Plowden report is probably the most thorough ever produced in England, covering every aspect of primary schools.

19. Flynn F.H. (1972). The case for homogeneous sets in mathematics. *Mathematics in School*, vol. 1, no. 2, pp. 9–11.

The reasons for setting and methods of doing it.

20. Jackman M.K. (1973) The case against homogeneous sets in mathematics. *Mathematics in School*, vol. 2, no. 1, pp. 16–18.

A response to Flynn's article, which supposedly used invalid arguments.

21. Brissenden T.H.F. (1973) Individualized learning and mixed ability groups in secondary mathematics. *Mathematics in School*, vol. 2, no. 6, pp. 16–18.

A discussion of homogeneous and heterogeneous sets in teaching.

22. Banks B. (1975) The Kent mathematics project and educational technology. *Mathematics in School,* vol. 4, no. 3, pp. 2–4.

A description, by its director, of the project and its application.

23. Banks B. (1976) Free choices. *Mathematics Teaching,* no. 75, pp. 17–20.

An account of a K.M.P. investigation about Euler's theorem.

24. Banks B. (1980) The K.M.P. and ed. tech. *Mathematics in School*, vol. 9, no.2, pp. 2–4.

A discussion of K.M.P. and age, ability, success, teachers, examinations and cost.

25. Gibbons R. (1975) An account of the Secondary Mathematics Individualized Learning Experiment. *Mathematics in School,* vol. 4, no. 6, pp. 14–16.

The author worked at Ladbroke mathematics centre where the S.M.I.L.E. scheme was developed.

26. Walker, R. (1977) Mathematics for schools: six years later. *Mathematics in School,* vol. 6, no. 3, pp. 2–6.

A description of the popular 'Fletcher maths.'

27. Rogerson A. (1975; 1978) S.M.P. 7–13. *Mathematics in School,* vol. 4, no. 1, pp. 4–6 & vol. 7, no. 5, pp. 4–6.

Two articles about the intentions and progress of an individualized learning scheme.

28. Graham J.D. (1976) Materials in a locally based curriculum development centre. *Mathematics in School,* vol. 5, no. 5, pp. 10–12.

A report on the revision of geometry material in the Birmingham Structured Mathematics Scheme.

29. H.M.S.O. (1964) *The Certificate of Secondary Education experimental examinations: mathematics; Examinations Bulletin no. 2.* Her Majesty's Stationery Office: London.

The experiment, the multi-choice test and the results. A two-section examination is suggested, with the first common to all schools and the second for each small group of schools.

30. H.M.S.O. (1965) *The Certificate of Secondary Education experimental examinations: mathematics 2; Examinations Bulletin no. 7.* Her Majesty's Stationery Office: London.

An account of the use, by a regional examinations board, of the ideas proposed in Bulletin no. 2.

31. M.A. (1968) *A report on mathematics syllabuses for the Certificate of Secondary Education*: Mathematical Association. Bell: London.

A small pamphlet analysing the content of mode I syllabuses and considering the complexities of mode III.

32. M.A. (1976) *A revised guide to mathematics projects in British secondary schools*: Mathematical Association. Bell: London.

This booklet gives brief factual details about sixteen projects.

33. Tall G. & Cahill M. (1979) The Schools Council and mathematical education. *Mathematics in School,* vol. 8, no. 2, pp. 6–8.

A summary of mathematics projects assisted by the Schools Council.

34. Howson A.G. (1978) Change in mathematics education since the late 1950s – ideas and realization – Great Britain. *Educational Studies in Mathematics,* vol. 9, no. 2, pp. 183–223.

A clear discussion of the content and process of curriculum change.

35. Bridge J.R. (1972) R.O.S.L.A. and after. *Mathematics in School,* vol. 1, no. 6, pp. 8–9.

How, and why, one headmaster has planned for the raising of the school leaving age.

36. eg. *Mathematics for General Education* (1976–77) Sets A to F. Macmillan Education: London

The Scottish Mathematics Appreciation Project Group has produced this final two year course for low ability pupils .

37. M.A. (1955) *The teaching of mathematics in primary schools.* Bell: London.
M.A. (1970) *A further report on mathematics in primary schools.* Bell: London.

Two comprehensive reports on principle and practice.

38. H.M.S.O. (1959) *Primary education.* Her Majesty's Stationery Office: London.

A handbook based on visits and discussions, which presents ideas and practices worthy of wider consideration.

39. Schools Council (1965) *Mathematics in primary schools*: curriculum bulletin no. 1. Schools Council: London.

This book contains an immense amount of practical advice for teachers.

40. H.M.S.O. (1965) *Primary education in Scotland.* Her Majesty's Stationery Office: Edinburgh.

The first report on post war Scottish primary schools, which classifies mathematics as a part of environmental study.

41. Watson F.R. (1976) *Developments in mathematics teaching.* Open Books: London (See chapter 9)

A discussion of recent changes in school mathematics, with five chapters of case studies.

42. Nuffield (1973) *Guide to the guides.* Chambers: Edinburgh; Murray: London; Wiley: New York.

A teachers' handbook for the Nuffield mathematics project.

43. Bell A.W. et al. (1978) *A calculator experiment in a primary school.* Shell Centre for Mathematical Education, The University: Nottingham.

A full discussion of an investigatory project.

44. Neill H. (1979) *The use of electronic calculators in the sixth form.* County of Durham Education Committee, Green Lane, Spennymoor: Durham.

A report based on work in three comprehensive schools.

45. M.A. (1965; 1967) *Experiments in the teaching of sixth form mathematics to non-specialists*: Mathematical Association pamphlets nos. 1 & 2. Bell: London.

Accounts of courses offered in academic schools.

46. See reference 41, chapter 12.

47. Sixth Form Mathematics Project (1975) *Presenting mathematics from the applicable point of view.* Macmillan/Schools Council: London.

An introduction, for the teacher, to the project and its series of books.

48. M.A. (1971) *Computers and the teaching of numerical mathematics in the upper secondary school*: Mathematical Association. Bell: London.

Ideas for use in teaching.

49. Bell A.W. & Morley S.A. (undated) *Sixth form mathematics courses for non-specialists*: A.T.C.D.E. National Association of Teachers in Further and Higher Education: London.

A pamphlet suggesting lower, middle and upper courses suitable for nearly all the new sixth formers.

50. Eyre R. & Dean P.G. (1978) The development of draughts by sixth form students. *Mathematics Teaching,* no. 84, pp. 39–42.

An account of an entertaining, instructive, investigative course where students do mathematics.

51. M.A. (1963) A symposium on modern mathematics: whole issue of journal. *Mathematical Gazette,* vol. 47, no. 362

Eight invited articles to give a clear, general picture of activity in Britain.

52. Howson A.G. ed. (1973) *Developments in mathematical education.* Cambridge University Press: Cambridge.

A survey of, and papers from, the 1972 international congress at Exeter.

53. Thom R. (1973) Modern mathematics: does it exist? In reference 52, pp. 194–209.

A balance sheet of things to retain, to amend and to eliminate.

54. Chapman L.R. ed. (1972) *The process of learning mathematics.* Pergamon: Oxford.

A book from a course of B.Ed. lectures which includes descriptions of four national projects.

55. Compare the two Mathematical Association guides: M.A. (1968) *A guide to mathematics projects in British secondary schools.* Bell: London.
M.A. (1976) *A revised guide to mathematics projects in British secondary schools.* Bell: London.

56. Hersee J. (1976) S.M.P., a disaster diverted? *Mathematics in School,* vol. 5, no. 1, pp. 2–3.

A reasoned reply to criticisms of modern mathematics.

57. Hodgkinson J. (1976) A personal view on S.M.P. *Mathematics in School.* vol. 5, no. 1, p. 3.

Teachers have experienced too much change in a short period of time.

CHAPTER 3

TEACHING MATHEMATICS TO PUPILS

Introduction

We all have some idea of what teachers do in school if only because we remember our own schooldays; our own teachers always seemed to be busy with a multitude of tasks in the corridors and playgrounds as well as in the classrooms. The teachers of today are just as busy with tasks, which all contribute to their pupils' education, but only some of these tasks are directly concerned with the actual teaching of mathematics.[1]

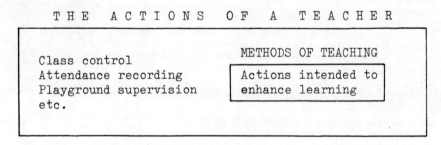

THE ACTIONS OF A TEACHER

Class control
Attendance recording
Playground supervision
etc.

METHODS OF TEACHING

Actions intended to
enhance learning

Figure 3.1 Isolating the methods of teaching from the other actions of a teacher

Each task is often referred to as an 'action of a teacher' and figure 3.1 shows that the methods of teaching have been chosen as those actions which are made with the direct intention of enhancing learning. It is probably obvious that an action such as 'playground supervision' should not be included but the exclusion of 'class control' needs some justification. This is an action which merely creates the conditions whereby a method of teaching may be used (though perhaps 'merely' is a rather weak adverb for such an important action as class control).

METHODS AND STYLES OF TEACHING

The methods of teaching mathematics, and the way that these methods are linked with the psychology of learning mathematics, are fully discussed in the next chapter. There, it is shown that the eleven main methods can be classified into three groups, namely, methods involving: (1) fixed responses by the pupils, (2) investigations by the pupils and (3) expositions by the teacher. A summary of these methods is given in figure 3.2. because it may help the reader of this present chapter, which considers the practice of teaching rather than the theory of teaching. In practice, a teacher frequently uses several methods of teaching during every mathematics lesson[2] and the combination and sequencing of these methods creates a teaching style for that lesson. For example, the normal style of one mathematician when teaching the pupils during G.C.E. Advanced-level lessons may

NAME OF METHOD			DESCRIPTION OF METHOD
Activity	Fixed responses by pupils	Rote learning	Repetition of facts, by writing or speaking
		Drill and practice	Demonstration of a drill, which pupils then practice by exercises
		Programmed learning	Teacher provides an effective sequence of activities, for pupils to reach set objectives
	Investigations by pupils	Directed discovery	Teacher sets goals, provides objects or ideas, and directs the activity as it progresses
		Guided discovery	Teacher sets aims and provides objects or ideas ; all these guide the pupils' activity
		Exploratory discovery	Teacher only provides objects or ideas, and the pupils explore them
		Free discovery	Discovery which is not initiated by the teacher
		Experimentation	Teacher or pupil states a hypothesis which pupils must prove to be true or untrue
	Expositions by teacher	Lecture	Teacher defines terms, expressions or symbols, breaks them into simple components which are explained, and finally summarizes
		Deductive	Teacher states a problem and then presents a correct sequence of steps which leads to a conclusion
		Inductive	Teacher considers particular examples, identifies their common properties, and states a generalization

Figure 3.2 A table showing the main methods of teaching mathematics

start with deductive exposition (i.e. giving correct solutions to homework questions), followed by inductive exposition (i.e. examples leading to a new generalization) and ending with guided discovery (i.e. the pupils investigating the generalization). If that same mathematician teaches some 13 year old pupils in another lesson, he is likely to use a different sequence of methods with more frequent changes from one method to another. Therefore, this teacher will have changed his teaching style to suit the pupils in a different class. If the same class of 13 year old pupils were taught by another mathematics teacher, the pupils would probably find that she, or he, uses another different style. This illustrates that each teacher should evolve a suitable teaching style for each lesson with a class and it is not enough just to take over a style which has been used by a previous mathematics teacher.

The actions of teachers and of pupils

It must be emphasized that the actions of a teacher are closely related to three other factors: the actions of pupils, the school environment and the mathematics curriculum.[3] This is represented by the tetrahedral surface in figure 3.3, where each face meets the other three along their common edges to represent the many points of interaction. The shaded face is uppermost because a teacher is responsible for controlling the situation. He has to assess the probable interactions, and then select an effective style of teaching which is modified by the actual interactions which occur during a lesson. The teaching style does not necessarily put the teacher in a dominant role and he may often expect the pupil to do a great deal of independent study. However, the teacher must realize that his job includes taking responsibility for choosing that particular style.

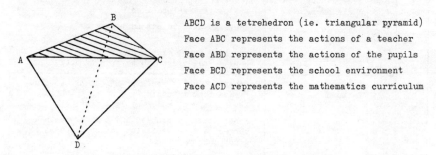

ABCD is a tetrehedron (ie. triangular pyramid)
Face ABC represents the actions of a teacher
Face ABD represents the actions of the pupils
Face BCD represents the school environment
Face ACD represents the mathematics curriculum

Figure 3.3 A teacher's actions relate to, and control, the three other factors

Methods, school structure and mathematics

A student who was soon to qualify for entry to the teaching profession spoke to me about her first secondary school post, which she had recently been offered and had accepted. She was looking forward to working in the mathematics department but 'their teaching methods were old fashioned' and did not employ the variety of approaches which she knew was possible for helping pupils to learn. What methods should she use when she started teaching?

My advice was that it would be rash to introduce radically different methods when she began because the 'old fashioned' methods were presumably part of the dominant social structure in the school. If, on arrival, she significantly challenged this structure then she was unlikely to gain the cooperation of the pupils and might even harm both their future and her own. From her description of the teaching, the school was efficiently organized on a system by which 'knowledge is rationally organized by the teacher and transmitted in terms of its examination efficiency'. (This quotation is from a book by Basil Bernstein, a sociologist at the London University Institute of Education.)[4] Professor Bernstein states that any shift from this social order resting on *domination* to one resting on *cooperation* (where the latter is more like the adults' social system) could only be made slowly. During this change, the introduction of other teaching methods, by her and like minded teachers, would be contributory factors. This change might be expected to improve the school's mathematics education in two ways: it could help the pupils to take more responsibility for their own learning and it could emphasize the changing nature of mathematics learning from a study of a predetermined body of knowledge to a process of mathematical enquiry. These two improvements would probably not be accompanied by a deterioration in the socially important examination results, if a gradual change were introduced.

Teaching styles change slowly

The style of mathematics teaching in many primary schools has altered a great deal since 1950. However, few teachers will be surprised to learn that our student had found a secondary school where mathematics is taught by 'old fashioned methods', especially as this does not mean that they are inappropriate methods. Their common use is illustrated by the following quotation from the survey, *Aspects of secondary education in England*, published in 1979. The teaching style which was seen in most school classrooms is summarized as:

> teachers explained, illustrated, demonstrated, and perhaps gave notes on procedure and examples. The pupils were led deductively through small steps and closed questions to the principle being

considered. There were few questions encouraging wider speculation or independent initiative.[5]

In many of these schools, where only about one-third of the courses are classified as traditional mathematics, even the introduction of new courses had not changed the traditional teaching style. This conservatism also exists in the U.S.A., where the 1975 National Advisory Committee report[6] showed that, despite the availability of new mathematics courses, their effective implementation in American schools was very slow. A conclusion which can be drawn is that teaching styles are slowly changing; there is a general trend in which investigational methods are used more frequently and teachers are becoming managers as well as instructors.[7]

Teachers who change their teaching styles

Teachers generally find it easier not to change their styles of teaching, which they have probably developed over a period of increasingly

Figure 3.4 'It's a new style of teaching. I've removed the blackboard, cut it into slates and given one to each pupil.'

successful years in a school. The two most common reasons for teachers changing their styles occur when teachers move to other schools and when their pupils are not learning enough mathematics. In the latter case, the teachers may introduce a new course or syllabus. With new courses it is interesting to realize that, while large amounts of money and thousands of man-hours of work have been used in developing these courses, their consequent adoption by school teachers has rarely been investigated. We therefore know very little about the process of changing from one style of teaching to another, but luckily a few teachers have written accounts of their own experiences and these accounts provide some guidance for other teachers. Two teachers who moved to schools where more cooperative social systems existed have described the results of their respective moves in the following ways. The first teacher wrote:

> As a primary school teacher in an unsympathetic school, I felt the demands of an institutional kind to be very heavy. There were ways of setting out to be adhered to; there was a timetable which seemed an intrusion into what it may have been possible to do with a class of children I had all day, there were end-of-term tests and a headmaster who reacted aggressively to abnormal results. I felt very strongly the conflict between these ideas and my own feelings about how necessary it was to work with children in a way which reflected who they were as well as what other people expected of them. It seemed as if most other teachers in the school were coping well enough with the system they worked in, but I felt unable to do justice to my beliefs and other people's expectations at the same time.
>
> Moving to a more flexible school, I thought that my feeling of pressure might be reduced but in fact, if anything, it was worse. If anything was possible then the temptation to try to do everything was enormous but impossible to realise. There seemed to be too many kids...
>
> In the end, of course, there are no master plans of organisation to cope with the different situations we encounter – none that work anyway. Talk of word card systems and so forth has always struck me as peripheral, but changes in teachers' effectiveness in the classroom often seem to follow a lessening of anxiety for them, which may come about in a variety of ways. I have been wondering, not for the first time, why I find help in other people's writing, and how it serves to reduce my anxiety.[8]

This teacher's ideals did not match those of his first school. The second teacher expressed similar views when she wrote:

On the whole, I had enjoyed my teaching at the Grammar Technical School. The streamed organisation had lent itself to a great deal of class teaching... Occasionally, I would introduce group work, making use of professionally manufactured work cards but this tended to be the exception rather than the rule. As time passed by, it became increasingly evident to me that more teaching than learning was going on and...I was – deep down inside me – dissatisfied by the lack of catering for the individual child...I was lucky enough to join the mathematics department at ...Fulford comprehensive school (which) divides each of its first three years into mixed ability classes. I admitted to the children that although I was not new to teaching, I was unfamiliar with the mixed ability organisation. This proved to be a good move...

It is certainly true that mixed ability teaching involves a great deal of hard work for the teacher in the evenings...I must say that never before have I experienced so much success in a classroom.[9]

The experiences of teachers (like the two just quoted) who alter their teaching styles by moving to other schools contrast greatly with the experiences of teachers who change their teaching styles while remaining in the same school. This is not easy for an individual teacher, but a group of mathematics teachers will be able to do so with relative ease. As well as sharing the work necessary to put a new teaching scheme into practice, they are able to discuss personal and other aspects of the situation. The group should make gradual changes, and the following example shows how a school introduced mixed ability teaching for 12 year old pupils. The introduction involved only half the classes in the first year, with the other classes being taught as before. The teachers made a success of this limited amount of mixed ability teaching before it was introduced for all the pupils of that age.[10]

A second example relates to a group of teachers introducing a different teaching style in one school, coinciding with the organizational change described in chapter 6. Several sixth form mathematics classes were regrouped when a new G.C.E. Advanced-level course was started. Before the change each teacher had taught a class of about eighteen pupils for six mathematics lessons a week. In most of those lessons he had used a traditional teaching style which involved: (a) a reminder or statement of the mathematical context, (b) the teacher defines and explains a general formula or property, (c) the teacher and pupils work through particular examples using the general formula or property, and (d) the teacher sets exercises. These exercises are set to test the general formula or property, rather than being chosen for their intrinsic interest or value; all these exercises are done by the pupils, with help available from the teacher. For the new course the teaching style differed only slightly yet significantly in two ways. Firstly, the pupils were more frequently taught by the inductive method which starts from particular examples and finishes with the general formula or property (i.e. steps (b) → (c) now became (c) → (b)). Secondly, as two lessons were private study periods, the pupils were given more responsibility for organizing their own learning, although this was closely monitored by their teacher and the other pupils during the two regular seminar periods when ideas and work were discussed. This new teaching style gave the pupils a much better preparation for the university courses to which most of them were proceeding. Also, the change of course and style benefitted the teachers concerned, who regularly met to discuss many details of their new teaching system.

In primary schools the introduction of discovery methods (which will be described in the next chapter) has been successfully made by many groups of teachers. There are personal accounts of the changes wrought by this introduction in the closing chapters of the Mathematical Association's 1970 *Further report on mathematics in primary schools*[11] and the Schools Council's 1965 *Mathematics in primary schools*.[12] However, it should not be imagined that so-called progressive methods have been allowed to completely replace more traditional ones.[13] In *Primary education in Britain*,[14] published in 1978, Her Majesty's Inspectors commend those schools which use a combination of didactic ('meaning to instruct') and investigational methods.

The characteristics of good teaching

Mathematics teachers may adopt new styles when they recognize the need for an improvement in their teaching, but an improvement cannot be assessed unless the desirable characteristics of good mathematics teaching are known. These characteristics apply to all stages of education and a good description of them was expressed by the Schools Council team which investigated mixed ability mathematics teaching in secondary schools. In their book, the team members list the following six desirable aspects:

Quality

(a) Sound mathematical content and variety of tasks.
(b) Suitability of tasks for pupils (appropriate level of difficulty, interest and relevance).

Continuity

(a) Continuity and development of the mathematical learning of individual pupils.

(b) Awareness by the teacher of individual pupil's progress.

Autonomy

Development of the pupil's ability to organize his own learning activities.

Discussion.

Mathematical discussion between pupils and between teacher and pupil.[15]

If we refer back to the example about a different teaching style with sixth form classes, it is probably obvious that the introduction of private study time and seminars gave greater opportunities for three of the aspects just listed, namely, discussion, autonomy and awareness. An assessment that these three aspects had improved, while the first three on the list had not deteriorated, showed that the teaching was better. With other classes in secondary and primary schools, better teaching may be achieved more easily by improving another of the aspects, for instance, by making the tasks more suitable for the pupils.

DIVERSITY

Changing the combination of methods

A pupil has to feel secure in his or her learning environment and I suggested earlier in this chapter that a sudden major change of teaching style could be an unsettling experience. There are only two ways to avoid this major change, and the satisfactory way is to reduce the use of one teaching method while increasing the use of another; this is obviously only possible if the two methods are used concurrently within one teaching style. The second way is to never make any change and this is unsatisfactory because the pupils themselves are changing both physically and mentally.[16] In this context, I am reminded of a secondary school where one man used almost the same teaching style with all his pupils. Whether he was teaching the first form or the sixth form, he employed a similar combination of drill and practice, directed discovery and deductive methods, and told the pupils exactly what they were to do and the answers they should reach. The outcome was that his pupils' examination results were consistently good at the end of each term and year, but rather a large percentage of his pupils chose to drop the subject after their G.C.E. examinations. This was not surprising because they had been taught to be motivated by examinations and not by their interest in the subject; once the examinations were finished then, for them, the study of the subject was also finished. These ideas lead me to suggest that a pupil receives a good mathematics education from a teaching style which includes:

1. a combination of at least two teaching methods during any lesson, and
2. a progressively changing combination of methods during a period of a term or more.

As an example we will consider teaching a pupil at various stages in his school career. For a 6 year old pupil, the teacher will use objects for the exploratory discovery method and will also talk with the pupil about the common properties of objects (i.e. the teacher will combine exploratory discovery and inductive methods). By the time the pupil is about 10 years of age, the teacher will have reduced the amount of exploratory discovery and introduced some guided and directed discovery. The inductive method will be used occasionally when, for example, the teacher lists common mathematical properties and writes a generalization on the blackboard, and there is likely to be some drill and practice so that the pupils learn to perform arithmetical calculations. When the pupil is 15 years old, the teacher may be asking many questions of the form 'What do you think about...?'. He is again making a greater use of the exploratory discovery method but its purpose now is to investigate mathematical ideas rather than objects. Drill and practice methods may now be used more extensively if the pupil will soon be taking a G.C.E. or C.S.E. examination, and the deductive method will have been introduced to present neat written solutions to mathematical problems. This example illustrates the various teaching methods used by a mathematics teacher who is attempting to satisfy his pupils' needs and expectations (see chapter 7).[17,18] Each teacher should have decided on a general plan which shows, or implies, his chosen combination of teaching methods and the ways in which that combination changes as the pupils become more mature. The teacher will then be able to follow that general plan, even though he will rarely have time to analyse the actual methods used in any group of lessons. One practical approach used by some teachers is to use certain books or activities rather than to think about using certain methods of teaching. Thus, a class may now be doing three exercises a week, instead of two, from a drill and practice text book, and may have started to do group projects suggested by a pack of guided discovery work cards. The teacher knows about the use of the text book and the work cards, and therefore by association knows that he is using more drill and practice and is introducing guided discovery, which is a correct combination of teaching methods for that part of his general plan.

Variation between teachers in a school

Variation of teaching style between teachers in a school should also be mentioned, because the fact that a group of teachers has agreed to use certain methods of teaching does not mean that they will all teach in exactly the same way. Chapter 5 considers mathematical differences between the sexes from which, for example, we might expect men teachers to put more emphasis on the visual-spatial aspects of mathematics. While such general trends may be true for all schools, the more important consideration in any individual school is the variety shown by teachers. This variety will give different mathematical experiences to the pupils despite the teachers supposedly using similar methods of teaching.

Variety in pupils' mathematical methods

There are strong indications from both primary[14] and secondary[5,10] school surveys that the most successful teaching uses various combinations of activities. This is not surprising when we consider the various ways by which pupils work at mathematics, even for such an apparently straightforward example as the mental addition of 25 and 27. In figure 3.5 the first pupil uses a way which shows his familiarity with the composition of numbers, whereas the second pupil uses a way which shows her familiarity with a method of adding

Figure 3.5 Two ways to mentally add 25 and 27

numbers. The first pupil chooses intuitively to replace 27 by 25 + 2 (whereas he might have chosen 24 + 3, 15 + 12, etc.) because the two 25s then combine easily to give 50 and the answer 52 is obtained quickly. The second pupil starts with the first number, 25, to which she methodically adds the next units digit, ie. 25 + 7, and then adds the tens digit, rather as with a sum written on paper. A pupil who is adding 25 and 27 chooses one of these two ways, or another equivalent way from the variety possible, because of previous teaching and because of his or her stage of mathematical development.

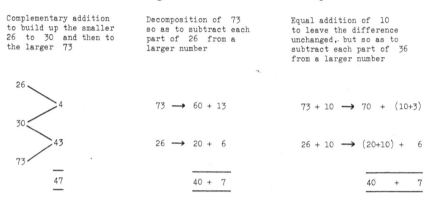

Complementary addition to build up the smaller 26 to 30 and then to the larger 73	Decomposition of 73 so as to subtract each part of 26 from a larger number	Equal addition of 10 to leave the difference unchanged, but so as to subtract each part of 36 from a larger number

$$73 \longrightarrow 60 + 13$$

$$73 + 10 \longrightarrow 70 + (10+3)$$

$$26 \longrightarrow 20 + 6$$

$$26 + 10 \longrightarrow (20+10) + 6$$

$$40 + 7$$

$$40 + 7$$

Figure 3.6 The structures of three ways by which to calculate 73–26

It is not only in mental addition that pupils use different ways to find the answer, and figure 3.6 shows three ways of subtracting 26 from 73. These ways are set out to emphasize their structure and are not set out in forms which pupils would normally be expected to use.[19,20,21,22]

These examples of addition and subtraction use only two from the many mathematical situations where the teacher will find the pupils using different but equally correct ways. The teacher should recognize, accept and build on these ways when planning further teaching.[23] Here, the teacher who tries to help the pupils to learn mathematics efficiently, may himself have to learn from the pupils. I know teachers who have regularly asked pupils to explain little pieces of mathematics to other pupils in their classes, and some of these explanations are now included in their own teaching. If we encourage individuality, we must accept pupils' various ways of solving many exercises and problems. This variety is advantageous because it shows pupils that mathematics can be used flexibly, with several paths leading to the solution.

Teaching the process or the tidy solution

It has often been said that mathematics is discovered inductively and that the steps of the process are then rearranged into a logical order so that they can be presented deductively. By such a rearrangement the mathematics is explained very clearly but the discovery process is hidden. In school there are occasions when both the process and the tidy solution should be taught. Nearly every teacher has been approached, at some time or other, by a pupil who said 'Can you help me with this?' and who then launched into a description of some problem. If the teacher were then pressed for time, he might have worked out a solution after school. His first solution would record his thoughts as he jotted down ideas, and solved parts of the problem. Probably, he would then have rearranged this record into a tidy solution which gave a clearer, methodical and logical explanation. The next day he would have been faced with the decision of which solution would be more useful to the pupil; should he explain the sequence of steps by which he had worked or should he explain the tidy solution? I feel that a good teacher will often explain some of the steps in his first rough work, in the hope that the pupil could then build on them and construct a tidy solution for himself. If the pupil failed to do this, the teacher would have to explain his own tidy solution. Traditional tidy solutions were the Euclidean geometry proofs, which many pupils found difficult to construct and which have now almost disappeared from school mathematics. It is interesting that this axiomatic study, whose decline was welcomed by many teachers, was replaced by a similar axiomatic study[24] of groups and vector spaces when modern mathematics was introduced. Even where teachers have recognized the mathematical tidiness and cohesion of these axiomatic systems, they do not seem to have successfully taught them to many pupils.[26] This may be because there are really very few secondary school pupils who can understand the rôle of axioms in mathematics, even though they are able to understand a tidy solution which uses this axiomatic structure.

Contemplation

It is unusual to include contemplation in a consideration of teaching mathematics but any teacher who encourages pupils to be interested in mathematics should realize that it is a necessary process. Contemplative thought by a pupil is not immediately obvious to either the pupil or the teacher, so for both of them the process is an act of faith. Only from the outcome can one sometimes know that there has been valuable contemplation instead of valueless time-wasting. For example, when a pupil is fiddling with something or staring into space, the teacher may sense that it is a period of contemplation and therefore will not interrupt. If the pupil reaches a conclusion or asks a significant question a few minutes later, the teacher knows that he has acted correctly. A teacher hopes that a pupil may gain two benefits from contemplation. The first is an intuitive understanding of the subject about which he has been thinking. This understanding comes from his linking separate concepts into a recognizable picture in his mind. The second benefit is an inspiration, or creative leap,[28] such as some mathematicians have[29] when they almost unconsciously discover the solution to a problem.

HOMEWORK

Private study in the evenings and at weekends used to be an almost universal feature of British grammar and public schools, their pupils having usually begun to do homework from an earlier age of about 9 years old. This early start is not now so common because of the virtual disappearance of the 11 + examination for grammar school entrance, but voluntary or compulsory homework is usually set for many pupils in comprehensive and other secondary schools. This homework is given by teachers who have to expend effort in three ways, namely to set homework, collect it and mark it.

Setting homework

When teachers set homework the quantity, level and topic must provide useful mathematical work for the pupils. With pupils of similar ability in each class, the most common method was to set several exercises which provided practice at the current topic being taught; those exercises would then be discussed at the start of the next lesson. This method is still frequently used but such immediate practice is not the only benefit to be gained from homework and a good teacher will probably use it in a variety of ways.[30] Sometimes, for example, revision exercises which relate to previous topics can be set to provide regular reinforcement of pupils' knowledge. Yet another way is to set homework which prepares the pupils for the topic which will be studied in their next lesson. This kind of homework might entail reading about the life of Pythagoras if the next lesson concerns Pythagoras' theorem, or it might revise factorization if that is a skill which will be needed for a more advanced topic. Preparatory homework might also be practical, as when pupils measure coins, tins and other circular objects if the next lesson will introduce the formula 'circumference = $\pi \times$ diameter'. As well as relating homework to past, present and future topics, it is possible to set homework on topics which are distinct from the classwork. This is a system which is especially suitable for the type of mixed ability teaching where the whole class does not work on a common topic at the same time. Such homework systems have been efficiently organized in some school mathematics departments by having pre-prepared homework assignments covering a whole term or year.[31] These assignments may vary from practice in basic skills through to small individual projects, but in total they provide one part of a planned mathematics curriculum.

Compulsory or voluntary homework

Homework may be compulsory or voluntary for the pupils and the voluntary system involves less work and stress for the teachers. At many schools, there are parents and pupils who think that homework is not necessary. In a compulsory system, there can easily be irritation as teachers try to collect subsequent homeworks from recalcitrant pupils, and the lesson time devoted to it can seriously interfere with the efficient teaching of mathematics. Conversely, a disadvantage of the voluntary system is the implication that this private study mathematics is unnecessary or unimportant, otherwise it would be compulsory. A voluntary system also encourages underachievement in many pupils, and would be unfair to pupils in the first years of secondary school when they had not had a chance to develop their self-discipline for study. These pupils should have either compulsory homework or no homework.

Marking homework

The teachers have to mark the homework collected, and marking with just ticks or crosses is rarely sufficient; it has been shown that pupils are likely to make better progress if a teacher writes comments which provide guidance and encouragement.[32] If the marking is not done promptly it cannot be returned while that work is fresh in the pupils' minds. Also, if homework is not returned in the lesson following its collection the pupils may feel let down by the teacher. This has been made clear to some of my student teachers, by pupils who made remarks like 'You're good, Miss, because you return our homework on time'. Of course, prompt marking is not so easy for a teacher with a full timetable but the following paragraphs show how good organization can help the teacher, without reducing the value of the homework to the pupils.

The organization of homework

The following suggestions for good organization can reduce the effort expended by the mathematics teacher. When the homework is selected, try to choose work which is suitable for the pupils and is also going to be easy to mark. For example, do not choose questions which require the manipulation of unnecessarily difficult fractions so that checking the pupils' calculations is likely to be complicated. Think also about the marking scheme so that, if the pupils expect a mark out of ten, you try to set five similar questions (for two marks each) rather than six as you may originally have intended. Having decided on the homework, give details to the pupils so that they are left in no doubt about what they should be doing. I have often seen this left to the very end of a lesson when a last minute instruction like '... and your homework is numbers 1 to 5 on page 124' is inviting confusion in a following lesson and extra work for the teacher. Some careful pupils will have done the correct homework, but there will almost certainly be others who could not find their hurriedly written note of the question numbers and maybe some lazy pupils who were bright enough to do only questions 1,2 and 5 instead of 1,2,3,4 and 5.

Efficiently organized homework does not waste valuable lesson time. For example, if pupils have separate classwork and homework books (or use file paper for homework) then classwork can continue while homework is collected. When marking, the teacher can save time by using the homework of the best pupils as an aid in marking similar work by other pupils. However, the greatest benefit comes from encouraging the pupils to write neatly and to set out their work carefully; not only does this make the work quicker to mark but many experienced teachers believe that their pupils thereby learn more mathematics. No research results seem to have been published to substantiate this belief, although some are available[33] about how the positive role of homework links it with better academic results and better behaviour in secondary schools. The explanation of this is that homework may have a 'symbolic importance in emphasizing the school's concern for academic progress' as well as providing the pupils with opportunities for improving their mathematics and developing their capacity for independent study.[34]

MISTAKES

In his *Lay sermon on a liberal education*, Thomas Huxley expresses the view that God's actions are '... always fair, just and patient. But also we know ... that he never overlooks a mistake.' A teacher who acted similarly would probably be very successful because the mistakes made by a pupil are often one of the best indications of the areas where mathematical understanding needs to be improved.[35,36,37,38] The word 'improved' has been chosen to emphasize that the teacher can only mould and add to something which already exists in the pupils' minds, just as in Piagetian terms a child can only develop mathematical concepts by accommodation (modification) and assimilation (absorption). Now it is obviously impossible to improve something if you do not know what is wrong with its present state, and this is why pupils' mistakes are so valuable; they indicate two kinds of faulty understanding, namely nonunderstanding and misunderstanding. These terms can be explained if understanding is thought of as a correct connection of a concept into its appropriate structure.[39] The meaning of this last sentence is probably not very clear but it should become clearer when we consider examples of faulty understanding.

Nonunderstanding

The first example refers to a pocket calculator which has keys for mathematical calculations. One key is marked $\boxed{\log}$ and its use gives the logarithm of any positive number; if I press the keys for $\boxed{2}$ and $\boxed{\log}$ the display shows 0.30103, if I press the keys for $\boxed{3}$ and $\boxed{\log}$ the display shows 0.47712, and so on. My younger son knows nothing about logarithms but he does know about the whole and decimal numbers. Therefore he understands the numbers he keys in and the numbers which the display shows, but can see no connection between them; this is a case of nonunderstanding. As he and I both know that he does not understand, it would be fairly easy for me to teach him about logarithms; he would then be able to correctly connect the two sets of numbers and this would have enlarged his mathematical understanding. Another clear case of nonunderstanding, which would be even easier to overcome, is the pupil who happens to see the factorial symbol (!) for the first time in a mathematical expression. He recognizes it as an exclamation mark but is quite unable to connect it with numbers. His teacher enables a connection to be made with the multiplication of positive integers by showing that

$$5! = 5 \times 4 \times 3 \times 2 \times 1$$

and the pupil's state of nonunderstanding has disappeared.

Misunderstanding

The teacher's next task is more difficult because he has to discover whether the above pupil has moved into a state of understanding or a state of misunderstanding. It is little use just asking the pupil 'Do you understand?' for he will almost certainly answer 'Yes' because a pupil rarely recognizes his own misunderstanding (whereas we have seen that he can recognize his own nonunderstanding). The teacher therefore probably tests for misunderstanding rather than for understanding, by a sequence of exercises as in figure 3.7. These exercises have been set out so that the first column summarizes the teacher's probable thoughts when selecting the sequence.

Teacher's thoughts	Test	Pupil's answer	True or False
Try for immediate success with tests like the example	6!	6x5x4x3x2x1	T
	8!	8x7x6x5x4x3x2x1	T
Try a sequence leading towards possible difficulties	3!	3x2x1	T
	2!	2x1	T
Try 1 as a special case	1!	1	T
Will he apply it to negative integers?	(-2)!	(-2)x(-1)	F
Misunderstanding by pupil			

Figure 3.7 A teaching sequence which searches for misunderstanding

At the bottom of the table is a false answer which has identified an area of misunderstanding, and the pupil's understanding can now be improved by a discussion showing that $(-2)\times(-1)$ is not a decreasing sequence (-1 is greater than -2) and does not end in 1, so it does not belong to the factorial pattern. This can lead the pupil to acknowledge that he cannot give a numerical answer when the factorial symbol follows a negative integer. He has now reached a stage where he connects factorials with multiplication, but only for positive integers greater than zero. If he now provides correct answers to questions like 4!, 9!, 13!, and also correctly answers that he cannot do $(-4)!$ and 0! then he probably now understands the factorials of positive integers greater than zero. This is enough for a start because he has achieved an understanding of a limited topic. It can be intelligently extended to deal with 0! or $\frac{5}{2}$! at some time in the future when understanding of these further factorials may be needed.

Understanding of further topics

We must be clear that it is always the *understanding of something* which is implied if any remark refers just to understanding. A pupil may understand the multiplication of fractions and misunderstand the division of fractions; when a teacher has that knowledge then he can begin to teach the pupil to understand the division of fractions. This is expressed more generally by saying that mathematics education is a process which includes teaching a pupil to gain a full understanding of some mathematical concept, symbol or experience and then teaching that pupil to gain a full understanding of some further mathematical concept, symbol or experience. This goal of a full understanding of a limited amount of mathematics must not be confused with, or allowed to deteriorate into, the goal of a limited understanding of a greater amount of mathematics. The reason for saying that the former goal is more valuable is that a full understanding of a limited amount of mathematics always provides the foundation for successful progress.

Error patterns

There are hardly any pupils who want to misunderstand mathematics but many pupils who do so, and the explanation often concerns error patterns. Let us consider the example of a pupil who understands the multiplication of integers and is trying to understand the multiplication of simple decimal fractions.

Examples by teacher	Thoughts by pupil
0·5 x 0·5 = 0·25 0·6 x 0·6 = 0·36 0·8 x 0·8 = 0·64 0·8 x 0·3 = 0·24	There is an easy connection with integer multiplication· because 5x5 = 25, 6x6 = 36, but every decimal fraction begins with a nought.

Figure 3.8 How a pupil can build up an error pattern

Figure 3.8 shows the first examples which might be given by a teacher and suggests a pupil's thoughts during this part of the lesson. This may be a quite able and hard working pupil who appreciates that learning mathematics involves the discovery of patterns of behaviour by numbers. He may not have been paying attention to everything said by the teacher, but he has thought about the examples on the blackboard or worksheet and has discovered a satisfying pattern.

Unluckily, he has discovered an error pattern, as is obvious from his thoughts shown in figure 3.8, because $2 \times 3 = 6$ but 0.2×0.3 is not 0.6, so the pattern fails in some multiplications involving 0.3, 0.2 or 0.1. However, as it succeeds in all the other multiplications of this type, eg. 0.7×0.9, the pupil may score a commendable fifteen marks out of twenty on his next homework, whereby the error pattern becomes reinforced as correct instead of being recognized as an error pattern. Such recognition is rarely achieved by the pupil and it is up to the teacher to consider possible errors, to ask questions which will show misunderstanding and then to correct it.[40] In the previous example, the teacher could have used a separate set of questions with answers below 0.1 (eg. $0.2 \times 0.2 = 0.04$, $0.1 \times 0.8 = 0.08$) to test for that possible error pattern. Sometimes, pupils' errors come from faulty reasoning. A teacher might be surprised to discover a pupil who had correctly calculated $0.2 \times 0.2 = 0.04$, then thought that it was wrong and replaced the answer by 0.4 because he 'knew that multiplication always gives a bigger number'. This is a common misunderstanding about the word multiplication, based on its earlier use with whole numbers and on its meaning in everyday speech.

Other commonly occurring error patterns can be discovered by studying the pupils' arithmetic reproduced in figure 3.9; the reader should try to explain the misunderstandings before reading the next paragraph.

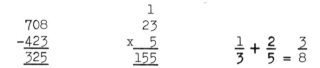

Figure 3.9 Three arithmetic error patterns

The three sums seem to show the following error patterns. In subtraction the smaller digit has been taken away from the larger digit in each column, so that a subtraction involving hundreds, tens and units has been performed as three separate subtractions involving units. The multiplication begins correctly with $3 \times 5 = 15$, the 5 is placed in the units column, but the ten is then added to the twenty before multiplication. The addition of fractions has been attempted by adding the numerators and adding the denominators, this misunderstanding probably being a generalization from adding whole numbers or from the correct pattern for multiplying fractions $(\frac{1}{3} \times \frac{2}{5} = \frac{1 \times 2}{3 \times 5} = \frac{2}{15})$. A pupil's error pattern must be discovered as soon as possib   by the teacher, and corrected before it is reinforced by repetition. Teachers, therefore, should always look closely at work where error patterns are likely to occur, such as certain sections of mixed ability work card schemes.

CONCENTRATION ON INDIVIDUAL PUPILS

Grouping and mixed ability teaching

Mixed ability classes have forced many teachers to think about pupils as individuals; the teachers consider the differences among the pupils in any mixed ability class and soon also look for these differences in all classes. This search for individuality is not a new idea; during the last hundred years, good mathematics teachers have been searching like this. Teachers who read this book might try to test their own perception of children by thinking about a group of pupils and then making two lists: one list of the mathematical similarities shown by those pupils and the other of the mathematical differences. These similarities and differences should not deal with generalities, but with details such as the kinds of understanding and spatial concepts which certain pupils have or how the members of a group are motivated (the details should include cognitive and affective aspects mentioned in chapter 5). Mathematical similarities and differences will exist among the pupils in every class, with similarities dominant in setted groups and differences dominant in mixed ability groups.

Teaching can be independent of the way the pupils are physically grouped, ie. sets, streams, bands, mixed ability, etc., as explained in chapter 6. For example, let us assume that a teacher has designed and produced a scheme called *Mixabmath* which he can use to meet the mathematics education needs of any 12 year old pupil. If he uses *Mixabmath* with a streamed group of pupils, who are relatively similar, then they are receiving mixed ability teaching, and if he uses it with a mixed ability group then they also are receiving mixed ability teaching. Although this successful scheme *Mixabmath* only exists in the imagination, it is easy to find an existing work scheme which is designed for mixed ability classes but is also used by pupils grouped in different ways. Thus, when it is realized that the type of grouping of pupils does not determine the style of teaching, it is clear that there is a difference between 'mixed ability teaching of groups' and 'teaching of mixed ability groups'.

We have just seen how a similar ability set could be taught using a mixed ability work scheme and it is just as true that a mixed ability class could be taught using text books and teaching styles which have been previously used with average ability pupils in setted groups. Mixed ability groups have actually been taught in this way in schools which could not afford new materials and where some mathematics teachers were neither interested nor trained in mixed ability teaching. However, such teaching was probably unsatisfactory for pupils and teachers alike.

The most satisfactory mixed ability teaching[41] employs a variety of materials and a variety of teaching methods.[42] In fact, it now seems illogical that any teacher could ever have attempted mixed ability teaching and yet used only one way of teaching ('Oh Sir, not another worksheet'); the acknowledged variety of pupils' learning styles and stages was surely most likely to need to be matched by using several different teaching methods.

Materials for mixed ability work schemes

The teaching of mixed ability groups has little chance of succeeding unless it is based on some organized work scheme.[43,45,46] A typical mathematics work scheme probably uses a selection of the following students' materials: work cards, work sheets, topic books, text books and apparatus. These materials have often been collected over a period of time and from various sources. Some materials will have to come from educational suppliers because teachers do not have the time and resources to construct a complete scheme. Any scheme which is purchased will always need to be modified to meet the special needs of individual schools.[47,48] This may be done by providing additional materials for use by higher and lower ability pupils, or by amending the prescribed learning style to match the cognitive styles of the pupils more closely.[49] With a typical scheme, in which pupils are regularly changing their work cards and apparatus, the teacher has more organizational work than with pupils in streamed or setted groups. He may frequently have to enter information on record cards and have to prepare assignment plans. These tasks are easier when the teacher becomes familiar with the scheme and the extra work is seen to be worthwhile if the pupils are busily learning mathematics.

Models of mixed ability teaching

In 1977 the Schools Council published a report[10] on current practice in mixed ability teaching of middle and secondary school mathematics. From the thirty two schools visited, they distinguished the six models of teaching described below. They found that the schemes at different schools used either short exercises or exploratory tasks or both. The short exercises aimed to develop concepts or techniques and the exploratory tasks were more open ended investigations. With the exercises or exploratory tasks, as shown in figure 3.10, the teachers' organization of their mixed ability groups was classified into three types X, Y or Z, of which the first two are also commonly used with streamed or setted groups of pupils.

Model	1. Exercises	2. Exploratory tasks
X Whole-class activity	All pupils study the same topic at the same time. Material is in the form of worksheets, work cards or topic work books.	Pupils are involved in various levels of investigation of a teacher-initiated problem or activity.
Y Group work	Small groups in the class work on different tasks from a text-book, topic book, worksheet or work card.	Small groups carry out different investigations or activities from a variety of sources.
Z Individualized schemes	Pupils work on materials from a structured scheme which is designed to develop concepts. The materials or tasks may be either sequences linearly or in a flow chart. Task assignment is systematic or teacher directed.	The pupil works individually, choosing his tasks, with guidance from the teacher, from a bank of investigations, not necessarily structured.

Figure 3.10 Six models of mixed ability teaching. (This figure is reproduced from the Schools Council report in reference 50.)

Individualized instruction

The third type of organization, which has just been mentioned, uses individualized instruction schemes. When these schemes are applied in their most extreme forms, each pupil works alone at an individual assignment from a syllabus which has been selected to match that pupil's special needs (i.e. the work, assignment, syllabus and needs are all four individualized). Slightly less extreme forms of individualized instruction,[51,53,54,55,56] having perhaps a common syllabus of work, have been enthusiastically supported by some people. This support led to schemes like the prestigious American 'Individually Prescribed Instruction – Mathematics' (I.P.I. – Math)[57] and the 'Secondary Mathematics Individualized Learning Experiment' (S.M.I.L.E.)[58] which is used in maybe 40 per cent of Inner London Education Authority secondary schools. Mathematics teaching has been helped by these schemes but, in operation, the schemes have often fallen short of people's original expectations about individualized instruction. This is because an operational scheme frequently becomes the determining factor and the pupils are fitted into it, rather like a handful of loose change into a coin sorting machine. Perhaps the most damning criticism made about some use of these schemes is that the only choice given to the pupils is their rate of working and this choice then allows some pupils to underachieve as seriously as they would have done in a streamed class. This criticism must be balanced against the acclaim of people who see the schemes used so that pupils really benefit; for example, such individualized instruction can be the only successful way of educating pupils who are not regularly attending school.

TEACHING THE SLOW LEARNERS

There is a need to understand, and to improve the mathematics education of, low ability pupils[59,60,61] and other pupils who have special educational needs. When these pupils attend ordinary schools (i.e. not special schools[62]), they probably receive special attention either as isolated pupils in mixed ability classes or as groups of slow learning pupils in remedial or withdrawal classes. Their teachers must expect to discover that some of the pupils are unable to start on a remedial mathematics course because they have a personal aversion to mathematics and also, maybe, to other subjects. Therefore a teacher with these pupils must start by trying to correct this aversion, which is often shown by the pupil being fearful or disruptive.

Fearful pupils

Sometimes pupils have a fear of mathematics which has been built up by their misunderstanding, nonunderstanding and failure during previous lessons, and this fear has to be resolved before any systematic learning of mathematics can be attempted. This therapeutic stage has two aims, to develop a confident relationship with the teacher and to bring success to the pupil. The mathematics teacher can try to interest the pupil in something from the wide variety of apparatus which is available. It is most important for the teacher to select apparatus which will enable the pupil to succeed. It really does not matter if the mathematical level is very elementary, or if the task is only marginally mathematical, provided the pupil succeeds and gains confidence. Then, and only then, can the therapeutic stage gradually begin to change into a normal remedial course.

Disruptive pupils

Teachers may find that a remedial class contains one or more disruptive pupils, who interrupt other people's work. With these pupils, the teacher's first actions may not be directed to teaching mathematics. If such a pupil is pathologically disturbed then the teacher obviously must cooperate with doctors from the school medical service, to devise a suitable form of instruction. However, *disturbed* pupils probably cause only a minority of the disruptions and the majority are caused by *disturbing* pupils, who act in this way because they are testing the authority and values of the teacher and school, or asserting their right to attention and respect. In treating these pupils, the first step is to begin to build up an atmosphere of mutual trust. In the book *Slow Learners*, based on her experience, Diane Griffin gives this advice on how to start:

> Some 'bottom stream' classes wait for the new teacher to indicate that he knows they are the 'thickies'. They accept this as true themselves, so why shouldn't the new teacher? It should not be surprising, therefore, if they act 'thick' either by passively showing no interest in anything or by behaving disruptively and noisily. Quite often they work hard to bring about what they feel is the normal state – the state of conflict!
>
> What does a new teacher do when confronted with this situation? The only viable thing to do is to be honest, to say, 'Look, I believe you are all individuals, all different and all important. I want to get to know you, to find out what you are good at and to learn with you.' It is my experience that most pupils instinctively recognise a sincere teacher and do respond to that kind of approach.[63]

Nearly every pupil is interested in, and good at, something. In learning about the pupil's interests, the teacher also learns about the pupil.

Patterns of diagnosis and treatment

The pupils who are learning to be less afraid of mathematics, or less disruptive, may join pupils with many other handicaps[64,65] to begin a normal remedial mathematics programme. The specific learning problem of each pupil should be diagnosed[66,67] by using personal knowledge and observation of the child as well as diagnostic tests.[68] Many pupils are likely to have common problems, such as limited powers of concentration. These common problems will lead the teacher to design all courses as sequences of low cognitive level activities which can be completed by a slow learner in ten or fifteen minutes.

Another common problem with slow learners is their need for attention and personal security, which can only be satisfied by a teacher who has the time to talk with them. This need may originate from their social or behavioural disadvantages, as well as from their academic disadvantages.[69] Whan a teacher studies the nature of pupils' academic disadvantage, he is likely to differentiate between the few pupils who have learning problems in mathematics only and the other pupils who have low academic achievements in all subjects. Although the teacher will encounter extra difficulties with the latter pupils because, for instance, they are also very poor readers, the teaching of the normal remedial course can be very similar for the whole class. This course is based on two principles, namely, that these pupils must be taught more slowly, and that they need more motivation, than most other pupils in the school.

Advice on teaching styles

The earliest national attempt to provide remedial mathematics teaching took place between 1963 and 1970, and was supported by the Swedish National Board of Education. This project provided and assessed special teaching[70] which was an effective means of helping disadvantaged pupils. In England in 1979, the 'Low Attainers in Mathematics' project was set up at Chelsea College, London. This project had the more limited aim of providing information and advice for teachers, and was much needed because of the small number of books[71,72,73] and articles[74,75,76,77,78] previously published in Britain. By early 1980, the project workers had visited a selection of primary, middle and secondary schools where they often found that teachers did not know about suitable text books and other resource materials which were already available.[79] Therefore, it seems that the teaching, for these low attainers, may be more efficiently improved by providing supportive in-service training than by producing more publications. To test this assumption, pilot in-service training schemes have been started.

In North America, more attention seems to have been given to ways of teaching mathematics to slow learners and we can benefit from these experiences. They are described in *The slow learner in mathematics*,[66] which was published by the National Council of Teachers of Mathematics in 1972, and also in the reports of two conferences held in Ohio and Leland.[80] The problems described in these three publications and in American teaching journals are rather similar to ours in Britain. Unluckily, it seems that relatively few teachers in any country are successfully solving these problems. It has been mentioned that some slow learners are physically handicapped children, with impaired sight or with impaired hearing. When these children attend ordinary schools, the teachers may need advice about suitable ways of teaching them. Regrettably, only a few books[81,82,83] and articles[85] are available which offer such specific advice about mathematics teaching.

Conclusion

This chapter has concentrated on the actions of teachers when they are trying to teach mathematics to their pupils. It has been shown that many different strategies can be used and every teacher must choose the best ones for his or her pupils. One simple strategy, which is often overlooked, is to see that nearly all the lesson time is used for education and very little time wasted.[86] Research has indicated that an important determinant of pupils' achievement in a topic is the amount of active learning time spent on that topic. However, observation in fairly typical classrooms has shown that pupils spend only 37 per cent to 74 per cent of the allocated time in actively learning.[87] A good teacher can often be distinguished by his or her ability to choose the right methods and style of teaching – and then to get on with it without delay.

Annotated References for Chapter 3

1. Shuard H. & Quadling D. (1980) *Teachers of mathematics: some aspects of professional life*. Harper & Row: London, New York.

   A book which comments on teachers' views of stages in their own careers.

2. Marland M. (1975) *The craft of the classroom*. Heinemann: London. See chapter 7.

   This book is subtitled 'a survival guide to classroom management in the secondary school.'

3. Begle E.C. (1979) *Critical variables in mathematics education*: Mathematical Association of America. Wiley: London, New York.

   Findings from a survey of the empirical literature; a broad ranging book.

4. Bernstein B. (1975) *Class, codes and control; volume 3: Towards a theory of educational transmissions.* Routledge & Kegan Paul: London, Boston. See p. 63.

   A sequence of essays which investigate the effect of class relationships upon institutionalizing codes in the school.

5. H.M.S.O. (1979) *Aspects of secondary education in England: a survey by H.M. Inspectors of schools.* Her Majesty's Stationery Office: London. See section 7.6.3.

   The report of a thorough investigation of the final two years of compulsory education in 384 schools (10% sample).

6. N.A.C.O.M.E. (1975) *Overview and analysis of school mathematics, grades K - 12.* National Advisory Committee on Mathematical Education, Conference Board of the Mathematical Sciences: Washington D.C.

   A report, with recommendations, on the health of American school mathematics.

7. U.N.E.S.C.O. (1973) *New trends in mathematics teaching; volume 3, 1972.* United Nations Educational, Scientific & Cultural Organization: Paris. See pp. 100-9.

   The first volume in an improved format which is informative and scholarly.

8. Delany K. (1979) Nine months later - a difficult delivery. *Supplement 22 of the Association of Teachers of Mathematics*, pp. 21-2.

   A personal expression of changing feelings about adequacy in the classroom.

9. Willmore H. (1974) From streamed teaching to mixed ability teaching in secondary school mathematics. *Mathematics in School*, vol. 3, no. 4, pp. 4-6.

   An account of personal adaptation to a new system.

10. Schools Council (1977) *Mixed ability teaching in mathematics.* Evans/Methuen: London. See p. 51.

    A valuable survey of current practice, which includes three case studies.

11. M.A. (1970) *A further report on mathematics in primary schools*; Mathematical Association. Bell: London.

    A comprehensive report on principles and practice.

12. Schools Council (1965) *Mathematics in primary schools*; Curriculum bulletin no. 1. Schools Council: London.

    This book contains an immense amount of practical advice for teachers.

13. Bennett S.N. (1976) *Teaching styles and pupil progress.* Open Books: London. See p. 54.

    A popular report on primary schools and their progressive/traditional teachers.

14. H.M.S.O. (1978) *Primary education in England: a survey by H.M. Inspectors.* Her Majesty's Stationery Office: London.

    An appraisal of mathematics and other subjects in 542 schools.

15. See reference 10, p. 21.

16. Trown A. (1978) Teaching style, mathematics and children *Mathematics Teaching*, no. 82, pp. 29–31.

An account of investigations which matched teaching methods with pupils' personalities.

17. Thomas A. (1974) Different ways of learning mathematics. *Mathematics in School*, vol. 3, no. 2, pp. 18–19.

An analysis of six ways used in primary schools.

18. Ward M. ed. (1979) *Mathematics and the 10 year old*; Schools Council Working paper no. 61. Evans/Methuen: London.

The report of a survey of topics, apparatus, strengths and weaknesses.

19. Davies H.B. (1978) A seven-year-old's subtraction technique. *Mathematics Teaching*, no. 83, pp. 15–16.

A bright boy invents the integer technique.

20. McIntosh A. (1978) Some subtractions: what do you think you are doing? *Mathematics Teaching*, no. 83, pp. 17–19.

Several accounts of childrens' attempts at subtraction.

21. Plunkett S. (1979) Decomposition and all that rot. *Mathematics in School*, vol. 8, no. 3, pp. 2–5.

The actual and potential use of written and mental algorithms.

22. Kilburn J. (1980) Taking ways. *Mathematics in School*, vol. 9, no. 3, pp. 14–15.

A discussion about ways of teaching subtraction.

23. Suydam M.N. & Dessart D.J. (1976) *Classroom ideas from research on computational skills*. National Council of Teachers of Mathematics: Reston.

How to help pupils who are learning to handle whole numbers and fractions.

24. Shibata T. (1973) *The rôle of axioms in contemporary mathematics and in mathematical education*. In reference 25, pp. 262–71.

Categorical and non-categorical theories and their relevance to school mathematics.

25. Howson A.G. ed. (1973) *Developments in mathematical education*. Cambridge University Press: Cambridge.

A survey of, and papers from, the 1972 International Congress of Exeter.

26. Krygowska A.Z. (1971) *Treatment of the axiomatic method in class*. In reference 27, chapter 3.

A thorough discussion based on work in Poland.

27. Servais W. & Varga T. eds. (1971) *Teaching school mathematics*. U.N.E.S.C.O. – Penguin: Harmondsworth.

A book presenting the current international situation in curricula and methods.

28. Tammadge A. (1979) Creativity. *Mathematical Gazette*, vol. 63, no. 425, pp. 145–63.

A discussion of creativity and its development in school pupils.

29. Krutetskii V.A. (1976) *The psychology of mathematical abilities in school children*. University of Chicago Press: Chicago. See pp. 44-6.

A very readable book about research applied to a theory of mathematical ability. The bibliography contains entries new to many Western readers.

30. Peterson J.C. (1971) Four organizational patterns for assigning mathematics homework. *School Science & Mathematics*, vol. 71, no. 7, pp. 592-6.

An article which provides a model, looking at the different ways of setting homework.

31. Abdelnoor J. (1978) How Slatyford school uses S.M.P. books in the organization of its mathematics teaching. *Mathematics in School*, vol. 7, no. 4, pp. 4-5.

A report of an individualized scheme which uses books and homework sheets.

32. Teacher comments and student performance: a seventy four classroom experiment in school motivation. *The Journal of Educational Psychology*, vol. 49, no. 4, pp. 173-81.

This study shows that encouraging comments on marked work are associated with higher achievement scores.

33. Rutter M. et al. (1979) *Fifteen thousand hours: secondary schools and their affects on children*. Open Books: London. See pp. 108-9.

A very interesting report on 1487 children as they progressed through 12 schools.

34. Austin J.D. (1979) Homework research in mathematics. *School Science & Mathematics*, vol. 79, no. 2, pp. 115-21.

A review of published research.

35. Sconyers J.M. (1976) The theorem that wasn't, or learning from a mistake. *Mathematics in School*, vol. 5,no. 5, p. 30.

An article showing the benefits gained from a mistake in matrix algebra.

36. Hart K. (1978) Mistakes in mathematics. *Mathematics Teaching*, no. 85, pp. 38-40.

A discussion of common mistakes by pupils, shown by the C.S.M.S. tests.

37. Kent D. (1978) Some processes through which mathematics is lost. *Educational Research*, vol. 21, no. 1, pp. 27-35.

Kent D. (1979) More about the processes through which mathematics is lost. *Educational Research*, vol. 22, no. 1, pp. 22-31.

Two sets of classroom anecdotes which show how pupils' mistakes can be used to lead to better teaching.

38. Küchemann D. (1978) Children's understanding of numerical variables. *Mathematics in School*, vol. 7, no. 4, pp. 23-6 & vol. 7, no. 5, p. 12.

Küchemann D. (1980) Children's understanding of integers. *Mathematics in School*, vol. 9, no. 2, pp. 31-2.

Three reports from testing 14 year old boys and girls.

39. Skemp R.R. (1979) *Intelligence, learning and action*. Wiley: London, New York. See chapter 10.

The statement of a model of intelligence, of which many mathematicians will approve.

40. Meyerson L.N. (1976) Mathematical mistakes. *Mathematics Teaching*, no. 76, pp. 38–40.

Explanations of why mistakes may be made and how they can be turned to advantage.

41. See reference 10, p. 63.

42. H.M.S.O. (1978) *Mixed ability work in comprehensive school*; Matters for discussion, no. 6. Her Majesty's Stationery Office: London. See pp. 111–15.

Reports from visits during 1975–77 to schools in England and Wales, with a series of subject papers including mathematics.

43. Prettyman P.A. (1975) *Mathematics*. In reference 44, chapter 10.

An account of the development of mixed ability teaching at Crown Woods school, London.

44. Kelly A.V. (1975) *Case studies in mixed ability teaching*. Harper & Row: London, New York.

Two groups of case studies: (1) headteachers and schools (2) teachers and subjects.

45. Vaughan B.W. (1975) The introduction of an integrated scheme for mathematics. *Mathematics in School*, vol. 4, no. 4, pp. 25–8.

A description of the whole process for a primary school.

46. Savins L. (1978) Mixed ability teaching: the practical implications of the teaching of mathematics in a large comprehensive school. *Mathematics in School*, vol. 7, no. 4, pp. 2–4.

This summary includes information about organization and schemes for less able and more able children.

47. Glennon V.J. (1976) Some issues in elementary school mathematics education in the United States. *The Irish Journal of Education*, vol. 10, no. 1, pp. 23–40.

The issues are formalism, individualized instruction, grouping, achievement, basics, free schools, metrication and calculators.

48. Romiszowski A.J. (1979) What's happened to individualised mathematics? *Programmed Learning and Educational Technology*, vol. 16, no. 2, pp. 146–50.

Many programmes have been written, so why has there been little success?

49. Glaser R. (1972) Individuals and learning: the new aptitudes. *Educational Researcher*, vol. 1, no. 6, pp. 5–13.

A discussion of the relationship between psychology and educational practice.

50. See reference 10, p. 37.

51. Gibby W.A. (1972) *The uses of programmed material in British schools and colleges*. In reference 52, pp. 286–309.

A discussion of the structure and application of this material.

52. Chapman L.R. ed. (1972) *The process of learning mathematics*. Pergamon: Oxford.

A book from a course of B.Ed. lectures, which includes descriptions of four national projects.

53. Larsson I. (1973) *Individualized mathematics teaching*. C.W.K. Gleerup/Lund: Sweden.

I.M.U. project results from Sweden.

54. M.A. (1974) *Mathematics, eleven to sixteen*; Mathematical Association. Bell: London. See pp. 169–71.

Guidance for the teacher who wishes to present a mathematical course in mathematics.

55. Crawford D.H. (1977) *The Fife mathematics project*. Oxford University Press: London.

Development, practice and evaluation of a mixed method of teaching mixed ability classes.

56. Davies B. & Cave R.G. eds. (1977) *Mixed ability teaching in the secondary school*. Ward Lock: London.

Two sociologists present theory and practice across the curriculum. Many useful references are included.

57. See discussion in reference 6.

58. Gibbons R. (1975) An account of the Secondary Mathematics Individualized Learning Experiment. *Mathematics in School*, vol. 4, no. 6, pp. 14–16.

The author worked at Ladbroke mathematics centre, where the S.M.I.L.E. scheme was developed.

59. Kelly A.V. (1974) *Teaching mixed ability classes*. Harper & Row: London, New York. See chapter 6.

A book which covers nearly all general aspects but with hardly any mention of mathematics.

60. Schools Council (1979) Brennan W.K.; *Curricular needs of slow learners*; Working paper no. 63. Evans/Methuen: London.

The report of a project studying the whole curriculum for slow learners between 5 and 16 years old.

61. H.M.S.O. (1980) *Aspects of secondary education in England: supplementary information on mathematics*. Her Majesty's Stationery Office: London.

This report contains detailed information about teachers, pupils, courses and schools.

62. H.M.S.O. (1978) *Special educational needs*: report of the committee of enquiry into the education of handicapped and young people. Her Majesty's Stationery Office: London.

The Warnock report; recommendations on how special education can be integrated into school and society.

63. Griffin D. (1978) *Slow learners*. Woburn Press: London. See p. 15.

This book about all slow learners has many messages for the mathematics teacher.

64. Johnson D.J. & Myklebust H.R. (1967) *Learning disabilities*. Greene & Stratton: London, New York.

Chapter 7 discusses problems and procedures with children who fail to learn mathematics.

65. Jones-Davies D.C. (1977) *Special pupils in mixed ability groups*. In reference 56, chapter 7.

Pupils with various handicaps and how an Extra Learning Centre can provide remedial help.

66. N.C.T.M. (1972) Lowry W.C. ed. *The slow learner in mathematics*; yearbook no. 35. National Council of Teachers of Mathematics: Reston. See chapters 2 & 9.

A book to provide methods and ideas of teaching the slow learner.

67. See reference 63, chapter 2.

68. Stockwell F.J. (1975) Remedial mathematics. *Mathematics in School*, vol. 4, no. 6, pp. 29–30.

A teachers' working party report, mainly about diagnosis.

69. Choat E. (1974) Johnnie is disadvantaged; Johnnie is backward; what hope for Johnnie? *Mathematics Teaching*, no. 69, pp. 9–13.

'Johnnie' is used to illustrate the problems of teaching mathematics to disadvantaged pupils.

70. Magne O. (1978) The psychology of remedial mathematics. *Didakometry*, no. 59. School of Education: Malmö, Sweden.

The rationale and development of a scheme for remediation of dyscalculia.

71. Ablewhite R.C. (1969) *Mathematics and the less able*. Heinemann: London.

A useful, but not very adventurous, book.

72. Williams A. (1970) *Basic subjects for the slow learner*. Methuen: London.

In this book, teachers are encouraged to expect a higher level of performance from their pupils.

73. See reference 63, chapter 4.

74. Berrill R. (1976) Mathematics and slow learners. *Mathematics in School*, vol. 5, no. 1, pp. 26–8.

A report of using tape recorders with ESN(M) pupils.

75. Pettican J. (1978) Mathematical games and puzzles for the handicapped. *Mathematics in School*, vol. 7, no. 3, pp. 4–5.

An account of five games and their use.

76. Womack D. (1978) On teaching the foundations of number. *Mathematics in School*, vol. 7, no. 1, pp. 28–30.

A discussion about pre-number activities and an account of teaching number in a special primary school.

77. Finlow D.J. & Winteridge D.J. (1978) Planning strategies for teaching the concept of number to E.S.N.(S) children. *Mathematics in School*, vol. 7, no. 2, pp. 9—12.

Learning characteristics and teaching strategies.

78. Wheatley C.L. & Wheatley G.H. (1979) Developing spatial ability. *Mathematics in School*, vol. 8, no. 1, pp. 10—11.

Three examples of spatial tasks which are suitable for some slow learners.

79. Lumb D. (1978) Mathematics for the less gifted. *Mathematics in School*, vol. 7, no. 2, pp. 2–7.

   Lumb D. (1980) Mathematics and the less gifted child in the middle years. *Mathematics in School*, vol. 9, no. 3, pp. 2–10.

   Two articles on their mathematical needs and available resources.

80. R.C.D.P.M. (1976) *Proceedings of the third national conference on remedial mathematics*; Research Council for Diagnostic and Prescriptive Mathematics. Department of Elementary Education, Kent State University: Ohio.

   S.M.S.G. (1964) *Conference on mathematics education for below average achievers*. School Mathematics Study Group, Stanford Junior University: Leland.

   Various papers were presented at these two conferences.

81. Frampton M.E. (1941) *Education of the blind*. Harrap: London.

   This book contains two short sections on mathematics in primary and secondary school.

82. R.N.I.B. (1973) *The teaching of science and mathematics to the blind*. Royal National Institute for the Blind: London.

   This includes articles about both primary and secondary school mathematics.

83. Payenbroek J. van (1972) *Arithmetic and mathematics: methodical and didactical aspects*. In reference 84, pp. 25–37.

   A general look at mathematics, and teaching it to overcome the special problems caused by deafness.

84. European Federation of National Associations of Teachers of the Deaf (1972) *Contributions to the education of the deaf: curriculum for the older pupils*. Rotterdam University press: Rotterdam.

   The proceedings of their second conference, held in Luxembourg, 9–10 October 1971.

85. See, for example, special journals for teachers of the deaf.

86. See reference 33, p. 184.

87. Bennett S.N. (1978) Recent research on teaching: a dream, a belief and a model. *British Journal of Educational Psychology*, vol. 48, no. 2, pp. 127–47.

   An article in which research findings support a model which emphasizes the importance of good classroom management.

CHAPTER 4

METHODS OF LEARNING AND METHODS OF TEACHING

Introduction

This chapter first illustrates that teaching has to satisfy and stimulate the thirst for learning, so that active learning and teaching are closely linked but are not identical. The link is made clearer by reference to psychological theories of learning, which lead to a discussion and analysis of the methods of teaching mathematics.

Capacity, learning and teaching

If each pupil's capacity for learning were fixed in the same way that a beer tankard's capacity for liquid is fixed, then the method of teaching could be regarded as a relatively simple operation – pour in a pint and that pupil is full. To carry the analogy further, think about a thirsty young man in a bar who asks for a beer. The bartender draws a pint which the man immediately drinks. The process may be repeated an unknown number of times, because the young man does not have a fixed capacity. What is known is that this capacity will generally increase if he forms the habit of drinking beer.

This story about drinking beer can be related to teaching and learning mathematics. The analogy would be that the beer which the young man drinks is mathematics which the pupil learns, and no one knows his or her capacity for learning. Before the 1950s, there was a common belief that we had each inherited a certain amount and type of intelligence which determined our capacity to learn. This capacity was measured by a person's Intelligence Quotient (I.Q.) and much of the research into this was pioneered by Sir Cyril Burt.[1] Further investigations during the last thirty years have not only discredited some of Burt's published results about inherited intelligence[3] but have also shown the amazing capacity of pupils to learn mathematics when they are given the right kind of teaching.[4] This is where the bartender comes into the picture, for he represents the teacher. The good bartender sells many pints of beer to the young man and knows about the different kinds of beer, but should also know when to stop serving him with any more beer. Similarly, the good teacher provides plenty of mathematics; he knows the different kinds, the methods of teaching and each pupil's capacity at any specific time. During the school year, every teacher should be able to stimulate the pupils' thirst for knowledge and help them to satisfy that thirst.

Learning, teaching and theories

We have reached the stage of considering a pupil who has a capacity for learning and a teacher who has a capacity for teaching. Although teaching and learning are closely related in schools, it is important to realize that a theory of teaching is not the same as a theory of learning. It is also important to distinguish between learning which is instigated and encouraged by a teacher and learning which occurs as part of a child's natural growth and development.

Without schooling, a child would take a long time to recognize triangles, because in family life he sees only a few triangular objects and numerous objects of many other shapes. A teacher will want to accelerate this recognition and so may give three different shapes only – circles, squares and triangles – made of rather similar materials. This teaching action quite likely originates from theories of how children naturally acquire concepts, rather than from theories of how they can best be taught these concepts. This is because, at present, mathematics teaching does not have a formulated theory of its own, so it has to depend on theories of general teaching and theories of mathematical learning, which will be discussed in chapter 5. However some attempts are now being made to connect theories of learning with theories of teaching mathematics. Readers are referred to the *Soviet studies in the psychology of learning and teaching mathematics*[5] and to the more modern book by Professor Hans Freudenthal[6] of the University of Utrecht, entitled *Weeding and sowing: preface to a science of mathematical education*, in which he is searching for a theory of teaching mathematics.

FIXED RESPONSE METHODS

Stimulus-response psychology

One group of theorists, who try to explain and predict people's simple responses during the process of learning, are the *associationist* psychologists. They studied simple actions and their consequences, and their best known term is *stimulus-response* (S-R). One meaning is that when a chosen stimulus (eg. 5×3) is given by the teacher, the pupil would immediately respond; if his response were correct it would be reinforced in some way such as praise and if it were wrong it would be corrected. The numerical example quoted above is of a very simple arithmetical skill only, but is rather important for teachers to know ways by which simple skills can be effectively learnt because their absence often puts a pupil at a disadvantage in later school mathematics.[7].

Rote learning

Such skills can be taught by *rote learning* i.e. by repetition of facts which are not understood, until they can be correctly written down or repeated as a parrot might repeat them. Sometimes this was the method by which multiplication tables were taught. The stimulus might be 'Say your three times table' and the correct response would be 'One three is three, two threes are six, ... ten threes are thirty.' This example demonstrates two disadvantages of such rote learning. Firstly, a pupil's response always starts at the beginning of the multiplication table so that he or she may have to recite 'One three is three, two threes are six, ... five threes are fifteen' before giving the correct response for 5×3. Secondly, while learning the table the pupil wastes progressively more and more time repeating facts which are already known in mastering the fewer facts which are still unknown. However these disadvantages may seem insignificant when compared with the time wasted by a child who always has to write down '3,3,3,3,3' (or even '111,111,111,111,111') and then laboriously add them together.

Drill and practice

Drill and practice can be a similarly instrumental method for teaching anything which is fundamentally a mechanical process. With subtraction, for example, a pupil can be given a drill which shows how to set it out and how to 'borrow one' from the previous column if need be, as in figure 4.1, and the pupil is then given several exercises on which to practise the drill. The pupil may do this practice either mechanically step by step or by thinking about its meaning. If a teacher includes a significantly different exercise (e.g. addition) amongst the subtraction exercises, the 'mechanical' pupils are identified as those who treat it like the other subtractions.

Although rote learning and drill and practice are commonly associated with teaching 'traditional' mathematics,[8] they are not absent from some present day classrooms. Some apparently modern

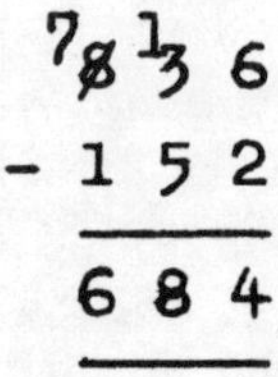

$$
\begin{array}{r}
{}^{7}\!\!\not{8}\,{}^{1}\!\!\not{3}\,6 \\
-\ 1\ 5\ 2 \\
\hline
6\ 8\ 4 \\
\hline
\end{array}
$$

Figure 4.1 A subtraction, using decomposition of the 8 (hundred)

mathematics is only traditional mathematics expressed in modern language; the exercise which was written as 'Evaluate 836 − 152' may now be written in a new text book as 'Perform the operation 836 − 152'. The pupils will do the exercises in the same way and a change of fashion is the only reason for that change in language.

Programmed learning and correct responses

Despite the criticisms already made, S–R learning should not be disparaged as there are occasions when teachers will find that they can use it effectively.[9] It was a basis for *programmed learning*,[11] which used carefully designed sequences of tiny units of work, through which pupils worked to achieve knowledge and understanding; each tiny unit was an effective stimulus and the correct response led to the next unit. Programmed learning has been successfully used by mathematics pupils[13] to obtain lower level educational objectives (i.e. knowledge and comprehension; see Bloom's taxonomy in chapter 8). Another occasion when S–R learning seems to be effective is for employees, e.g. craftsmen, whose work includes the solution of a limited range of mathematical calculations; the stimulus of any problem within that range triggers the correct solution as a response. On both these occasions, S–R learning has been associated with a high rate of success by the learner and this success is necessary as it seems to satisfy a basic expectation of pupils. Nearly all mathematics teachers know the satisfaction which pupils gain from giving correct verbal responses[14] or doing a page of correct practice exercises, and know how this can motivate them for the next piece of mathematics.

The right amount of practice in each stage

The amount of practice which each pupil receives has to be suitably judged by a teacher, and this is more difficult to judge with learning mathematics than it is with learning physical skills. If a child were being taught to ride a bicycle, the parent would not expect it to learn immediately and might start by holding the back of the saddle. Support like this gives the child confidence while it is learning basic skills but once these are learnt it does not need such support; in this example, the child may get annoyed if the parent continues to hold the saddle. The child now wants to practise progressively more difficult cycling skills.

Learning mathematics is rather similar. The teacher has to be prepared to give help as each successive curriculum stage is practised. If the teacher does not allow the pupil enough practice he will not be ready to move on to the next stage, so subsequently he will probably fail to learn that next stage, and so on throughout the sequence of lessons. This is the situation which has occurred when a pupil ends the year saying 'If only the teacher gave me time to learn...'. Conversely, there are teachers who give pupils too much practice, expecting them to do pages of exercises of the same type and feeling pleased because the pupils worked quietly all through a lesson, even if their mathematics has not progressed.

Somewhere between these unsuccessful extremes of too little practice and too much practice, lies the choice where the pupil has enough practice to learn new ideas or revise old ideas. The amount of practice required by older or more able pupils may be much less than the amount required by those who are younger or slower to learn. The important goal is to give all pupils that amount of practice which they need to allow them to move confidently on to the next stage in the teaching.

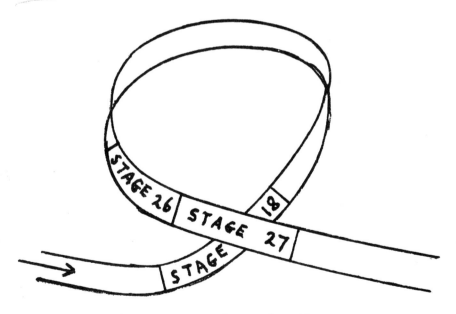

Figure 4.2 Progressive stages in teaching

Progressive stages in teaching

Progressive stages in teaching should not be considered as sections of a straight line, because that representation would restrict our teaching style. For example, Piaget believes in learning by accommodation whereby new experiences modify existing concepts, so that there has to be some way of going back to previous learning. Experienced mathematics teachers use a similar process when they start a lesson by saying 'Does anyone remember the lessons last term when we used...?' Therefore our representation of progressive stages in teaching has to allow a stage to recall earlier stages, as in figure 4.2, where stage 27 touches stage 18 and might also need to touch other stages. The best term to describe this is 'a spiral process.'

Progress and activity methods

An earlier section has shown that practice is not for its own sake but is to consolidate each stage of learning mathematics. Such progressive learning often comes from both rote learning and drill and practice methods.[9] Almost every pupil who uses these methods manages to gain new knowledge and understanding, which shows that the methods cannot involve only thoughtless repetition and reproduction.

To learn anything a pupil has to use mental activity, which is often supported by physical activity, so I classify all effective teaching as being by *activity methods* and do not restrict the term to teaching which uses some type of apparatus. That restriction is rather artificial because handling objects and writing are both physical activities, and there are times when writing on a piece of paper is just as valuable as cutting it into shapes.

INVESTIGATORY METHODS

Gestalt field psychology

Chapter 5 discusses the theories of Piaget and Bruner, who are classified as *Gestalt field* psychologists. These psychologists believe that understanding is developed by a pupil who meaningfully relates a new experience with previous experiences which have already been assimilated. Obviously, the methods of teaching based on these theories provide a great contrast to those based on the stimulus-response theories, and the major task of the teacher changes drastically. Instead of providing a stimulus (and teaching the pupil to make the correct response) he is now faced with the need to provide an investigatory activity (and teaching the pupil to relate experiences in a mathematical way).

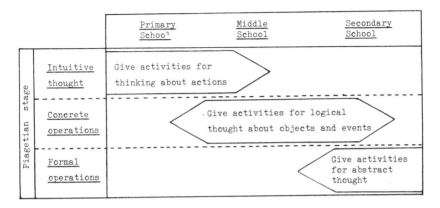

Figure 4.3 The kind of activities which teachers should provide for average pupils, based on Piagetian theory

The activity provided by the teacher must obviously be carefully chosen if the teaching is to be effective and two sets of guidelines, about matching and grouping, are now suggested to facilitate this careful choice. In the first set, the activities are matched to the developmental stages of the pupils. Piaget's theory is the most popular among mathematics teachers and it leads to broad guidelines as shown in figure 4.3. From this figure, for instance, 'activities for logical thought about objects and events of which the pupil has direct concrete experience' can be used at any time from upper primary school through to secondary school.

The second set of guidelines groups the activities into theoretical cycles by which topics can be taught and learnt.[15,16] Each cycle generally begins with some physical activity and passes through stages to reach a logical or formal conclusion, which is then available for use within the next learning cycle in a progressive sequence of topics. The two cycles proposed by Bruner and Dienes (see chapter 5) are shown in figure 4.4. Dienes' work was specifically concerned with mathematics teaching and applications of his cycle are given in his book *The six stages in the process of learning mathematics.*[17]

Discovery methods of teaching

The two cycles of activities represented by figure 4.4 illustrate *discovery* methods of teaching. This term is often used by teachers to imply that their school uses modern methods of teaching but the words must be used more precisely if they are to be a part of any discussion about improving teaching.[18] Firstly, let us consider the verb 'to discover'.[19] It is only possible to discover something which is already in existence, although that existence has previously been

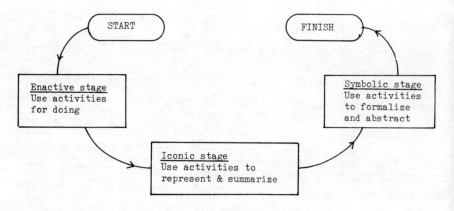

(a) Teaching activities for Bruner's three stages

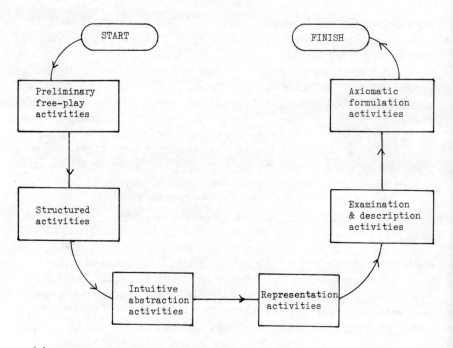

(b) Teaching activities for Dienes' six stages

Figure 4.4 Theoretical cycles of activities for teaching and learning mathematics

unknown to the discoverer. For example, Christopher Columbus discovered America but the land was already in existence. This typifies the discovery of a physical object but many mathematical discoveries are made in the mind. For example, in a lesson a pupil might investigate a set of geometric shapes and write out a table as in

SHAPE	NAME OF SHAPE	F NO. OF FACES	V NO. OF VERTICES	E NO. OF EDGES
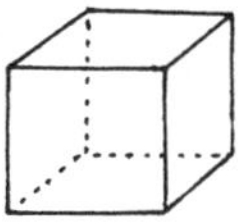	Cube	6	8	12
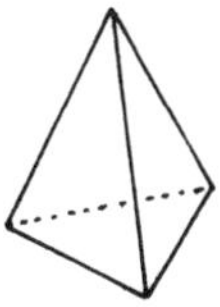	Tetrahedron	4	4	.6
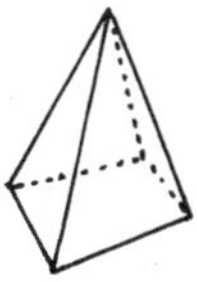	Square based pyramid	5	5	8

Figure 4.5 Part of a table of facts about certain solids

figure 4.5. Then, it is possible that the pupil would suddenly discover that, for many such shapes, the numbers have a special relationship which can be expressed as:

no. of faces + no. of vertices − no. of edges = 2
or   F   +   V   −   E   = 2

This relationship is known by other people but their knowledge of it does not prevent the pupil discovering it for himself or herself. In fact, forgetful people sometimes have the pleasure of discovering the same thing twice, which emphasizes that individual discovery in learning is frequently rediscovery of knowledge.

There are also recorded instances of concurrent discovery, when two people in different places discover the same thing at the same time. Euclidean geometry has been mentioned several times so far, and this is the place to mention non-Euclidean geometry because it provides a good example of concurrent discoveries. In the 1820s, when several mathematicians were concerned about Euclid's parallel lines axiom, Karl Gauss (a German), Nicholas Lobachevsky (a

Russian) and John Bolyai (a Hungarian) each discovered independently that Euclid's axiom did not depend on the other axioms and that it could be replaced by alternative parallel line axioms.[20]

These examples of rediscovery and concurrent discovery show that the discoveries made by an individual can be independent of all those made by other people. In school this means that all the pupils in one class may make the same discovery during the same lesson. Of course, this concurrent discovery of mathematics is unlikely to happen unless it has been pre-arranged by the teacher. Let us now consider how this pre-arrangement can be achieved by using any of the four discovery methods of mathematics teaching, namely, directed discovery, guided discovery, exploratory discovery and, last but not least, free discovery.

Directed discovery

The method of teaching by *directed discovery* can be explained by describing a lesson in one school. The teacher will have given every pupil a copy of the partially completed table shown in figure 4.5. He will also have put out on the desks several physical models of nine shapes (including the cube, tetrahedron and square based pyramid). He will direct the pupils to investigate the numbers of faces, vertices and edges on these shapes and to fill in six more lines of the table. While they are doing this, the teacher will walk around the classroom giving instructions to pupils who are not certain about the next thing to do. Near the end of the lesson, the teacher will probably go to the blackboard and write 'Discover a formula to connect the number of faces, vertices and edges. Check that this formula is true for every shape you have used.' At the close of the lesson, pupils who have not managed to discover the formula will probably be told to write:

$$F + V - E = 2$$

This *directed discovery* method contains a small element of discovery and requires very little initiative from the pupils. They are being prodded along a pre-determined path and their sole element of choice is the order in which they investigate the other six shapes. Even those pupils who discover the correct formula will not gain much personal satisfaction because most of the thinking has been done by the teacher. However it is not a wasted lesson for the pupils, who will probably have valuable practice in following instructions and will finish the lesson with a neat and complete table as proof of some activity on their part.[21] Although they did not all discover the formula, which is an ideal start to learning it, they will all have correctly written it down for use in the future.

Guided discovery

In *guided discovery* the teacher starts the lesson with a statement or question which suggests the right way of thinking about, and investigating, a situation. The pupils then start work and may come to the teacher for more guidance during the lesson. The use of this method in a school can again be illustrated by a classroom where the nine geometric shapes are put on the desks, but the pupils are not directed stage by stage. The teacher starts the lesson by saying 'Discover some relationships between the faces, vertices and edges of these shapes.' The pupils then handle and compare them. Some pupils will try placing the shapes in a meaningful sequence, discussing this with fellow pupils and then jotting down ideas in writing. Other pupils will follow different paths of action which either lead somewhere, or nowhere apparent, by the end of the lesson.

This *guided discovery* method allows some pupils to make significant mathematical discoveries but others just discover that they have failed to discover anything worth recording. This method therefore brings more success to some pupils and less success to others, when compared with directed discovery. After the start of the guided discovery lesson, the pupils have to use their own initiative in making a mathematical investigation so that they are expected to act as mathematicians rather than as typical school pupils. They could not do this without suitable preparation from previous activities which would have taught them, for instance, about the selection and recording of data.

This guided discovery lesson probably uses more apparatus than the corresponding directed discovery lesson, as most pupils will compare several shapes, instead of investigating each shape in turn. These pupils are also working at harder mathematics; such a comparison of the faces, vertices and edges of two or more shapes is a higher level of mathematical activity than just investigating one shape because pupils have to do two simultaneous tasks, to select (numerical) facts and form relationships between them.

Considering the outcomes of this guided discovery lesson, the teacher cannot expect all the pupils to have methodically written down the names of all nine shapes during the lesson, or to have all discovered the same relationship. At the end of the lesson he might make the pupils share their knowledge to provide a fairly common basis for future discussion and work. This sharing means that most pupils will have been told some of the knowledge, because a varying amount will have been discovered. The teacher must decide in what ways this lesson is better, or worse, than an expository lesson in which he tells selected facts to pupils.

Exploratory discovery

In the *exploratory discovery* method, the teacher structures the learning activity by providing or approving the objects or ideas which the pupils use, but does not give any instructions even as to the aim of the lesson. He is then available to give help to any pupil who asks for it. This is a more open ended method [22] than guided discovery and it is typically used in the early stages of a teaching cycle as in figure 4.4 so that pupils may explore the properties of some objects or ideas. Another common use of exploratory discovery is in projects, when pupils are working either individually or in small groups.[23,24]

Exploratory discovery can be a very interesting method for the teacher to use because, during it, he has many opportunities to discover how the pupils learn when they are not restrained. These opportunities can help him to devise better teaching strategies for use with other teaching methods.[25]

Free discovery

Free discovery comes from the natural curiosity of the pupil, about any objects or ideas. It is not initiated by the teacher but he does have a teaching rôle to play. He must show interest, give encouragement and provide advice if he thinks that it will help the pupil to learn more from that discovery.

A summary of the main methods of teaching mathematics

While these four discovery methods[26] are fresh in our minds let us consider their relationship to the other main methods of teaching mathematics. The discovery methods, together with experimentation, are the methods of *investigations by pupils* which are shown in figure 4.6 as coming between *fixed responses by pupils* and *expositions by teachers*.

A comparison of the four discovery methods

Although the explanations of these discovery methods have been illustrated by starting with geometric shapes, which are objects, it must be stressed that all four methods are just as useful when starting with ideas. In the summary of these methods in figure 4.6, they are placed in the chosen order because the sequence from directed discovery to free discovery has these properties:

1. an increasing element of pupil initiative
2. a decreasing probability of pupil discovery
3. a reduction in the equality of pupils' attainments
4. the teacher's rôle changing from director to adviser

NAME OF METHOD			DESCRIPTION OF METHOD
A c t i v i t y	Fixed responses by pupils	Rote learning	Repetition of facts, by writing or speaking
		Drill and practice	Demonstration of a drill, which pupils then practice by exercises
		Programmed learning	Teacher provides an effective sequence of activities, for pupils to reach set objectives
	Investigations by pupils	Directed discovery	Teacher sets goals, provides objects or ideas, and directs the activity as it progresses
		Guided discovery	Teacher sets aims and provides objects or ideas ; all these guide the pupils' activity
		Exploratory discovery	Teacher only provides objects or ideas, and the pupils explore them
		Free discovery	Discovery which is not initiated by the teacher
		Experimentation	Teacher or pupil states a hypothesis which pupils must prove to be true or untrue
	Expositions by teacher	Lecture	Teacher defines terms, expressions or symbols, breaks them into simple components which are explained, and finally summarizes
		Deductive	Teacher states a problem and then presents a correct sequence of steps which leads to a conclusion
		Inductive	Teacher considers particular examples, identifies their common properties, and states a generalization

Figure 4.6 A table showing the main methods of teaching mathematics

5. the teacher's image changing from one who knows everything to one who has to search for information
6. a decreasing efficiency in transmitting knowledge
7. an increasing difficulty in assessing and planning progress towards a defined end point.

Experimentation

It has been mentioned that the investigation methods include discovery and *experimentation*. An experiment is a procedure for testing a hypothesis, so this method starts with a hypothesis which is stated by either the teacher or the pupils. The teacher often knows that this hypothesis is either true or untrue but the pupils have to investigate its truth by devising a proof which suits their level of mathematical development. Some young teenagers are intrigued by formulae which appear to generate prime numbers and a teacher might propose a hypothesis about Mersenne's formula, $2^p - 1$, where p is replaced by a prime number. (Note that the first prime numbers are 2, 3, and 5; thus Mersenne's formula gives $2^2 - 1 = 3$, $2^3 - 1 = 7$,

$2^5 - 1 = 31$, where 3, 7 and 31 are also prime numbers.)[28] Pupils could fairly easily design experiments, which might use pocket calculators or computers, to test whether the formula always gives a prime number.

The experimentation method of teaching could also be used to study geometry, for instance when pupils investigate areas. The teacher might start the lesson by showing either figure 4.7 or figure 4.8 on the overhead projector screen. The pupils could then use squared paper and scissors to investigate the truth of the associated hypotheses.

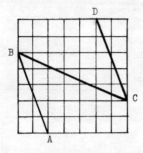

A square of area 7x7=49   Rearrangement of the four parts to form
is cut along AB, BC and CD   a parallelogram of area 10x5=50

Hypothesis: as area = base x perpendicular height
              then   49=50

Figure 4.7 An untrue hypothesis for the experimentation method

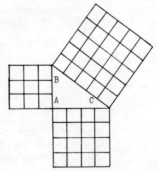

The triangle ABC, right angled at A, has sides of
length 3,4 and 5 units.   On the sides are drawn
squares with areas 9,16 and 25 square units, and
we notice that 9+16=25

Hypothesis: for every triangle ABC, right angled
             at A, $AB^2+AC^2=BC^2$

Figure 4.8 A true hypothesis for the experimentation method

EXPOSITORY METHODS

Exposition by the teacher

In the 1960s and 1970s investigative methods were fashionable with many primary teachers and some secondary teachers, most of whom searched for a suitable balance between these new methods and the traditional methods. *Exposition by the teacher* contains three of these traditional methods which have always been popular with mathematics teachers. Although there has been a decline in their use with primary and middle school pupils, they are still the predominant methods used with older pupils who are presumed to have developed to Piaget's 'formal operations' stage.

The following four reasons may be why these expository methods are popular with teachers. Firstly, they are mathematically neat and complete as each lesson contains a presentation and explanation of mathematics which lead to a conclusion. Secondly, they boost the teacher's self esteem as he is the fount of knowledge. Thirdly, a teacher can get satisfaction from presenting a complete syllabus in a sequence of lessons. Finally, the teacher himself has often successfully learnt school mathematics in this way and expects his pupils to do likewise.

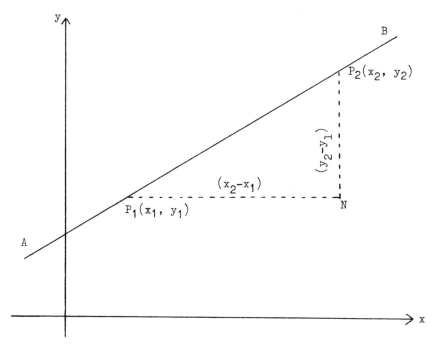

Figure 4.9 A blackboard diagram for the lecture method of teaching

Expository methods transmit information in only one direction, which is from the teacher to the pupils. This goes on fairly continuously over a period of time which may be for just a few minutes or may occupy most of a lesson. During this time the pupils should be thinking about the spoken information, and it is difficult for them to do this if they are also making notes about the information. The pupils will have more freedom to think about the mathematics if the teacher has a clearly stated and understood policy about notes. This might be to hand out any necessary notes at the start of a lesson or later, to pause every now and again during the exposition so that the pupils can make notes, or to give a reference to certain text book pages which contain the information. These general remarks about exposition by the teacher apply to the following three methods: the lecture method, the deductive method and the inductive method.

Lecture Method

The *lecture method* has three phases: (1) definitions of the terms, expressions or symbols which form the subject of the lecture; (2) explanations of the definitions just mentioned. Each individual definition must be broken down into simple components so that the pupils can understand them; (3) a summary which brings these components together so that the whole subject is understood by the pupils.

As an example of the three phases, consider a teacher lecturing about the gradient of a straight line graph. He could start with figure 4.9 drawn on the blackboard and would use the following main points in the lecture method.

Phase 1:
 definition

$$\text{Gradient of line} = \frac{(y_2 - y_1)}{(x_2 - x_1)}$$

Phase 2:
 explanation

A line has a constant gradient
On AB, choose any two points P_1 and P_2
P_2 has coordinates (x_2, y_2)
P_1 has coordinates (x_1, y_1)
From the right angled triangle P_1NP_2
  $P_2N = (y_2 - y_1) = $ difference in y coordinates
  $NP_1 = (x_2 - x_1) = $ difference in x coordinates

Phase 3:
 summary

Gradient of line AB = Gradient of segment P_1P_2
$$= \frac{\text{difference in y coordinates}}{\text{difference in x coordinates}}$$
$$= \frac{(y_2 - y_1)}{(x_2 - x_1)}$$

The deductive method

Deduction is probably the most neat and complete form in which mathematical reasoning is presented (see 'teaching the process or the tidy solution' in chapter 3). When using the *deductive method*, the teacher starts by stating a problem which explains a situation and requires a conclusion. School mathematics commonly uses problems of this kind which say 'given that certain things are true then prove this conclusion'. If this method is used with the intention of giving the pupil a relational understanding (see chapter 5) then the teacher must be careful to explain the situation in clear and simple terms, before logically using agreed rules of inference to move step by step to the conclusion.

A secondary school teacher frequently uses the deductive method when explaining how examination questions should have been answered by the pupils. The pupils may then copy down this answer and are perhaps impressed by this demonstration of the power of mathematics and the skill of their teacher.

The inductive method

When using the *inductive method*, a teacher considers a number of particular examples and focuses the pupils' attention on common

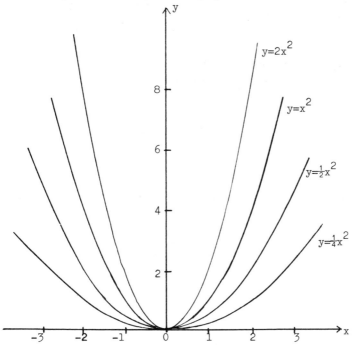

Figure 4.10 The parabolic graphs of four particular equations

properties which are present in all these examples. The teacher then states a generalization which is likely to be true for all other similar examples (and he has to explain what is meant by similar). An example of using the inductive method at school is to plot the particular graphs $y = \frac{1}{4}x^2$, $y = \frac{1}{2}x^2$, $y = x^2$ and $y = 2x^2$ as shown in figure 4.10. These graphs have the common properties that they all pass through the origin of the coordinate axes and that the x axis is a tangent to every graph. It is therefore likely that these common properties will be true for the graph of the equation $y = ax^2$ for every value of $a \rangle 0$.

Pupils will often find that the inductive process helps[29] them to solve a problem because when they consider particular simple cases then a pattern begins to appear. It is therefore important that teachers use the inductive method for two purposes, to make generalizations and to emphasize the process by which they have been reached.

Conclusion

All the methods of teaching mathematics have now been considered. Mathematics teachers in schools have often found it easier to discuss impersonal issues like the content of the curriculum rather than the personal issue of the methods which they are using in their teaching. They appreciate the value of analysing a mathematical problem by using familiar symbols, graphs, etc., and this chapter has suggested a vocabulary which can be used to analyse the process of teaching. If teachers begin to think about the style of their teaching and discuss it with their colleagues and pupils, then their teaching is likely to improve.

Annotated References for Chapter 4

1. Burt C. (1954) *Age, ability and aptitude*. In reference 2, chapter 1.

   In this chapter, Sir Cyril recounts educational developments since 1913.

2. University of London Institute of Education (1954) Studies in education, no. 6: *The problems of secondary education today*. Evans: London.

   The texts of a special series of lectures.

3. Hearnshaw L.S. (1979) *Cyril Burt: psychologist*. Hodder & Stoughton: London.

   An investigation of Burt's research, with the aid of his diaries.

4. Krutetskii V.A. (1976) *the psychology of mathematical abilities in school children*. University of Chicago Press: Chicago.

   A very readable book about research applied to a theory of mathematical ability. The bibliography contains entries new to many Western readers.

5. N.C.T.M. (1969-75) Kilpatrick J. et al. eds. *Soviet studies in the psychology of learning and teaching mathematics.* National Council of Teachers of Mathematics: Washington.

Fourteen volumes which are a valuable source of information.

6. Freudenthal H. (1978) *Weeding and sowing.* Reidel: Dordrecht.

An attempt to found a theory of teaching mathematics by observing and analysing learning processes.

7. S.M.P. (1974) *Manipulative skills in school mathematics.* School Mathematics Project: London.

A pamphlet which discusses the need for certain specified skills.

8. Wilson G.M. (1951) *Teaching the new arithmetic.* McGraw Hill: New York. See chapter 9.

Originally published in 1939, this book considers arithmetic to be a tool used by children and adults.

9. Sobel M.A. (1970) *Skills.* In reference 10, chapter 11.

Suggestions of how to develop skills alongside understanding.

10. N.C.T.M. (1970) Rosskopf M.F. ed. *The teaching of secondary school mathematics*; yearbook no. 33. National Council of Teachers of Mathematics: Washington.

Curriculum influences, aims and applications.

11. Gibby W.A. (1972) *The uses of programmed material in British schools and colleges.* In reference 12, pp. 286-309.

A discussion of the structure and application of this material.

12. Chapman L.R. ed. (1972) *The process of learning mathematics.* Pergamon: Oxford.

A book from a course of B.Ed. lectures which includes descriptions of four national projects.

13. Ausubel D.P. & Robinson F.G. (1971) *School learning; an introduction to educational psychology.* Holt, Rinehart & Winston: London, New York. See p. 336.

A presentation of Ausubel's theory, which focuses on classroom learning and teaching.

14. Ewbank W.A. (1977) Mental arithmetic - a neglected topic? *Mathematics in School,* vol. 6, no. 5, pp. 28-31.

Reasons for using mental arithmetic and examples of its use.

15. Servais W. & Varga T. eds. (1971) *Teaching school mathematics.* U.N.E.S.C.O. - Penguin: Harmondsworth. See pp. 23-4.

A book presenting the current international situation in curricula and methods.

16. Glenn J.A. ed. (1977) *Teaching primary mathematics; strategy and evaluation.* Harper & Row: London, New York. See pp. 14-17.

Recommendations for producing successful teaching and learning.

17. Dienes Z.P. (1973) *The six stages in the process of learning mathematics.* National Foundation for Educational Research: Slough.

Three studies which illustrate the stages described early in the book.

18. Deans J.F. (1972) *A note on discovery*. In reference 12, pp. 241–53.

A discussion of ideas expressed by many people.

19. Freudenthal H. (1973) *Mathematics as an educational task*. Reidel: Dordecht. See chapter 6.

A good book for the good mathematician.

20. Kline M. (1962) *Mathematics; a cultural approach*. Addison-Wesley: London, Massachusetts. See chapter 26.

An interesting book which stresses the wide significance of mathematics.

21. Kuper M. & Walter M. (1976) From edges to solids. *Mathematics Teaching*, no. 74, pp. 20–3.

An account of directed discovery teaching using rectangles and boxes.

22. Grossman R. (1975) Open ended lessons bring unexpected surprises. *Mathematics Teaching*, no. 71, pp. 14–15.

Infants and teachers explore numbers.

23. Curtis T.P. (1975) Two sixth form investigations. *Mathematics Teaching*, no. 73, pp. 40–3.

Computer based team work on numerical mathematics.

24. M.A. (1980) *The use of pupil's projects in secondary school mathematics*. Mathematical Association: Leicester.

A booklet about the content, supervision and assessment of pupil's projects.

25. Haylock D.W. (1978) An investigation into the relationship between divergent thinking in non-mathematical and mathematical situations. *Mathematics in School*, vol. 7, no. 2, p. 25.

Creativity, related to success in open ended activities.

26. Biggs E.E. (1972) *Investigational methods*. In reference 12, pp. 216–240.

Biggs E.E. (1973) *Investigation and problem solving in mathematical education*. In reference 27, pp. 213–21.

Two articles about teachers and children using investigations.

27. Howson A.G. ed. (1973) *Developments in mathematical education*. Cambridge University Press: Cambridge.

A survey of, and papers from, the 1972 International Congress at Exeter.

28. MacDivitt A.R.G. (1979) The most recently discovered prime number. *Mathematical Gazette*, vol. 63, no. 426, pp. 268–70.

A note which traces the history of Mersenne prime numbers.

29. Wills H. (1970) *Generalizations*. In reference 10, chapter 10.

The kinds of generalization, their employment and use.

CHAPTER 5

THEORETICAL ASPECTS OF LEARNING MATHEMATICS

Introduction

A knowledge of teaching methods should be linked with a knowledge of the way children learn mathematics. This chapter therefore first considers the familiar situation in school, and then shows how this can be related to theoretical aspects of learning. In school, pupils have a succession of mathematics lessons and study a sequence of topics. Over a period of weeks or years, the teacher has to plan each lesson so that the pupil develops his or her mathematical learning. If this is to be efficient and enjoyable, the teacher must consider three important aspects of learning.

Firstly, each lesson or topic is dependent on some skills and understanding which the pupil has already learnt. These may have been learnt during the previous lessons in school, or during the natural development of the child outside school. For example, a pupil who is trying to collect a set of triangular red objects must have previous understanding about triangular shapes and the colour red. He selects these two concepts of triangular and red from the immense stock of knowledge which he has built up.

Secondly, the sequence of learning can be varied, provided it meets the needs of the pupil and of the mathematics topic. For example, if a pupil chooses to collect rectangular objects before collecting triangular objects, or vice versa, either sequence is acceptable. However, an understanding about triangles and rectangles must precede any attempt to understand polygons. By handling, making and drawing triangles and rectangles the pupil will realize that these figures all have straight sides which form the complete perimeter.

These two common properties may then be used to build up ideas about polygons. This example illustrates how 'hierarchy' enters into psychological theories about learning as the concepts of triangular and rectangular are of the same order but the concept of polygonal is a higher order concept.

Thirdly, at later stages of development, the mathematics which has been learnt is greater than the sum of the mathematics contained in the separate lessons or topics. Compare this to building models with a Meccano set, where the plates, strips, wheels and bolts can be combined to make a toy car. On another day this motor car can be partly or wholly dismantled but the memory of it will be retained and the parts of the Meccano set can then be used to construct more models. In a similar way, when learning mathematics, a pupil who combines several particular topics in different ways may find that the common properties become apparent and a generalization can be made. This generalization will then be remembered as well as the separate topics. This resemblance between mathematics and Meccano is especially apt for those people who enjoy playing with mathematics.

This introduction, with three considerations of:

1. development from one set of topics to the next topic,
2. possible variety of sequence of topics, and
3. the whole being greater than the sum of the topics,

may now help the reader to study the psychology of learning mathematics. This psychology will be expressed by theories and the purpose of a theory is to represent the important parts of some situation. Each theory is a language and people who know that language can talk about the ways they teach and the ways their pupils learn.[1]

The study of the psychology of mathematics education

By analogy with the above introduction:

1. There are a number of theories of learning, and the reader should expect to find that they describe similar developmental stages of learning. This is not surprising when it is realized that they may be applied to the same children learning mathematics.
2. With these theories of learning, different readers of this book will choose to vary the sequence of study. For each theory there must be a foundation, such as the idea of a concept[2,3,4] which was introduced earlier in this chapter. Theories usually propose hierarchical stages by which learning is built up and provide suitable distinctive names for these stages, but it should be

noted that two authors may give different meanings to the same word. As no theory provides absolute truth, teachers often choose to support the theory which closely suits their own teaching. Individuals have a similar freedom to consider the following outlines, and then use the references to study any theory which, at some time, they choose.

3. It will be shown that a pupil who learns separate topics in mathematics, without understanding how these topics relate to one another, has a restricted form of learning. In a similar way, students who want to find out more about the psychology of learning mathematics need to know how the separate theories can be linked. The following pages therefore describe a route through the theories. This may be used in the same way as a holiday journey, starting anywhere, travelling quickly or slowly, exploring theories, and leaving at any place.

The psychology of general education

A study could start with educational psychology books published in the 1950s and 1960s[5,6] which provide a valuable historical picture, although today's teachers will translate some conclusions into different actions. For example, the statement that 'at 11 years of age, two broad aptitudes are discernible – an aptitude for academic, bookish learning, and an aptitude for visual-practical-mechanical attainments'[7] could have been used to support the 1960s British school system which selected about 25 per cent of the most academically able children to go to grammar schools. This statement now suggests the need to develop both aptitudes in upper primary and lower secondary education. A second example is the sentence 'Differences due to sex were very marked, boys being much more practically minded than girls.'[7] This conclusion might only have been used to confirm the need for boys, but not girls, to have practical training but actually it has led to a more detailed study of the psychology of sex differences.[8] These differences are not merely due to different forms and rates of psychological development but are also due to experiences within the family and at school.

This last sentence illustrates how the psychology of education has been changing, from an interest in rather fundamental and isolated learning processes to an interest in both the learning and teaching processes when the child is influenced by societal behaviour and by the school curriculum. The earlier interest, of course, has provided a solid base on which later workers have been able to build, but even then the move from earlier laboratory-type situations has not been easy. The child is influenced by so many factors, especially during the many hours spent out of school, that it is difficult to decide why or how a child has developed a certain skill or understanding.

FOUR CONTRIBUTORS TO MATHEMATICS EDUCATION

Piaget

The difficulty of discovering the processes of learning is especially evident in elementary mathematics education, as the child's everyday life provides numerous mathematical experiences. In this field of study, Professor Jean Piaget is one of the first researchers who made a substantial contribution[9] through his lifetime's work in Geneva. He is also a leader in changing such research from a measurement of the differences between individuals at one time, towards measurement of the differences in one individual between different times.

Since the early 1920s Piaget has been investigating many aspects of the development of young children, using the verbal responses which they made to questions. This 'clinical' method lacked a statistical basis and, for years, was not accepted by many other psychologists. Acceptance was also hindered because the incomprehensibility of his writings led educators to misuse his ideas, but books are now available which provide teachers with an interpretation in clear and relatively simple language.[10,11] These books have encouraged many teachers to apply his ideas to their teaching and, of course, this increased application has highlighted some inadequacies in his theories.[12,13]

In the last thirty years, Piaget's work on the child's concepts of number, space, volume, weight and time[14] has had a major influence on mathematics education. His research shows that these concepts are constructed from a series of experiences. He claims that two forms of construction are possible, *accommodation*, which is a modification of the existing concept and *assimilation*, which is an absorption of new experiences.

In Britain, Piaget's theories were first applied in primary schools. When a young child is learning mathematics, he has to develop these concepts of number, space, etc.[15] Piaget showed that this intellectual development passes through five qualitatively different stages, and the teacher must also provide suitable work which builds on experiences from the earlier stages. Even then, some children will never reach the final stage for all the mathematical concepts which they learn.

The stages are: (1) sensory-motor, birth to 2 years, when the child learns to organize his actions, (2) pre-conceptual thought, 2 to 4 years, when the child's concepts lack the generality of accepted concepts, (3) intuitive thought, 4 to 7 years, when a child can think about actions, but cannot make mental comparisons, (4) concrete operations, 7 to 11 years, when the child can think logically about objects and events of which he has direct concrete experience, and (5) formal operations, 12 years onwards, when the person has a capacity for abstract thought, for example to think logically about mathematical relations.

Using accommodation and assimilation during these five stages, the learner is forming his or her own representation of reality. Piaget insists that the learner must actively participate in the work in order to develop a 'construction' of reality rather than merely accepting a 'copy' of reality.

The validity of applying Piaget's Swiss research results to British children has been confirmed, although there is not agreement on every detail,[17,18] but research has only lately attempted to similarly study older children. Since 1974 the 'Concepts in Secondary School Mathematics and Science' project at Chelsea College, London, has been extending Piaget's work in order to identify a developmental hierarchy of understanding.[19,20,21] In 1978 an associated study, the 'Chance and Probability Concepts' project at Loughborough University of Technology, was started.[22] From the results of these two projects, the researchers hope to construct an 'overall concept map' which can be used as a guide when reforming any secondary school mathematics curriculum.

Bruner

For many years, Professor Jerome Bruner was the director of the Center for Cognitive Studies at Harvard University and he is renowned for his ideas on the efficient organization of learning.

The sequential stages of intellectual development which Piaget claims are necessary, are similar to those proposed by Bruner.

We would suggest that learning mathematics reflects a good deal about intellectual development. It begins with instrumental activity, a kind of definition of things by doing them. Such operations become represented and summarized in the form of particular images. Finally, and with the help of a symbolic notation that remains invariant across transformations in imagery, the learner comes to grasp the formal or abstract properties of the things he is dealing with.[23] (See figure 4.4 on p. 70.)

These three stages, which Bruner calls *enactive, iconic* and *symbolic*, are different *systems of representing reality* which may all be used by adults and older children while they are learning some piece of mathematics. Therefore, they are stages in the function of learning which cannot be translated directly into Piaget's stages of cognitive development at different ages.

Participation, through 'learning by discovery', is one important aspect of Bruner's belief.[24] He is not satisfied with pupils learning a body of mathematical knowledge; he also wants them to think like mathematicians. For example, he expects an older pupil with mathematical ability to solve a problem in the way he has discovered mathematicians solving problems, i.e. by thinking in the symbolic stage, but reverting at times to using iconic stage images to aid his solution. Incidentally, this reversion emphasizes that Bruner's three stages of development are not completely sequential. It will interest some teachers to study a pupil who is solving a problem, seeing the rough notes which are made during the process or talking to him about the method of solution. Just as a teacher is pleased when marking a correctly learnt exercise, he is also rewarded by evidence of original mathematical thinking by his pupils. These pupils could be sixth formers who have learnt to use advanced mathematics, or they could be ten year olds who have discovered number patterns.

Dienes

After his education in Britain, Zoltan Dienes worked at the University of Sherbrooke, Quebec, for many years and is an acknowledged leader in designing apparatus which encourages children to develop their mathematical learning by discovery methods. His theory of learning relies in part on ideas of Piaget and Bruner. He describes mathematical learning as 'being pre-eminently one of construction of predicates followed only afterwards by a critical, i.e. logical examination of what has been constructed'.[25] This is confirmed by his experiments with two types of mathematical tasks, one type emphasizing constructional properties and the other emphasizing logical properties. These experiments led Dienes to become an enthusiastic proponent for reversing the teaching sequence which had traditionally been followed. Instead of the teacher starting with a formal definition and examples, which the pupils then use while doing exercises, Dienes considers that learning should start with applications which the pupils actually experience and progress to a formal mathematical summary.

For this new teaching sequence, Dienes designed apparatus and planned its use by pupils who are learning concepts of arithmetic and algebra, and concepts of function, scalars, vectors and matrices. While using this apparatus, the pupils are performing mathematical processes as they pass through Dienes' six stages of learning; therefore they are acting as mathematicians as well as gaining mathematical concepts.[26,27] The first stage is preliminary free play which allows the pupils to become familiar with basic geometrical or numerical properties of some apparatus, for example discovering that certain pieces fit together in a satisfying way. The second stage is several structured games with rules and objectives, which leads to the third stage where each pupil abstracts the common structure between the games. In the fourth stage, this intuitively understood structure is represented by a graph or in some other diagrammatic form. This diagram is examined and described using some suitable language in the fifth stage, which leads to a formulation of axioms and mathematical proofs in the final stage. (See figure 4.4. on p. 70.)

Skemp

The last three theories, those of Piaget, Bruner and Dienes, have contained an upper level stage of logico-mathematical learning. A similar level occurs in Professor Richard Skemp's theory. Skemp is a mathematician and educational psychologist at the University of Warwick and in his popular Penguin book, *The psychology of learning mathematics*,[28] he contrasts an upper level reflective intelligence with a lower level intuitive intelligence which automatically classifies external data. In Skemp's terms, *schemas* are formed by fitting together concepts to integrate existing knowledge and assimilate new knowledge. He writes that reflective intelligence enables a learner to reflect on his current schemas in order to set up new schemas. These new ones may be of a higher order and may be more immediately useful. This can be illustrated by considering that a pupil has formed a schema while learning to add and multiply natural numbers, i.e. the numbers 1,2,3,4, etc. Once the pupil understands this as a whole, and is not just able to correctly perform some particular additions and multiplications, then he can use it as a building block to set up a higher order schema which also uses negative numbers. In Skemp's more developed theory,[29] when a person correctly makes these new connections between some concept, e.g. the negative numbers, and an appropriate schema (which already exists in his brain) he is thereby experiencing understanding.

In 1976, Skemp described two kinds of understanding[30] used in mathematics, which when compared with the earlier simple ideas of understanding arithmetic[31] illustrate the advances made in both psychology and mathematics education. The first kind is *instrumental understanding* or rules without reasons, for example 'I have learnt, and can use, the formula that area is length times breadth.' This kind is commonly known as mathematical 'skill', whereas a detailed description is 'the ability to apply an appropriate remembered rule to the solution of a problem without knowing why the rule works'. The second kind is *relational understanding* which includes knowing both how and why, for example 'Each little square is a unit area and I can fit rows of them into this larger rectangle to cover the area. Therefore I know that area is length times breadth and I can use this formula.' Relational understanding can be described as 'the ability to deduce specific rules or procedures from more general mathematical relationships'.

Probably we will all teach pupils who only have an instrumental understanding of area and therefore wrongly use $A = lb$ to find the area of a triangle. This mistake will not be made by the pupil with relational understanding of area, who may also be able to discover the correct formula $A = \frac{1}{2}lb$. This does not mean that instrumental understanding is bad, for there are times when it is an ideal tool. However, relational understanding of many schemas should be learnt by pupils of average and above average mathematical ability. I like to think of relational understanding as a friendship with mathematics (see figure 5.1), which is a much warmer relationship than a knowledge of mathematics.

Figure 5.1 We've made friends with maths

These ideas about different kinds of understanding interested many psychologists and mathematicians[32,33,34,35,36,37] They agreed not only that instrumental understanding and relational understanding are two kinds but that a third kind also exists. This is *formal understanding*, which is 'the ability to connect symbolism and notation with relevant ideas which combine into chains of logical reasoning'. These three kinds of understanding, if exclusive, can be represented by the vertices of a triangle (see figure 5.2). Then each point on, or inside, the triangle represents some quantitative combination of the different kinds of understanding (of a mathematics topic) which a person might have at a certain time. For example, the point I represents a solely instrumental understanding, such as that of a pupil who is correctly applying a set of rote-learned rules to solve an equation. Any point on the line IR represents some combination of instrumental and relational understanding and the centre, C, of the triangle represents an equally-balanced understanding of each kind. It is never true that one combination of the different kinds of understanding is intrinsically better than any other combination. Every mathematics topic has many uses and applications; its particular use and application by some person determine the most appropriate combination of formal, instrumental and relational understanding.

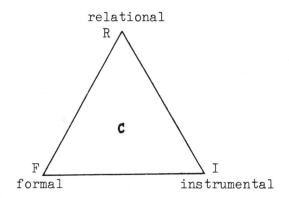

Figure 5.2 The suggested three kinds of understanding

OTHER FACTORS IN LEARNING MATHEMATICS

The work of Piaget, Bruner, Dienes, Skemp and their colleagues has been of great help in improving the effectiveness of mathematics education for many pupils. It has also been complemented by other investigations of the following factors in learning mathematics: the unequal development of boys and girls, their motivation, the rôle of instruction, mathematical ability, emotional involvement and the special nature of mathematics as a subject.

The psychological and sociological development of boys and girls

Two paragraphs earlier, we were considering different kinds of understanding, and there seems little doubt that more of the able girls than boys delight in including perfect instrumental understanding within their achievements. Many boys play down the importance of accuracy of technique and presentation in favour of a delight in relational and intuitive understanding.[38] This is supported by a comparative study of the G.C.E. Ordinary-level mathematics examination achievements of boys and girls who had apparently had very similar classroom instruction, as they were taught in the same mixed schools.[39] The examination papers contained both multiple choice and free response questions, but the examination results strongly favoured the boys, for only on a few multiple choice questions did the girls achieve at least parity with them.

The G.C.E. O-level examination only caters for the more able pupils but a similar sexual pattern probably exists for pupils of all abilities. As part of a research study which started at Sheffield City Polytechnic in 1975, almost all the 12-13 year old pupils in several comprehensive schools were tested for mathematical achievement. The results of individual test items indicate that girls try to apply known rules to recognized situations, whereas boys use more independent processes, e.g. intuitive thought, and are better at devising the solutions to problems.[40,41,42] Other somewhat similar studies have shown achievement differences between the sexes at the age of 10 years, and these differences have been shown to increase during adolescence.[43,44,45,46] As most of these boys and girls have received similar mathematics teaching in mixed classes, then their differences in achievement must be attributed to their differences in ability or differences in attitude.

Comparisons of boys with girls have shown that they have very similar mathematical abilities up to about 9 years of age.[47] After that age, it has been fairly clearly established that, partly from genetic factors, boys develop a greater visual-spatial ability while girls are developing a greater verbal ability than the other sex develops. This ability difference is a factor which can produce differences in achievement but it is probably less important than attitude difference. With the latter, a child's mathematical development is thought to be influenced by three social sex-linked factors: direct parental reinforcement, simple imitation and the child's concept of itself as a member of society.[48]

An example of the first is that many parents consider mathematics to be a masculine subject, so they expect boys to understand it but are ready to make excuses for girls who cannot. Therefore, at the age when school mathematics ceases to be compulsory, a comparatively higher percentage of girls drop the subject. With those who continue it to G.C.E. Advanced-level it has been shown that, although the fathers often influence the choice, the girls' attitude to mathematics comes mainly from their mothers' feelings about the subject.[49] In ways like this, adults subconciously help to shape children to fit into the existing adult society. Children also experience the social pressures of fellow pupils, which contribute to the second and third factors previously mentioned. Both in single sex schools and in mixed schools, many pupils seem to applaud or accept mathematical success for teenaged boys but tend to condemn it for girls. This may be linked with the personalities of girl mathematicians, who were shown by one study to be more intelligent, radical and 'masculine' than a comparable group of sixth form pupils who were studying French.[49] Although these may be the personality traits of most girl mathematicians now leaving school, girls with different qualities might become equally good mathematicians in schools which set out to encourage them. Schools with efficient and committed men and women teachers may be able to redress the present inbalance, wherein girls' attitudes to mathematics deteriorate over a period of secondary schooling when there is often an improvement in the attitudes of boys.[50]

Motivation

A few sentences before this, the social pressure of fellow pupils was mentioned and this is one factor in the motivation of a pupil. Most motivational factors seem to fall naturally into two groups,[51] the *biogenic* motives (e.g. hunger and pain-avoidance) which have a very marginal relationship with learning mathematics and the *sociogenic* motives (e.g. group-membership and expectation of success) which have a very direct relevance to good learning. Their apparent importance may be judged by the well founded view that 'the level of (a student's) performance is 50 per cent the result of differences in true ability and 50 per cent the results of differences in the strength of motivation'.[53] Success, experienced by teachers or by pupils, is a major factor in mathematics education. Success motivates people and failure disheartens them.

Instruction

Almost everyone will agree that it is desirable for a mathematics teacher to have good personal attributes and to provide good instruction when developing a pupil's mathematical understanding.[54] In studies of streaming in schools (see chapter 6) it has been shown that a pupil's level of future attainment is related to the level which the school and teacher expect, as well as to the level which the pupil has already reached. Therefore the pessimistic teacher should not look at theories of psychological development as an excuse for limited attainment, for example, that a group of pupils would never understand the concept of area. In contrast, there are optimistic teachers who use the theories like a map which shows the route that most pupils can follow if they are give the correct instruction.[55] Some of these optimistic teachers are enthused by love of their subject while others may be conforming with pedagogic ideas or national ideology. The last occurs in the U.S.S.R. where instruction is considered to have a major influence on the pupil's mathematical development[56] and any genetic component is considered to be relatively unimportant.

Ability

Most mathematics teachers distinguish between pupils' mathematical ability and general ability. In the Western world, there is reasonable agreement that general ability has these three components: solely genetic (contributing perhaps 65 per cent of the total), solely environmental (23 per cent) and genetic-environmental due to intelligent parents usually providing superior environments (12 per cent).[57] Teachers know, from working with pupils, that this general ability is linked with mathematical ability, although the links are as yet ill-defined. Since the 1920s, it has commonly been thought that mathematical ability has two distinct aspects,[58] namely, one for learning, selecting and reproducing mathematics and the other for creative mathematical work. People have unsuccessfully attempted to use factorial analyses to break down these two aspects into more detailed factors, and also to relate these two aspects to general ability, but our knowledge is still in the rather vague state represented by figure 5.3. Dr. Ruth Rees, of Brunel University, is one researcher who has recently tried to refine the 'learning, selecting and reproducing' area of figure 5.3. In her study of difficulties in learning mathematics she investigated two factors, a general mathematical ability (in which straightforward problems stimulate a response which always leads to a solution) and an inferential mathematical ability (which is needed to solve non-creative problems of a more abstract nature). Most workers who use mathematics, e.g. craftsmen, pharmacists and salespeople, only need this general mathematical ability which seems to be closely linked with general ability.

Mathematical ability is the subject of a stimulating and extensive book about U.S.S.R. psychological research between 1955 and 1966. The book is now available in translation[59] and provides very full details, for example, of a collection of test problems and the technique of interviewing testees to discover the nature of their mental activity. The researchers have used an interesting variety of non-traditional techniques, concentrating on the process of learning mathematics rather than on terminal objective tests, and the results

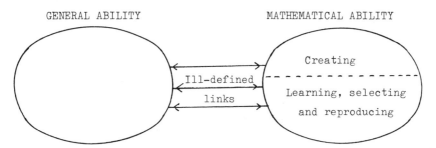

Figure 5.3 A representation of general and mathematical ability

advance our knowledge of the understanding of mathematical abilities. The consideration it gives to the needs of growing children is beyond any previously available in Britain.[60]

The phrase 'has mathematical ability' usually describes a child who has an above average talent for mathematics,[62] which is probably supported by a good or excellent general ability. Even for a gifted child, this talent is often recognized only by a mathematician, who should foster and encourage it. Characteristics which the teacher may recognize are suggested in a 1977 discussion booklet about gifted children in middle and comprehensive schools.

> The ability to calculate and the ability to reason about geometrical shapes were traditionally signs of mathematical giftedness; are there other less explicit indicators? Mathematical potential may be revealed by beautifully precise communication. Gifted pupils can have a wide vocabulary and a gift for selecting the appropriate word. ... They may detect ambiguity or imprecision in the teacher's mathematical language. Gifted young mathematicians want to generalize, ... what will happen, they will ask themselves, or their friends, or a teacher:
>
> - if we change the numbers?
> - if we work in a different base?
> - if we used letters instead of numbers?
> - if we turned it upside down, or reflected it, or enlarged it?
> - if we did it in three dimensions instead of two?
> - if we tried it with irregular figures as well as regular ones?
> - if we imagined it drawn on a balloon?
>
> There may also be a delight in logical fantasy; it is no coincidence that Lewis Carroll was a mathematician. Mathematicians often play chess and they are often musical.[63]

The child with little mathematical ability is likely to be weak in other subjects and talents, such as vocabulary and imaginativeness, but this is not necessarily so. Each child has his or her individual group of abilities.

> If ability is regarded only in terms of aptitude for learning, then a number of different kinds of aptitude can be distinguished. ... Imagination and originality, in the eyes of many, are qualities different in kind from intelligence as measured by standardized tests. Recognition of ability demands that these qualities are also taken into account ... Above all it appears that motivation and the will to achieve underwrite the effort of those who put talent to the greatest use.[64]

In this passage David Hopkinson, an H.M.I., is reminding us that the theoretical aspects of learning mathematics must go beyond a study of latent abilities to include a study of the emotional factors which lie within the *affective domain*.

Liking mathematics; the affective domain

Liking mathematics is certainly linked with being successful at mathematics, and, for pupils, success is usually linked with receiving a good mark, or a complimentary remark, for correct answers and for good work. These rewards are given by the teacher and affect the pupil's attitude towards mathematics, which is one of his, or her, emotional factors. We all have our own general idea of the meaning of the word *attitude*, but if we are to assess it and talk about it, there has to be a more clearly defined theory.[65]

As the study of attitudes to mathematics has only begun to gain momentum since 1960,[66] the results only offer pointers. A pupil's attitude to mathematics is an amalgamation of attitudes to specific factors of mathematics, which can be recorded on a scale ranging from strong approval to strong disapproval. Examples of such factors are the pupil's *perception of the mathematics teacher* and *self concept in mathematics* to which I have already referred, although some people may feel it more important to measure a pupil's *attitude towards algebra* or some other part of the subject material. One unresolved problem with assessing these specific factors is that the recorded change in any pupil's attitude, over a period of time, may be affected by his different interpretation of the words used; for example, does a pupil at ages 10, and then 15, years interpret the word 'algebra' in the same way? Some other attitudinal factors were indicated by a British study which found that 16 year old pupils chose to study more mathematics because they liked the subject rather than because they found it easy to learn, and that pupils with a mathematical bias preferred a symbolic mode of presentation of the work, whereas arts-biased pupils preferred a verbal mode of communication.[67]

Certain other conclusions about attitudes are likely to be generally true for British pupils, although often based on research from the U.S.A. As many experienced teachers may expect, attitudes to mathematics develop most around the ages from 8 to 13, and these attitudes will often remain for the rest of a person's life. It is therefore most important that pupils receive good mathematics education during these middle school years, especially as attitude has been shown to be a reliable predictor for later success or failure with school mathematics. This does not mean that all grossly under-achieving pupils are doomed to a lifetime of mathematical failure, as some pupils' attitudes improve with sympathetic and skilful teaching.[68] The most effective approach is to start from those parts of mathematics where the pupil can confidently succeed, thus deflating the *anxiety* about mathematics which so often appears as one factor in the attitude of people who are 'no good at the subject'. Linked with anxiety are socio-cultural factors such as the *expectations* of parents, teacher, or peers (described in chapter 7) and personality factors such as *introversion, creativity, intuition, perseverance* or *motivation*.

In the determination of any person's attitude to mathematics,[69] similar factors can be combined in groups which identify distinct characteristics. One such set of characteristics suggested for secondary school middle ability pupils,[70] is:

A. Representing commitment, interest and application to mathematics;
B. Tending to see mathematics as an algorithmic, mechanical and somewhat stereotyped subject;
C. Tending to see mathematics in an open-ended, intuitive and heuristic setting.

While A is probably linked with a pupil's general attitude to school and learning, it will be noticed that B and C require a measurement of the pupil's view of the mathematics itself.

THE NATURE OF MATHEMATICS

In this discussion of the development of mathematics learning, we have so far mainly considered the learner. As learning must demand some kind of matching between the learner and the subject, it is now time to consider the nature of the mathematics itself.

One must also invoke an understanding of the structure of knowledge and inquiry within the particular subject matter discipline whose mastery is sought. For example, if one perceives 'mathematics' as basically a body of strategies, heuristics, or methods of inquiry, then clearly an approach to instruction calculated to optimize process learning is most advisable. If mathematics is seen as a compendium of subject-matter understandings (e.g. arithmetic facts, computational algorithms, specific postulates or theorems), an approach which optimizes subject matter mastery would be preferred.[71]

It should be realized, however, that Shulman is referring only to the mathematics which is to be learnt in school. The nature of this mathematics is well discussed[73] in *The process of learning mathematics* where Dr. Baron writes of its growth and its existence as an invented creation which is related to the physical universe. In the same book, it is interesting to contrast this with the previous chapter, where 'some healthy entertainment'[75] by a university professor demonstrates that much about the nature of mathematics is not relevant for the majority of mathematics teachers. They will find relevance, for example, in applications of logic to mathematics education[76,77,78] and of mathematics to everyday experiences.[79]

We know that everyday life has been changing, and that the curriculum has also been changing. It would be wrong to imagine that the nature of mathematics, or at least our view of that nature, has remained fixed.[81] It has been wisely suggested that there are eight forces which 'influence and activate mathematical evolution, (1) cultural stress, both environmental and hereditary...(2) symbolization, (3) diffusion, in the anthropological sense, (4) abstraction, (5) generalization, (6) consolidation and diversification, (7) cultural lag and resistance, and (8) a process of selection.'[82] Other sections of this book show that mathematics teaching and learning are also affected by these forces, but here we will consider the three which are mathematically most important, namely, generalization, abstraction and symbolization.

Generalization

Generalization can be considered either as a process or as a statement. In this, it reflects two contrasting views of school mathematics, either as a creative activity or as a body of knowledge. Generalization is the process by which a mathematician passes from understanding one structure to understanding another structure which includes the former as a part; or it is the statement that certain structures have a particular property which can be extended to a finite or infinite number of other structures.[84,85] An application in school is that pupils may be encouraged to use an abacus when learning to understand the addition and subtraction of small whole numbers and then this helps them to build up a more general understanding of the denary system of numbers. Once this generalized structure is understood it may be used in place of several earlier structures; for example, pupils no longer need to know the separate facts that $3 + 2 = 5$, $30 + 20 = 50$, $300 + 200 = 500$, etc. This demonstrates that greater generality goes hand in hand with greater simplicity for the mathematician.

Abstraction

Abstraction is the process of identifying the essential core in one or more mathematical structures by ignoring the details which are, in some sense, superfluous. Once this essential core has been studied to discover its mathematical properties, the results can be applied to any other structure which has the same essential core. An example of two such similar structures is given by the mathematical joke that 'a topologist is a person who cannot tell the difference between a ring doughnut and a tea mug'. A mathematically superfluous detail is the materials of which they are made, so we may mould the ring doughnut from soft clay. As shown in figure 5.4 it may be remodelled

Figure 5.4 Turning a ring doughnut into a tea mug

into a tea mug without breaking its surface, so the obvious fact that the ring doughnut only has one surface is also a true fact for the tea mug. Most readers will now appreciate one common fact, or property, of these two structures. In school, pupils use sets of mathematical shapes, equations, etc., which provide many opportunities for them to practice abstraction.

Symbolization

Symbolization is a way in which we can carry out processes like generalization and abstraction, using rules to manipulate defined symbols. Mathematical symbols, which include words, figures and special signs, are also used to communicate messages to other people and we are all familiar with this on work sheets or in text books. Nearly everybody should be able to read, speak and understand those symbols which occur in their everyday life.[86,87] It has already been said that mathematics should be considered as a changing subject and the symbols in use today have developed over the centuries to meet the needs of developing mathematics and evolving society. If pupils study these changes, maybe using Karl Menninger's book[88] *Number words and number symbols*, it may help them to understand the nature of today's mathematics.

Conclusion

This chapter has shown that the present theories of learning mathematics have been influenced by developing ideas about the nature of mathematics and the psychology of learning. These present theories have been described, using examples of actual learning in schools.

Annotated References for Chapter 5

1. Hilgard E.R. (1964) *A perspective on the relationship between learning theory and educational practices.* Chapter 17 in Hilgard E.R. (1964) *Theories of learning and instruction*: Sixty-third yearbook of the National Society for the Study of Education. Chicago University Press: Chicago.

   The contribution of experiments and theories of learning to the technology of education.

2. Heritage R.S. (1975) What is a mathematical concept? *Mathematical Education for Teaching*, vol. 2, no. 1, pp. 19–22; Heritage R.S. (1976) Schematic analysis and mathematics teaching. *Mathematical Education for Teaching*, vol. 2, no. 3, pp. 25–32.

   Two articles which identify and link concepts used in school.

3. Rosskopf M.F. ed. (1975) *Childrens' mathematical concepts*. Teachers College Press: New York.

   Six summaries of research on symmetry, topology, area, limit, function·and logical inference.

4. Fischbein E. (1977) Image and concept in learning mathematics. *Educational Studies in Mathematics*, vol. 8, no 2, pp. 153–65.

   A discussion about models being able to initiate and generate learning.

5. Katz D. (1951) *Gestalt psychology*. Methuen: London.

   A late book on this theory of psychology.

6. Lovell K. (1958) *Educational psychology and children*. University of London Press: London.

   A balanced presentation of early ideas.

7. Peel E.A. (1967) *The psychological basis of education*. Oliver and Boyd: Edinburgh (See p. 198 & p. 197).

   The revised edition of a 1956 publication on aspects of development and learning.

8. Maccoby E.M. & Jacklin G.N. (1975) *The psychology of sex differences*. Oxford University Press: Oxford.

   A survey of actual and theoretical differences in intellectual performance and social behaviour. There is a superb annotated bibliography.

9. Piaget J. (1950) *The psychology of intelligence*. Routledge and Kegan Paul: London.

   Intelligence; its use, development, socialization and relation with perception and habit.

10. Beard R.M. (1969) *An outline of Piaget's developmental psychology*. Routledge and Kegan Paul: London.

    An account for teachers of the major features, using examples from Piaget's work.

11. Boyle D.G. (1969) *A students' guide to Piaget*. Pergamon: Oxford.

An account of Piaget's developmental psychology and its relevance for children's education.

12. Freudenthal H. (1973) *Mathematics as an educational task*. Reidel: Dordrecht (See appendix 1).

A suitable book for the good mathematician.

13. Ashton P.T. (1975) Cross-cultural Piagetian research; an experimental perspective. *Harvard Educational Review*, vol. 45, no. 4, pp. 475–506.

This article raises doubts about the invariance of stage sequence. A full reference list is included.

14. Piaget J. & Szeminska A. (1952) *The child's conception of number*. Routledge and Kegan Paul: London.

Piaget J. & Inhelder B. (1956) *The child's conception of space*. Routledge and Kegan Paul: London.

Two books which deal directly with mathematical development.

15. Steffe L.P. & Smock C.D. (1975) *On a model for learning and teaching mathematics*. In reference 16, pp. 4–18.

The model discussed has three phases: (1) exploration, (2) abstraction and representation and (3) formalization and interpretation.

16. N.C.T.M. (1975) Steffe L.P. ed. *Research on mathematical thinking of young children*. National Council of Teachers of Mathematics: Reston.

A presentation and discussion of six empirical Piagetian based studies related to primary school aged children.

17. Lovell K. (1961) *The growth of basic mathematical and scientific concepts in children*. University of London Press: London.

Piagetian theories applied to British children.

18. Shayer M. et al. (1976) The distribution of Piagetian stages of thinking in British middle and secondary school children. *British Journal of Educational Psychology*, vol. 46, no. 2, pp. 164–73.

Shayer M. & Wylam H. (1978) The distribution of Piagetian stages of thinking in British middle and secondary school children: II; 14 to 16 year olds sex differentials. *British Journal of Educational Psychology*, vol. 48, no. 1, pp. 62–72.

Two articles based on a survey using class-tests of Piaget's original tasks.

19. Hart K. (1978) The mathematics research of the C.S.M.S. project at Chelsea College. *Mathematical Education for Teaching*, vol. 3, no. 3, pp. 3–12.

A discussion about tests to measure understanding of topics common to many secondary school courses.

20. Hart, K. ed. (1980) *Children's understanding of mathematics*. John Murray: London.

Conclusions from the C.S.M.S. project. A most interesting book.

21. Küchemann D. (1978) Children's understanding of numerical variables. *Mathematics in School*, vol. 7, no. 4, pp. 23–6 and vol. 7, no. 5, p. 12.

Küchemann D. (1980) Children's understanding of integers. *Mathematics in School*, vol. 9, no. 2, pp. 31–2.

Three reports from testing 14 year old boys and girls.

22. Piaget J. & Inhelder B. (1975) *The origin of the idea of chance in children*. Routledge & Kegan Paul: London.

Fischbein E. (1975) *The intuitive sources of probabilistic thinking in children*. Reidel: Holland.

Two books about concepts of probability.

23. Bruner J.S. (1968) *Toward a theory of instruction*. Norton: New York (See p. 68).

A reprint of his famous 1966 Harvard University Press book.

24. Bruner J.S. (1973) *Beyond the information given*. George Allen and Unwin: London.

A collection of major papers on cognition, development and education, with a bibliography of his publications from 1939 to 1972.

25. Dienes Z.P. (1960) *Building up mathematics*. Hutchinson: London (See p. 40).

The theory and practice of building up mathematical concepts with primary school pupils.

26. Dienes Z.P. (1964) *Mathematics in the primary school*. Macmillan: London.

The presentation of novel mathematical situations by which pupils learn mathematics.

27. Dienes Z.P. (1973) *The six stages in the process of learning mathematics*. National Foundation for Educational Research: Slough.

Three studies which illustrate the stages described early in the book.

28. Skemp R.R. (1971) *The psychology of learning mathematics*. Penguin: Harmondsworth.

The ways in which pupils understand mathematics and its basic concepts.

29. Skemp R.R. (1979) *Intelligence, learning and action*. Wiley: London, New York.

The statement of a model of intelligence, of which many mathematicians will approve.

30. Skemp R.R. (1976) Relational understanding and instrumental understanding. *Mathematics Teaching*, no. 77, pp. 20–6.

Practical and theoretical aspects of meanings of the word 'understanding'.

31. Williams J.D. (1964) Understanding and arithmetic – I: the importance of understanding. *Educational Research*, vol. 6, no. 3, pp. 192–201.

Williams J.D. (1964) Understanding and arithmetic – II: some remarks on the nature of understanding. *Educational Research*, vol. 7, no. 1, pp. 15–36.

Two articles dealing with psychological and practical aspects.

32. Byers V. & Herscovics N. (1977) Understanding school mathematics. *Mathematics Teaching,* no. 81, pp. 24–7.

A proposed tetrahedral model of mathematical understanding.

33. Backhouse J.K. (1978) Understanding school mathematics - a comment. *Mathematics Teaching*, no. 82, pp. 39-41.

Understanding from the point of view of 'knowing'.

34. Godfrey R. (1978) Understanding school mathematics - classroom reality. *Mathematics Teaching*, no. 83, pp. 40-1.

Support for the tetrahedral model of understanding.

35. Meyerson L.N. & McGinty R.L. (1978) Learning without understanding. *Mathematics Teaching*, no. 84, pp. 48-9.

Four examples from secondary school mathematics.

36. Buxton L. (1978) Four levels of understanding. *Mathematics in School*, vol. 7, no. 4, p. 36.

The four levels discussed are rote, observational, insightful and formal.

37. Skemp R.R. (1979) Goals of learning and qualities of understanding. *Mathematics Teaching*, no. 88, pp. 44-9.

A synthesis of ideas about mathematical understanding.

38. Blackwell A.M. (1940) A comparative investigation into the factors involved in mathematical ability of boys and girls. *British Journal of Educational Psychology*, vol. 10, nos. 2 & 3, pp. 143-53, 212-22.

These articles review earlier researchers and describe a set of tests used with 100 boys and 100 girls aged $13\frac{1}{2}$ to 15 years.

39. Wood R. (1976) Sex differences in mathematics attainment at G.C.E. Ordinary level. *Educational Studies (Carfax)*, vol. 2, no. 2, pp. 141-60.

An analysis of answers to both multiple choice and free response questions.

40. Preece M. (1979) Mathematics: the unpredictability of girls? *Mathematics Teaching*, no. 87, pp. 27-9.

A discussion of some differences found between secondary school aged boys and girls.

41. Preece M. (1980) *Learning difficulties in mathematics with particular reference to girls*: report of a B.P. research project. Sheffield City Polytechnic: Sheffield.

A summary of the first years of research.

42. Isaacson Z. & Freeman H. (1980) Girls and mathematics - a response. *Mathematics Teaching*, no. 90, pp. 24-6.

Comments on Preece's article in reference 40.

43. Hilton T.L. & Berglund G.W. (1974) Sex differences in mathematics achievement - a longitudinal study. *Journal of Educational Research,* vol. 67, no. 5, pp. 231-7.

An investigation from 1961-1967 of sex-typed interests.

44. National Assessment of Educational Progress (1975) *Math. fundamentals: selected results from the first national assessment of mathematics: Mathematics Report 04-MA-01.* United States Government Printing Office: Washington D.C.

The title describes this report.

45. Kellaghan T. et al. (1976) The mathematical attainments of post-primary school entrants. *Irish Journal of Education*, vol. 10, no. 1, pp. 3–17.

The results of objective tests based on the content of the primary curriculum.

46. E.C.S. (1980) *The women in mathematics*. Education Commission of the States: Suite 300, 1860 Lincoln Street, Denver, Colorado 80295.

A study of 3000 pupils at ages 13 and 17.

47. Fennema E. (1974) Mathematics learning and the sexes: a review. *Journal for Research in Mathematics Education*, vol. 5, no. 3, pp. 126–39.

The results of thirty six research studies of American children from ages 3 to 18.

48. See reference 8, chapter 10.

49. Stamp P. (1979) Girls and mathematics: parental variables. *British Journal of Educational Psychology*, vol. 49, no. 1, pp. 39–50.

An investigation of parental influence on two groups of girls who studied mathematics or French in the sixth form.

50. Preece M. (1979) Learning difficulties in mathematics with particular reference to girls. A paper for the Spring meeting of *The Psychology of Mathematics Education Workshop*, Shell Mathematics Unit, Chelsea College, London.

'By the end of the year the mean attitude ratings for the boys and girls had diverged significantly'.

51. Rosenberg H. (1970) *The art of generating interest*. In reference 52, chapter 6.

An exploration of the psychological bases and the techniques.

52. N.C.T.M. (1970) Rosskopf M.F. ed. *The teaching of secondary school mathematics*: yearbook 33. National Council of Teachers of Mathematics: Washington.

Curriculum influences, aims and applications.

53. Atkinson J.W. & Rayner J.O. (1978) *Personality, motivation and achievement*. Wiley: London, New York.

A discussion of recent developments.

54. Butler C.H. & Wren F.L. (1941) *The teaching of secondary mathematics*. McGraw Hill: New York.

The first half of this book includes a discussion of the improvement of instruction.

55. Wheeler D. (1977) On not discouraging ourselves. *Mathematics Teaching*, no. 81, pp. 6–7.

There is a need for optimism if mass education is to work.

56. N.C.T.M. (1969–75) Kilpatrick J. et al. eds. *Soviet studies in the psychology of learning and teaching mathematics*. National Council of Teachers of Mathematics: Washington.

Fourteen volumes which are a valuable source of information.

57. Vernon P.E. (1979) Intelligence testing and the nature/nurture debate, 1928–1978: what next? *British Journal of Educational Psychology*, vol. 49, no. 1, pp. 1–14.

A reply to common criticisms of I.Q. testing and a discussion of the present position.

58. See reference 38.

59. Krutetskii V.A. (1976) *The psychology of mathematical abilities in school children.* University of Chicago Press: Chicago.

A very readable book about research applied to a theory of mathematical ability. The bibliography contains entries new to many Western readers.

60. Peel E.A. (1971) *Psychological and educational research bearing on mathematics teaching.* In reference 61, pp. 152-4.

An interesting summary, with references.

61. Servais W. & Varga T. eds. (1971) *Teaching school mathematics.* U.N.E.S.C.O.-Penguin: Harmondsworth.

A book presenting the international situation in curricula and methods.

62. Stanley J.C. et al. eds. (1973) *Mathematical talent; discovery, description and development.* John Hopkins University Press: Baltimore.

The proceedings of a symposium on research in early childhood education.

63. H.M.S.O. (1977) *Gifted children in middle and comprehensive secondary schools*: Matters for discussion no. 4. Her Majesty's Stationery Office: London See p. 71.

Giftedness is defined and its place in school and subject considered.

64. Hopkinson D. (1978) *The education of gifted children.* Woburn Press: London See pp. 39-40.

A book about all gifted children but also with special reference to mathematics education.

65. Hoyles C. (1975) Attitudes and motivational factors in mathematics learning. *Mathematical Education for Teaching*, vol. 2, no. 2, pp. 33-8.

Starting from the deficit and growth needs of Herzberg's theory, the author has used interviews to identify affective factors.

66. Aiken L.R. (1970) Attitudes toward mathematics. *Review of Educational Research*, vol. 40, no. 4, pp. 551-96.

Aiken L.R. (1976) Update on attitudes and other affective variables in learning mathematics. *Review of Educational Research*, vol. 46, no. 2, pp. 293-311.

Two reviews of articles and theses, with many references.

67. Kempa R.F. & McGough J.M. (1977) A study of attitudes towards mathematics in relation to selected student characteristics. *British Journal of Educational Psychology*, vol. 47, no. 3, pp. 296-304.

A 1975 study on over 300 pupils in first year sixth form.

68. Magme O. (1978) The psychology of remedial mathematics. *Didakometry*, no. 59. School of Education, Malmö, Sweden.

The rationale and development of a scheme for remediation of dyscalculia.

69. Hall E. (1978) *Using personal constructs*: Rediguide no. 9. Thomas K.C. (1978) *Attitude assessment*: Rediguide no. 7. University of Nottingham School of Education: Nottingham.

Two research guides which explain about measuring people's attitudes.

70. P.M.E.W. (1975) *Psychology of Mathematics Education workshop report*; 13 June 1975. Centre for Science Education, Chelsea College: London See p. 4.

Two papers on attitude and motivation to mathematics.

71. Shulman L.S. (1970) *Psychology and mathematics education.* In reference 72, p. 70.

An interesting summary published for the N.S.S.E.

72. Begle E.C. (1970) *Mathematics education; yearbook 69.1 of the National Society for the Study of Education.* University of Chicago Press: Chicago.

The new curriculum in mathematics: educational and psychological problems and solutions.

73. Baron M.E. (1972) *The nature of mathematics – another view.* In reference 74, pp. 21–41.

The view of a lecturer from a College of Education.

74. Chapman L.R. ed. (1972) *The process of learning mathematics.* Pergamon: Oxford.

A book from a course of B.Ed. lectures.

75. Kilmister C.W. (1972) *The nature of mathematics.* In reference 74, pp. 1–20.

Mathematical proof, truth, and a historical sketch-pad by a pure mathematician.

76. Mercer J.A. (1972) *The role of logic.* In reference 74, pp. 66–86.

The applications of logic and proof, rather than the philosophy.

77. See reference 12, chapter 19.

78. O'Brien T.C. (1972) Logical thinking in adolescents, *Educational Studies in Mathematics*, vol. 4, no. 4, pp. 401–28.

A study of high school students' ability to recognize and use four forms of implication.

79. Hawkins D. (1973) *Nature, man and mathematics.* In reference 80, pp. 115–35.

The kinds of mathematics which are needed by children.

80. Howson A.G. ed. (1973) *Developments in mathematical education.* Cambridge University Press: Cambridge.

A survey of, and papers from, the 1972 International Congress at Exeter.

81. Dubbey J.M. (1970) *Development of modern mathematics.* Butterworths: London.

A chronological development from pre-history to the present, which describes mathematical topics and schools of thought.

82. Wilder R.L. (1972) *The nature of modern mathematics.* In reference 83, p. 40.

Mathematics is a science, developing new concepts and methods.

83. Lamon W.E. ed. (1972) *Learning and the nature of mathematics.* Science Research Associates: Chicago.

The development, pedagogy, psychology and communication of mathematics.

84. Wills H. (1970) *Generalization.* In reference 52, chapter 10.

The kinds of generalizations, their employment and use.

85. Plumpton C. (1972) *Generalization and structure.* In reference 74, pp. 87–121.

A discussion which uses examples from sixth form pure and applied mathematics.

86. Harkin J.B. & Rising G.R. (1974) Some psychological and pedagogical aspects of mathematical symbolism. *Educational Studies in Mathematics*, vol. 5, no. 3, pp. 255-60.

Difficulties with ambiguous, synonymous, archaic, inappropriate and contradictory symbols.

87. Woodrow D. (1976) Words, signs and symbols. *Mathematical Education for Teaching*, vol. 2, no. 3, pp. 19-24.

Symbolic expression is a common feature of mathematical activity but there is little information about how and when we learn to use symbols.

88. Menninger K. (1969) *Number words and number symbols*. Massachusetts Institute of Technology Press: Cambridge (Mass), London.

A cultural history of nearly every aspect of numbers throughout the world.

CHAPTER 6

GROUPING AND ORGANIZATION

Introduction

Pupils need to be grouped so that their education can be organized in an appropriate way. In fact, grouping and organization influence mathematics teaching more than most people realize. This chapter will describe the various methods of grouping and also the uses of these groups in the organization of mathematics teaching and learning. To start with grouping, let us consider a typical G.C.E. mathematics fifth form which is, in many ways, similar to its counterpart in other schools following a broadly similar curriculum. We shall call this group the 'fifth form G.C.E. class'. This title gives useful, but limited, information which might be sufficient for someone who is enquiring about the organization of mathematics in the school. However, anyone who is to teach that class needs more explicit information, for example about smaller groups of pupils in that class or even about individuals, before he or she can successfully do so.

The previous paragraph mentioned a fifth form class, containing perhaps twenty five pupils, as one particular group but it must be realized that groups may be of any size. They may be much larger, as in a school which has several hundred pupils who all wear the same uniform. On the other hand, a remedial mathematics group may contain only four pupils.

METHODS OF GROUPING PUPILS

Grouping by age and sub-grouping by ability, interest, etc.

The British system of primary and secondary education is dominated, and even restricted, by an overriding concern for the age of pupils and almost the only exception which has been considered is the early transfer of gifted pupils to a higher class or school.[1] We are so used to this system that we accept the restriction as a normal phenomenon. I remember an American exchange-teacher who wanted to enrol his $12\frac{1}{2}$ year old daughter at a local British school for two years. He was amazed when, just because of her age, she was expected to join a second year class and he protested that the headteacher had not fully considered his daughter's previous education. He emphasized that his daughter had never before studied French or algebra and had probably studied different topics from British pupils in other subjects. Moreover, she had started school at 6 years of age, a year later than British children, and would re-enter the American system when they returned home. However, the headteacher was adamant that the girl went into a second year class because of her age; any other details were considered irrelevant.

In some schools, these other details may be considered relevant, as is shown in community schools where adults are encouraged to join classes where they and the younger pupils learn together. Normally, however, grouping by age comes first and then further grouping by interest, ability, aptitude, etc. may follow. A mathematics teacher should be aware that grouping by ability (see chapter 5) may use either the *mathematical ability* of pupils or their *general ability*. (This general ability is often measured by a combination of three separate assessments in mathematics, English and verbal reasoning.) The following pages will show that special ability in the subject is considered when setting pupils, general ability is considered when

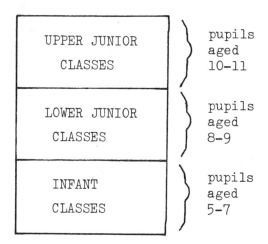

Figure 6.1 Vertical grouping in a primary school

streaming pupils, and either kind is used for other ability groupings, e.g. mixed ability.

Nine methods of grouping will now be defined or described, using familiar examples from primary and secondary school. Because most of the readers of this book are likely to be interested in mathematics, and because the study of patterns is an important part of doing mathematics, diagrams will be used to emphasize patterns in the groupings.

Vertical grouping

Vertical grouping occurs when all the pupils within an age range of two years or more are grouped together. They can then be taught by one or more teachers.

An example of vertical grouping in a primary school is illustrated by figure 6.1. (Primary schools sometimes use the name 'family grouping' as an alternative to 'vertical grouping'.) If there were about ninety pupils in one of these vertical groups, they would then be regrouped into three classes, using one or more of the following grouping methods.

Random ability grouping

Random ability grouping occurs when, without measurement of ability, pupils are assigned to convenient sized working groups.

An example of random ability grouping comes from a five-form entry comprehensive school. All the pupils in the first year can be randomly assigned to classes by writing 1,2,3,4,5,1,2,3,4,5,1,2,3, ... etc. alongside their names on an alphabetic list so as to form the five classes. As there is no regular link between each pupil's position on the alphabetic list and that pupil's ability, this simple procedure for random ability grouping might, by chance, produce mixed ability groups of pupils.

Mixed ability grouping

Mixed ability grouping occurs when the ability (and maybe the aptitude) of the pupils is assessed, and then the pupils are assigned to convenient sized working groups so that each group contains pupils with a wide range of ability and aptitude.[1]

An example of mixed ability groups within a class is when every working group of four or five pupils is selected to contain one of the brightest pupils, one of the weakest, and two or three across the range in between brightest and weakest.[2] This grouping aims for social cooperation as well as academic development, and it can enable the brightest pupil to set a high academic standard for the group and to help the less able members to learn about mathematics.

Banding

Banding occurs when all the pupils within an age range are assessed by reference to ability and are then grouped in bands, so that each separate band:

(1) contains pupils of mixed ability, although maybe not from the full range of ability

(2) generally contains enough pupils for two, three or four classes.

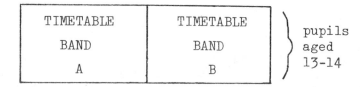

TIMETABLE BAND A	TIMETABLE BAND B

pupils aged 13-14

Figure 6.2 An example of banding, linked with timetable organization

Figure 6.2. illustrates banding when pupils are assigned to two parallel, full ability range, bands to facilitate timetable organization and to make team teaching possible. For example, in a six form entry school, there will be three classes in band A and three classes in band B. In either band, the three classes will always have mathematics lessons at the same time which makes team teaching simple to operate. Also, if mathematics lessons for band A classes do not coincide with lessons for band B classes, only three sets of apparatus are needed and a group of only three teachers needs to be concurrently available.

UPPER BAND GCE	MIDDLE BAND CSE	LOWER BAND NO EXAM

pupils aged 15-16

Figure 6.3 An example of banding, linked with public examinations

Figure 6.3. illustrates a rather different application of banding, when 15 year old pupils are separated into three bands. There is a smallish upper ability band whose pupils will take the G.C.E. Ordinary-level examination and a small lower ability band whose pupils will not take any public examination. All the remaining pupils, who will take the C.S.E. examinations, are in a large middle band. There may be only two classes in the upper band and one in the lower band, while the middle band may contain enough pupils to be regrouped into three classes.

These last three methods of grouping (random, mixed and banding) have all been based on groups of mixed ability pupils although in the last example, linked with public examinations, none of the three mixed ability bands contains pupils from the full range of ability. The next two methods are solely based on groups of similar ability pupils.

Streaming

Streaming is a similar ability grouping which extends over two or more years of school. At the start, pupils are assessed by reference to general ability (and aptitude). From this assessment, each pupil's name is placed on a list which ranks pupils from those with the highest ability down to those with the lowest ability. This list is then divided into several parts to assign the pupils to their respective working groups. These groups are used for almost all subject teaching.

5A	5B	5C	5D	5E
4A	4B	4C	4D	4E
3A	3B	3C	3D	3E

} pupils aged 13–16

Figure 6.4 General ability streams (A, B, C, D, E) in a secondary school

Figure 6.4. illustrates an example of streaming during the third, fourth and fifth years at secondary school. For each year there are five classes, with the A stream pupils having the highest general ability and the E stream pupils having the lowest general ability. Most pupils will remain in one stream for all three years, as is implied by the name 'streaming'.

Setting

Setting is a similar ability grouping which extends, usually, for one school year. At the start, the pupils are assessed by reference to mathematical ability. From this assessment, each pupil's name is placed in a list which ranks pupils from those with the highest ability to those with the lowest ability, and this list is then divided into several parts to assign the pupils to their respective mathematics sets.

Figure 6.5 Mathematical ability sets in a primary school

An example of setting in a primary school which has a basic mixed ability group structure (see figure 6.5.) is when 9 year old pupils are reorganized into sets for the next year's mathematics teaching only. This is known to be a common primary school practice and the 1978 H.M.I.s' primary school survey found that 72 per cent of mathematics classes had been formed by setting or streaming.[3]

Friendship grouping

Friendship grouping occurs when friends come together to form groups, as happens naturally in the school playground. In the classroom, a teacher may state the maximum and minimum numbers in any group, before allowing the pupils to select their own groups. Friendship between pupils is important to them so that these groups will often naturally produce good working relationships. Even some poorly motivated pupils will work at their mathematics to keep their group together. When friendship groups are formed, the teacher must be prepared to influence their membership to avoid one pupil being isolated and thereby identified as being friendless.[4]

Interest grouping

Interest grouping brings pupils together to work at a common interest. These groups are most often used with investigational methods of teaching (see chapter 4) and are usually formed by a combination of the decisions made by pupils and teacher. For example, although the pupils are allowed to choose a mathematics topic which interests them, the teacher ensures that each pupil is following a progressive sequence of topics. The presence of an isolated pupil is not undesirable with mathematics interest grouping; it does not identify that pupil as a social outcast because it is not a social grouping, and it does not identify that pupil as a poor mathematician because some good mathematicians will probably choose to work alone.

Sex grouping

Sex grouping occurs when girls and boys are segregated into single sex schools, classes and other educational groups. Earlier in this century some sex grouping was common for all pupils, except the very youngest, and evidence of this can still be found on old school buildings in many places. There are even old primary school buildings which still have the original three entrances with the words 'boys', 'girls' and 'mixed infants' carved above the doors which lead into the playgrounds. In primary education, sex grouping is now rare and out of 22 685 British primary schools in 1976[5] only fifty were solely for boys and forty five for girls. About one fifth of the 4173 secondary schools were still single sex, despite the swing towards a higher percentage of mixed secondary schools. This swing came with comprehensive education, when for example a large comprehensive school was formed by amalgamating neighbouring boys' and girls' schools. Such amalgamation into mixed schools often brings social and administrative benefits but there is no evidence that mixed classes are better for mathematics teaching and learning. As is shown in figure 6.6, in almost all secondary school mathematics lessons the boys and girls seem to work in separate groups. This apparently natural wish to be segregated seems to be further emphasized in the upper secondary school, where it has been found[6] that girls attending mixed schools are less likely to choose sixth form mathematics than are girls attending girls' schools.

Figure 6.6 In a mixed secondary school, the boys and girls often choose to work in separate groups

The same grouping methods in schools and L.E.A.s

For the nine methods of grouping which have just been described, most of the examples have been about schools and classes. Although that is the context in which teachers usually think about grouping, the same methods of grouping are also applied by Local Education Authorities (L.E.A.s). These L.E.A. groupings are used to determine which pupils enter which schools, and must influence which pupils are in any class. Therefore, the different methods practised by L.E.A.s will now be considered and teachers of mathematics should recognize the same grouping patterns which have already been seen within schools and classes.

Banding is often used to facilitate the transfer of pupils from many primary schools to several secondary comprehensive schools. In the final year at primary school every pupil's general ability is assessed and his or her name (i.e. not the actual pupil) is placed in an upper, middle or lower ability band. Each secondary school must then accept a balance of pupils across the three bands, thereby ensuring a reasonably mixed ability entry into every secondary school. This example of banding within an L.E.A. is illustrated in figure 6.7 and a comparison with figure 6.3. will show the same grouping method applied within a school.

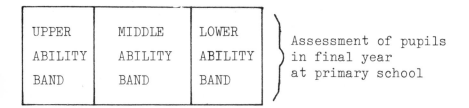

Figure 6.7 An example of banding, to transfer pupils from LEA primary to secondary schools

Streaming is used by those L.E.A.s in which nearly all the high ability pupils attend grammar schools and all the middle and lower ability pupils attend comprehensive schools, except for pupils with significantly different mental, sensory, physical or emotional characteristics who attend special schools.[8,9] This is illustrated in figure 6.8, which has three columns (streams over several years) like the five columns seen in figure 6.4. One social effect of these last two examples of banding and streaming is to extend the catchment area from which pupils are drawn for any one school. In an L.E.A. with a policy of neighbourhood schools, most pupils attend the school nearest to their own homes so that the catchment areas are relatively small. This can produce schools where most pupils belong to one class or ethnic group, and the mathematics teaching has to be appropriately organized.

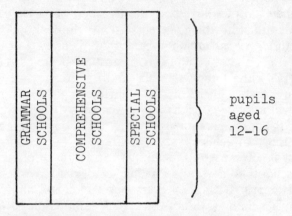

Figure 6.8 General ability streams in LEA secondary schools

As a last example of the same grouping methods in schools and L.E.A.s, we will consider vertical grouping. Figure 6.1 has shown its application in a primary school and the same pattern is evident in figure 6.9 which illustrates schools within an L.E.A.

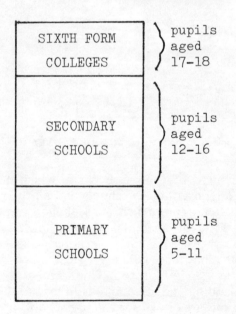

Figure 6.9 Vertical grouping in an LEA

USING GROUPINGS

Sequences of groupings

This chapter began by considering a group with the title 'fifth form G.C.E. class'. It was then realized that a teacher who was unfamiliar with the group needed to know more than the mere title to understand how to successfully teach the group. The class title, indeed, is only a start to such understanding and the teacher needs to place those pupils in the context of the school, its catchment area and the Local Education Authority's policy for grouping. One way a teacher can do this is to follow the sequence of groupings which has brought the pupils to his or her class. There are usually good reasons why some of the separate groupings, already described in previous pages, have been combined into that sequence. With an understanding of those reasons and a knowledge of any further suitable groupings within the class, the teacher should be better prepared and able to select a teaching style which will suit these pupils.

Equivalent outcomes from sequences of groupings

Despite possible variety in the sequences of groupings, the main desired outcome does not change; it is that pupils should learn mathematics. It has been found that this outcome may be difficult to achieve after certain sequences of grouping; for instance, when some low ability 14 year old pupils are in a strongly academic setting system. However, many equivalent outcomes are achieved in schools which use different sequences of groupings and it is certain that the sequence cannot wholly determine the outcome. An illustration of this certainty comes from considering how a primary school pupil who is given a collection of red or blue triangles and circles, sorts the collection into four different sets. The outcome can be achieved in two ways: either by the sequence which firstly groups them into red shapes and blue shapes and then, secondly, into separate sets of red triangles and red circles, blue triangles and blue circles respectively; or by the sequence which firstly groups into triangular shapes and circular shapes and then, secondly, subdivides each of these. In both ways the result or outcome is the desired one, namely that the pupil has sorted the collection into its four different groups.

The rearrangement of groups to meet individual needs

A sequence of groupings may lead to classes of a suitable size, but when a teacher looks at the characteristics of the pupils in each class he may decide that some rearrangement must be made to satisfy the needs of individual pupils. This rearrangement is often made, without changing the group sizes, by a straightforward interchange of pupils between groups. Five common reasons for moving a pupil from one group to another are: (1) to retain friendship groups whose members have previously worked well together, (2) to place a timid pupil in the same group as his supporting friend, (3) to create a social or academic balance between groups, (4) to separate two pupils who have shown that they have a bad influence on each other, and (5) to separate a pupil from a teacher who either cannot control, or cannot effectively teach mathematics to, that pupil.

MIXED ABILITY OR SIMILAR ABILITY GROUPS?

Of the nine different grouping methods already described in this chapter, five are linked with pupils' abilities. Their measurement enables a teacher to place the pupils in a mixed ability group or in a similar ability group. There are obviously advantages and disadvantages linked with both these groupings and the best method of combining the groupings, at each stage of a pupil's development, is still being sought by many mathematics teachers. For example, teachers often decide to use one of the three following groupings with 13 year old pupils in a school: (1) mixed ability groups in every class, (2) banding by selecting two highest ability classes, one remedial class, and perhaps three mixed ability classes from the remainder of the pupils, or (3) setting. Decisions such as these should be made by considering the ways in which mixed ability and similar ability groupings affect the pupils, and the ways these groupings affect the teachers.

Outcomes for the pupils

A pupil who has not done well enough at school mathematics will often be at a serious disadvantage when he leaves secondary school and will perhaps be unable to start an apprenticeship or to enrol for a higher education course. He may find that he is restricted in his choice of job and may sometimes find it difficult to get a job at all. The next chapter will show that pupils expect their years of primary and secondary education to prepare them for jobs, or for more education. Mathematics is therefore a high-status subject where the outcomes are very important for nearly all pupils. These outcomes cannot be ignored when decisions are being made about grouping methods in school mathematics. For lower-status subjects, which all pupils should experience but in which the outcomes are less important, the choice of a particular grouping method is not nearly as critical. The few pupils who must obtain a leaving qualification can often be specially taught during their final years at school.

Let us now compare two outcomes for the pupils, namely, the attainments in mathematics and the achievements in personal development (e.g. liking school or more specifically liking mathematics lessons) which result from different groupings. The following paragraphs compare these outcomes for those pupils who have been taught in mixed ability classes and those who have not. Therefore there are two outcomes and two groupings as shown in figure 6.10. For each column (outcome) it would be possible either for both forms of grouping to be equally successful or one form of grouping to be better and the other worse. Those teachers who support the introduction of mixed ability grouping hope to find that it is superior to similar ability grouping for at least one outcome. Moreover, they certainly hope to discover that mixed ability grouping is not worse for either outcome.

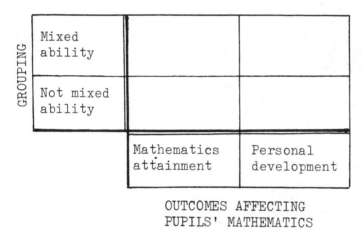

OUTCOMES AFFECTING
PUPILS' MATHEMATICS

Figure 6.10 The four variables used when considering grouping and outcomes

Of the research which has been done into methods of grouping and mathematics teaching and learning, we need only consider reports from large scale research programmes. These results should be generally applicable to similar situations in other schools. Three recent studies of pupils at secondary school satisfy these requirements. The first is the Banbury school study[10,11] of about 2000 pupils, the second is the Stirling study[12,13] of almost 5000 pupils and the third is the National Child Development study (N.C.D.)[14,15] of about 6000 pupils. In these three studies, the details vary slightly. For instance, the Banbury study tested pupils who either had or did not have mixed ability grouping for the whole of a two year period (11 to 13 years old) and the N.C.D. study tested pupils who had or did not have mixed ability grouping during the year when aged between 12 and 13. Both studies followed the pupils through to the age of 15. Another variation is that the Banbury study dealt with one school, the Stirling study dealt with two individualized learning schemes, and the N.C.D. study was of previously selected children, so that each grew from a different element (the school, the curriculum, the pupils) in the education system.

Despite the similarities and differences of the three studies, the general results from them are almost the same. From measures of the mathematics attainment of pupils of any ability, the main evidence is that having or not having mixed ability teaching is equally effective. However, a small effect shown by the Banbury long term study is that mixed ability grouping produced fewer bottom grades in C.S.E. and G.C.E. Ordinary-level examinations. Most measures of personal development are not significantly different for either grouping but there is some evidence that, where there is a difference in personal development, mixed ability grouping will produce the more favourable measure for a low ability pupil, or the less favourable measure for a high ability pupil.[16] In the Banbury study there was one marked tendency which must be mentioned, although it does not directly bear on mathematics education, namely, that the mixed ability grouping produced more effective integration between younger pupils of different abilities and backgrounds. However, when the pupils were two years older, their friendship patterns seemed to be unaffected by the previous forms of grouping.

To conclude this section on the outcomes for pupils in mixed ability and similar ability groups, I wish to emphasize two points. Firstly, there are very similar conclusions from other research about school grouping methods.[17,18] Secondly, although research studies have found no consistently significant difference between groupings they incidentally have emphasized that, to learn mathematics, pupils need able and experienced teachers.

Outcomes for the teachers

We have just referred to the pupil outcomes from three main studies of mixed ability grouping and it is interesting that, of these three, only the Stirling study investigated the outcomes for mathematics teachers. This study tried to discover how the teachers felt when in charge of a mixed ability class. One of the principal findings was that the new style of teaching often placed these teachers in a deep seated conflict situation. This was not an external conflict, as sometimes happens between pupils and teachers, but an internal conflict between the teachers' own beliefs and actions. Some of my students have talked about such internal conflicts experienced during teaching practice, for example when a student who believed in social cooperation had threatened to place three boys in detention after school, or when another student had taught some pupils a mathematics topic which she believed to be without value for them. These internal conflicts can be a constant source of worry to young teachers, and anyone who intends to remain in teaching must resolve the problems sufficiently well to avoid such worry. Older teachers may experience similar worries when they are faced with a changed style of teaching. It is often too late in life for these teachers to adopt an alternative career and therefore they need help in resolving their conflicting feelings.

Except for this Stirling study, nobody seems to have been interested in the way different groupings of pupils affect the teachers. In fact, the teachers' feelings have almost been ignored. This apparent lack of interest is evident in two major reports about grouping. The outcomes for the teacher are limited to one paragraph in the Schools Council book on mixed ability teaching in mathematics[20] and to three pages in the book about the Banbury study.[21]

Because there is so little hard evidence the following comments are indications, rather than facts, about outcomes for teachers. Teachers recognise their mathematics to be a high-status subject and the academic success of their pupils is important to the self-esteem and reputation of most mathematics teachers. The latter point was illustrated by one of my sixth form pupils when I wished him success in his forthcoming examination. He replied 'I'd better succeed, sir, for your reputation is at stake as well as my future.' We may conclude that a mathematics teacher is unlikely to choose to use a new grouping method if it might give a lower academic outcome for the pupils and thus reduce the teacher's self-esteem and reputation. Another reason for not choosing to change is the extra work which is involved. A teacher has to put a great deal of effort into all his work but he usually has to put extra effort into teaching the lowest ability pupils in any age range. In schools where pupils are setted or streamed, those 'extra effort lessons' are obviously easier to bear when they are timetabled between relatively easier lessons – it is like putting in a burst of speed during a cross country run. With low ability pupils in every mixed ability group, some teachers feel that too many lessons require this extra effort and that they are trying to sprint all the way. That is not the way to do well in a long distance race and it may not be the way for a teacher to get job satisfaction.

It is impossible to conclude that mixed ability grouping should be used for mathematics lessons in all schools in Britain; conclusions can only be made about individual schools. In any school, the mathematics teachers should decide which pupils are to be taught in mixed ability groups, which pupils are to be taught in similar ability groups and which pupils are to be taught in groups formed by any other method. The decision must benefit the teachers as well as the pupils; I am certain that the pupils' immediate needs must not always take priority, as the school must retain good mathematics teachers and also attract new ones.

THE RÔLE OF THE SENIOR MATHEMATICS TEACHER

I have found no accurate record to show when the first senior mathematics teacher was appointed. It was probably soon after 1840 when the Grammar Schools' Act enabled school governors to introduce mathematics teaching into their schools. Since then thousands of these appointments have been made by headteachers, delegating their responsibility for school mathematics to an experienced teacher of the subject. By 1980 we are in a situation where all schools, primary and middle and secondary,[22,23,24] are encouraged to appoint a teacher with special responsibility for mathematics. In different schools this teacher may be known as the 'Coordinator for Mathematics', the 'Head of the Mathematics Department' or the 'Senior Mathematics Teacher', but I will use the last term.

Although qualified in mathematics, the senior mathematics teacher has rarely had special training in management and leadership, which are considered in the following paragraphs. When describing the specific administrative qualities needed, three broad assumptions are made: firstly that the mathematics department conforms with the general philosophy and organization of the school, secondly that work can be partially delegated to other teachers of mathematics, and

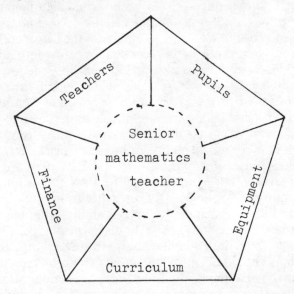

Figure 6.11 The five constituent responsibilities of a senior mathematics teacher

thirdly that the responsibility is shared with others, for example, that a pupil's progress in mathematics concerns the pupil, parents, year tutor, class teacher and senior mathematics teacher.

The overall responsibility of the senior mathematics teacher can be separated into five constituent responsibilities, namely for teachers, pupils, curriculum, finance and equipment[25] as shown in figure 6.11.

Responsibility for the mathematics teachers

The senior mathematics teacher is the leader and organizer of the group of mathematics teachers in the school and has responsibility both for their personal development and for their teaching. Obviously, a senior mathematics teacher does not encourage good teachers to leave the school but there will always be some members of staff who will expect to move to more senior posts as the next step in their careers. A teacher, for example, may be applying for a more senior post, either in administration or in mathematics, and will be at an advantage if he or she has previously been given some opportunities for organizing people and activities. These can be provided by the senior mathematics teacher delegating some responsibility and allowing other teachers to organize some part of the curriculum; perhaps the computer education, the mathematics club, a work card scheme or the syllabus in part of the school. Another way in which the senior mathematics teacher may foster the personal development of teachers is by assessing teachers' needs for gaining further professional qualifications and by encouraging teachers to attend suitable courses in mathematics or general education. These courses will not only provide further qualifications for the teachers but should lead to better mathematics teaching in the school and thus benefit the pupils as well.

The main function of a mathematics teacher is to provide his or her pupils with a sound mathematics education. Therefore the actual teaching which is done must be very carefully monitored by the senior mathematics teacher. This is possible because he receives a great deal of objective and subjective evidence about the achievements, strengths and weaknesses of each of his teachers. This evidence comes from the teacher, from colleagues, from pupils, and from the standard of work done by the pupils and the teacher. The senior mathematics teacher needs to discuss such evidence with the teacher concerned and then decide how that teacher may be given the best kind of support to improve his teaching. This support must not usurp the teacher's personal responsibilities, for example, support can help him to control a class but it must not take control out of his hands. A teacher often finds it easier to accept help from someone less obviously in authority than the senior mathematics teacher. This might be given by another experienced mathematics teacher whose age and status more nearly match those of the teacher being supported.[26]

A different kind of support will be given by other teachers, in ways such as voluntarily taking over classes when the regular teacher attends meetings at the local teachers' centre. This is most likely to happen when the teachers all belong to a cordial, united group. In my experience, mathematics teachers seem to naturally group together in many school staffrooms. Therefore, many senior mathematics teachers will find it easy to develop these natural groups by introducing regular mathematics staff meetings. These will be most valuable if the teachers not only discuss the successes and problems of pupils but also discuss the curriculum and styles of teaching.

Matching teachers and pupils on the timetable

While considering the responsibility of the senior mathematics teacher for the teachers, we must think how he or she assigns teachers to different classes on the timetable. It is customary for pupils, during their years at a school, to be taught mathematics by several teachers. This, I think, is a good system which ensures that most pupils learn the maximum amount of mathematics. I do not look on the system as a means of sharing the best teachers but as a recognition of the ways in which different teachers use their various talents and interests. Some will naturally emphasize the history of mathematics while others will enthusiastically introduce its present day applications.

The traditional way of organizing teaching was based on a slowly changing staff and classes consisting of stable groups of pupils. As each class moved up the school, it changed its teacher after each period of one or two years. A class, for example, could have Miss Brown for the first two years, Mr. Smith for the third year and then Mrs. Green for the two further years. This traditional pattern allows the pupils sufficient experience of different teachers' styles of teaching without there being numerous changes of teacher. Another way in which pupils can be taught by two or more teachers is to use a type of team teaching[27,28] where each teacher is responsible for part of one year's curriculum.

This reference to team teaching demonstrates that some schools have moved away from the rigid pattern of one teacher doing mathematics with one class for a fixed number of minutes every day. It is interesting to discover[29] the flexible time allocations for mathematics in one group of primary schools, where nearly 40 per cent of headteachers apparently did not advocate regular times or days for mathematics lessons, provided that the pupils did enough mathematics while in a teacher's class.

Obviously it is easier for a senior mathematics teacher to reorganize groupings of pupils and styles of teaching within a flexible timetable structure than within a rigid one. It is nevertheless possible within a rigid structure, as the following example shows. I once worked in an academic sixth form college where we decided to introduce both a new style of teaching and a new syllabus. This had to be organized to fit into the existing timetable structure without employing any more teachers. It was achieved by changing from traditional class teaching to another pattern using lectures and seminars. Previously, three teachers each taught six periods a week (i.e. eighteen periods in total) but, in the new pattern, the three teachers each led five seminars a week and one teacher gave two lectures (i.e. $3 \times 5 + 1 \times 2 = 17$ periods in total). This new scheme therefore used seventeen periods of teaching time, but we also held a weekly staff meeting (the eighteenth period) during which we evaluated the new scheme and planned work for the following weeks.

Each pupil attended the two lectures and two of the fifteen seminars, and did private study for the remaining two timetabled periods in the week. Therefore, the pupils now had four, instead of six, taught periods each week and I had to estimate whether this would be detrimental to their progress. This was not simple to demonstrate, but I used 'periods per week per pupil' of teacher contact time as a reasonable unit of measure. (N.B. One unit is equivalent to one period a week of individual tuition for a pupil). Under the old scheme, each pupil was in a group of about eighteen for six periods a week; therefore his teacher contact time was $6 \div 18 = 0 \cdot 333$ periods per week per pupil. Under the new scheme, each pupil was in a group of about seven pupils for two seminar periods a week, and in a group of about fifty four pupils for two lecture periods a week; his teacher contact time was therefore $2 \div 7 + 2 \div 54 = 0 \cdot 323$ periods per week per pupil. On that basis, the pupils could be expected to do as well under this new scheme and, when we were used to the new syllabus, the examination results seemed to confirm this. We had therefore successfully introduced a new system within a rigid timetable structure.

A previous section mentioned the different talents of mathematics teachers in a school. One responsibility of the senior mathematics teacher is to take strengths and weaknesses into account when trying to match a teacher with pupils in his classes. Perfect matching will never occur, of course, but pupils who are learning statistics should be taught by a teacher whose strengths include statistics and a teacher who is good with the slow learners should be given the opportunity to teach them. In this way, the teachers and pupils are more likely to be satisfied and successful. It appears, however, that there are secondary schools which may be less concerned with success and satisfaction than with equality, because schools sometimes advertise Scale One posts where 'every member of the Mathematics Department will teach across the full range of age and ability'. Such a system is admittedly better than one where the probationer teacher is given low ability and difficult classes for most of the week, but I do not think that it is necessarily fair either to the teachers or pupils. I have known teachers who successfully taught difficult pupils, and enjoyed doing so, and it would have been unfair to separate such well matched teachers and pupils. Therefore, I think that a school's mathematics teachers should be assigned to classes so that, as far as is possible, (1) pupils have the best opportunity to learn mathematics, (2) teachers and pupils enjoy their work, (3) teachers gain the experience which they will need for promotion and to improve their teaching and (4) the assignment is seen to be equitable rather than equal.

Responsibility for the pupils

It seems that, in general, the senior mathematics teacher delegates most of his responsibility for pupils' day to day learning and behaviour to the class teachers, and then adopts a supervisory rôle. This should be an active supervisory rôle, as illustrated in this report about checking teachers' work:

Staff were asked whether there was any check on whether they set homework. Schools varied from 10 per cent to 100 per cent in the proportion of teachers who said that checks were made. A high proportion was associated with a better academic outcome. Teachers were also asked if anyone was aware if staff arrived late for school. Again, schools varied in the proportion saying that people were aware – from 56 per cent to 100 per cent. Lack of awareness of staff punctuality was associated with poor attendance by the children. The checking of both homework and punctuality was usually an informal process rather than a formal procedure. But in the more successful schools teachers reported that senior colleagues knew what was happening.[30]

Responsibility for the curriculum

The mathematics pupils' progress over periods of a year or more is not the responsibility of the class teacher, but of the senior mathematics teacher. This responsibility is closely linked to his responsibility for the curriculum (see chapter 8) and while the senior mathematics teacher is monitoring pupils' progress he is gaining the information to help him decide which mathematics courses should be offered in the following years. Many courses will remain the same, but discussion is needed about other courses which will change and about new courses which will be introduced.[31] In my experience, this discussion in a school should involve as many mathematics teachers as possible if the new and changed courses are to be successful.[32] This experience is supported by these two reports, one about new courses in mathematics:

> It is unwise to take such a step without a reasonably united and enthusiastic team. The head of department must expect to provide a considerable measure of support, guidance and advice to his members of staff as they attempt to learn new techniques and to adopt new roles[33]

and the other about courses in all subjects:

> Schools where most teachers planned jointly tended to have better attendance and less delinquency. Of course the group planning took many different forms – from fully integrated courses to the more usual method of the head of department providing guidance on the general format of the courses from year to year, but leaving individual teachers to plan the details independently. It was striking, however, that in the less successful schools teachers were often left completely alone to plan what to teach, with little guidance and little coordination with other teachers to ensure a coherent course from year to year.[30]

It is not enough for the senior mathematics teacher to see that the school curriculum is progressive from year to year. He or she must also see that it follows on from pupils' mathematics in their previous schools and that it provides a good foundation for any further study or work.

Responsibility for the finance

The senior mathematics teacher must try to ensure that there is enough money available to provide the equipment which is needed to teach mathematics well. He must, initially, make out a good case for the mathematics teaching to receive a fair share of the annual school equipment allowance. This allowance varies greatly from L.E.A. to L.E.A. but averaged about £20 per pupil in 1979. That sum, divided between subjects, is barely enough to pay for consumable items like duplicated worksheets and for the replacement of some pieces of apparatus.

In a year when the pupils also need a new set of mathematics books there are probably other pupils in the school who need new text books for other subjects. Thus the senior mathematics teacher may have to convince some other teachers, including the headteacher, that the mathematics books must have priority. It may be easier to convince other teachers in a primary school, where almost everyone teaches mathematics, than in a secondary school where battle lines tend to be formed on a departmental basis. In a secondary school, the senior mathematics teacher must be prepared to argue the case with others, like the senior English teacher who says '... surely you can teach mathematics for another year using the present books, whereas our G.C.E. English syllabus contains a new novel which we must buy.' The senior English teacher may still view mathematics as an unchanging subject which needs new teachers but not new books, and he must be educated about the changes of teaching method and syllabus content which have taken place.

A convincing argument is more likely to be presented if a previous departmental meeting has discussed various alternative teaching strategies and decided why the new mathematics books are necessary. For instance, they may be needed because of a changed syllabus, or because they are the only way to teach effectively in a poorly staffed department, or because many of the present copies have fallen to pieces after two to twenty years use (and this last argument is stronger if the department has an efficient recording system for its equipment).

Another school source of finance may be the Parent Teacher Association (P.T.A.) which might pay for both capital and current equipment. P.T.A.s often aim to link each fund-raising event with the purchase of an indentifiable object, and some senior mathematics teachers have used these Associations to obtain computing equipment or to obtain complete individualized work schemes. Such equipment is unlikely to appear unless the initiative is taken by the senior mathematics teacher. He or she must consult other mathematics teachers to decide about any suitable equipment which is needed. Details about it, including its cost, should be given to the school's P.T.A. representative as soon as those details are known, because at some future committee meeting the P.T.A. Chairman is likely to ask the unannounced question 'what can we buy the school this year?' and then expect an immediate reply. A P.T.A. will usually consider buying any item of extra equipment which improves the school, while the L.E.A. provides the necessary basic equipment.

If teachers wish to buy course materials, then the L.E.A. mathematics adviser may provide some money, especially if the course will strengthen a school's mathematics teaching which compares unfavourably with that in neighbouring schools. Money may also be available for an experiment with newly published course materials, if the teachers are prepared to share the knowledge they gain with other schools in that L.E.A.[34]

Responsibility for the equipment

The senior mathematics teacher's responsibility for selecting, obtaining and maintaining mathematics equipment is closely linked with his responsibilities for curriculum and finance. The wide variety of equipment used by teachers is illustrated by the chapter sub-headings from the 1971 U.N.E.S.C.O. source book on *Teaching school mathematics.*[35] It lists and gives details of drawings and diagrams, geo-boards, three-dimensional models, space frames, moving models, films, algebraic aids, logical materials, calculating machines and textbooks. This list is by no means exhaustive as it does not include, for instance, library books or computers.

Once the school has been provided with a wide range of equipment for teaching mathematics, the two following problems arise: firstly, the storage of the equipment and secondly, how the schools can provide suitable spaces for the equipment to be efficiently used. These problems have led to the introduction of mathematics rooms, laboratories and areas which will be considered in the next section.

MATHEMATICS ROOMS, LABORATORIES AND AREAS

Mathematics classrooms

In most primary schools, each mathematics teacher (who will also teach other subjects) has his or her own classroom. It is ideal if middle and secondary school mathematics teachers also have their own classrooms or, if that is not possible, if certain classrooms in the school are specially allocated for mathematics teaching.

This insistence on each school having mathematics rooms is related to three trends in mathematics teaching and learning. Firstly, school mathematics has become less of an abstract study and more closely linked to objects and events in everyday life. It is therefore not sufficient for pupils to rely on their mathematics books which can be carried from room to room. These pupils need to have mathematics lessons in rooms where mathematical objects and ideas have been collected and displayed. This mention of display leads to the second trend, which is the change from pupils learning mathematical knowledge to pupils performing mathematical activities. If pupils have drawn interesting mathematical diagrams, then they should be encouraged to display these drawings around the walls of their mathematics rooms. The third trend is the growth of investigatory methods of teaching. These require apparatus which cannot be easily transported between numerous rooms in a school; if the apparatus is stored in a few specialist mathematics rooms then the teaching is likely to be more efficient.

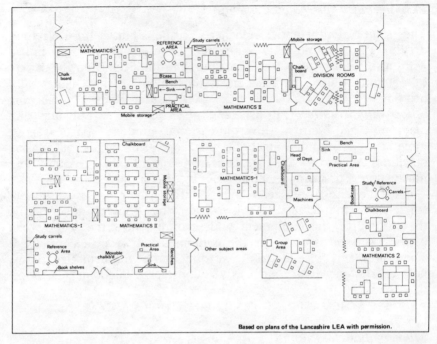

Based on plans of the Lancashire LEA with permission.

Figure 6.12 Three designs for secondary school mathematics areas. Reproduced from Mathematics in School, vol. 2 no. 5 p. 31

Mathematics laboratories

Mathematics laboratories[36] started to be introduced into schools in the 1960s, usually by the conversion of an existing room. A mathematics laboratory is described in the 1968 Mathematical Association booklet[37] as a combination of a classroom, a workshop, a calculating machine room, a study, a reference library and a store room. Such a laboratory can be very useful as the centre of mathematics learning in a school because it provides a place for staff and pupils to study, a place where the mathematics club meets or a place where apparatus is available. However, it cannot serve all these functions simultaneously and the concentration of resources in one place means that those resources are not easily available for the many pupils who could benefit. These are probable reasons for very few schools now having mathematics laboratories.

Mathematics areas

Even if few schools have mathematics laboratories, there are many schools which have special mathematics areas (see figure 6.12). An area may consist of the mathematics teachers' classrooms, grouped with a study/library, an open plan work area, a computer education room or a resource store.[38,39,40,41] Such an area certainly seems to help teachers to work together and make mathematics a well organized subject.[42] All the pupils recognize that this is the special mathematics area and the mathematically inspired pupils (who are not all mathematically gifted) often look on the area as their home base.

Conclusion

This chapter has discussed the groupings and organization which take place in Local Education Authorities and in schools, so that pupils can be taught mathematics as effectively as possible. It has been shown that the senior mathematics teacher has to play a vital rôle, all the time supporting and being supported by his or her team of mathematics teachers. The next chapter discusses the expected outcomes from these groupings and organization.

Annotated References for Chapter 6

1. H.M.S.O. (1978) *Mixed ability work in comprehensive school*: Matters for discussion no. 6. Her Majesty's Stationery Office: London. See p. 38.

   Reports from visits during 1975–77 to schools in England and Wales, with a series of subject papers including mathematics.

2. Bridges D. (1976) The social organisation of the classroom and the philosophy of mixed ability teaching. *Cambridge Journal of Education*, vol. 6, no. 1/2, pp. 15–23.

   The ways in which teachers' problems are rooted in social philosophy.

3. H.M.S.O. (1978) *Primary education in England; a survey by H.M. Inspectors*. Her Majesty's Stationery Office: London. See p. 31.

   An appraisal of mathematics and other subjects in 542 schools.

4. Kelly A.V. (1974) *Teaching mixed ability classes*. Harper & Row: London, New York. See chapter 4.

   A book which covers nearly all general aspects but with hardly any mention of mathematics.

5. H.M.S.O. (1976) *Statistics of education; schools*. Her Majesty's Stationery Office: London.

   One volume of the comprehensive annual statistics.

6. H.M.S.O. (1975) *Curricular differences for boys and girls*; Education survey no. 21. Her Majesty's Stationery Office: London.

   A survey of the subjects studied by primary and secondary school pupils in mixed and single sex schools.

7. Yates A. (1971) *The organization of schooling; a study of educational grouping practices*. Routledge & Kegan Paul: London.

   A discussion, using research results, of grouping pupils into schools and into classes.

8. Jenkins K.R. (1975) The partially hearing unit. *Journal of the Society of Teachers of the Deaf*, no. 20, pp. 23–5.

   This article summarizes the different types of provision for special educaton, and considers the particular contribution of a unit in an ordinary school.

9. Cave C. & Maddison P. (1978) *A survey of recent research in special education*. National Foundation for Educational Research: Slough.

   A review undertaken for the D.E.S.

10. Newbold D. (1977) *Ability grouping – the Banbury enquiry*. National Foundation for Educational Research: Slough.

    A statistical, but fairly readable, report on social and academic outcomes from grouping arrangements.

11. Postlethwaite K. & Denton C. (1978) *Streams for the future*? Pubansco: Banbury School, Banbury, Oxfordshire.

    A report of the progress of pupils who had been taught in mixed or similar ability groups for the first two years in secondary school.

12. Morgan J. (1977) *School mathematics under examination; 1, Affective consequences of an individualised learning programme*. Dime Projects, Education Department, University of Stirling, Stirling.

    The development of a suitable reporting system and its use to assess Scottish project materials.

13. Giles G. (1977) *School mathematics under examination; 2, A comparison of the cognitive effects of individualised learning and conventional teaching*. Dime Projects, Education Department, University of Stirling, Stirling.

    The results of a comparative study sponsored by the S.E.D.

14. Fogelman K. et al. (1978) Ability grouping in secondary schools and attainment. *Educational Studies*, vol. 4, no. 3, pp. 201–12.

    Some results from a longitudinal study which takes account of many background variables.

15. Essen J. et al. (1979) Some non-academic developmental correlates of ability grouping in secondary schools. *Educational Studies*, vol. 5, no. 1, pp. 83–93.

    These results from the N.C.D. study show little difference between the effectiveness of mixed ability, streamed or setted groups.

16. Kerry T. (1978) Bright pupils in mixed ability classes. *British Educational Research Journal*, vol. 4, no. 2, pp. 103–11.

    A discussion of the need for identification and special treatment of bright pupils, based on a small group of schools and teachers.

17. Goldberg M. et al. (1966) *The effects of ability grouping*. Teachers College Press: New York.

    This study of 3000 children shows that ability grouping, of itself, has no important effect on academic achievement.

18. Corbishley P. (1977) *Research findings on teaching groups in secondary schools*. In reference 19, chapter 1.

    Schooling over 50 years; a summary of results in Britain and America.

19. Davies B. & Cave R.G. eds. (1977) *Mixed ability teaching in the secondary school*. Ward Lock: London.

Two sociologists present theory and practice across the curriculum. Many useful references are included.

20. Schools Council (1977) *Mixed ability teaching in mathematics*. Evans/Methuen: London. See p. 30.

A valuable survey of current practice, which includes three case studies.

21. See reference 10, section 6.

22. M.A. (1976) *Mathematics in middle schools*. Mathematical Association: Leicester. See p. 5.

A report from the 5–13 sub-committee, with reprinted articles from *Mathematics in School*.

23. M.A. (1976) Mathematics for the first two years in secondary school. *Mathematics in School*, vol. 5, no. 2, pp. 2–5.

Advice on resources, organization and courses.

24. M.A. (1977) Maths in middle schools; matters arising. *Mathematics in School*, vol. 6, no. 3, pp. 27–8.

A report of a discussion which considers the senior mathematics teacher's rôle in one school.

25. Hall J.C. (1978) Secondary school heads of mathematics. *Mathematics in School*, vol. 7, no. 3, pp. 29–30.

A summary of the results of an investigation into the views of teachers.

26. Dean P.G. & Gleason J.L. (1976) Advice, assistance and inspection in the U.S.A. *Trends in Education*, vol. 1976, no. 1, pp. 45–8.

This article describes formal evaluation, informal intervisitation and the buddy system.

27. See reference 4, chapter 3.

28. Warwick D. (1976) *Team teaching*. Hodder & Stoughton: London.

There are chapters, and references, to the theory and practice in schools but without special mention of mathematics.

29. Bennett S.N. (1978) Recent research on teaching; a dream, a belief and a model. *British Journal Educational Psychology*, vol. 48, no. 2, pp. 127–47. See p. 131.

An article in which research findings support a model which emphasizes the importance of good classroom management.

30. Rutter M. et al. (1979) *Fifteen thousand hours; secondary schools and their effects on children*. Open Books: London. See pp. 136–7.

A very interesting report on 1487 children as they progressed through 12 schools.

31. Dunford J. (1979) Objectives into practice. *Mathematics in School*, vol. 8, no. 1, pp. 12–13.

Advice on how to introduce changes into the curriculum.

32. Harvey N. (1974) Mathematics in a comprehensive school. *Mathematics in School*, vol. 3, no. 1, pp. 7–9.

A senior mathematics teacher describes the mathematics curriculum and organization.

33. See reference 20, p. 51.

34. H.M.S.O. (1979) *Local authority arrangements for the school curriculum*; Report on the Circular 14/77 review. Her Majesty's Stationery Office: London. See section A5.5.

.A summary of L.E.A. replies on many aspects of the curriculum; it includes comments and bar graphs about four questions on school mathematics.

35. Servais W. & Varga T. eds. (1971) *Teaching school mathematics*. U.N.E.S.C.O.-Penguin: Harmondsworth. See chapter 2.

A book presenting the current international situation in curricula and methods.

36. See reference 35, pp. 119–20.

37. M.A. (1968) *Mathematics laboratories in schools*; Mathematical Association. Bell: London.

Most of this booklet is descriptions of laboratories in specific schools.

38. Birtwistle C. (1973) The secondary school mathematics area. *Mathematics in School*, vol. 2, no. 5, pp. 30–1.

Ideas about the provision of a suitable area, and three suggested designs.

39. Shaw R. (1973) Equipment for the mathematics room. *Mathematics in School*, vol. 2, no. 6, pp. 30–1.

The result of teachers' votes about designing and equipping a room.

40. Chorlton J. (1979) Open plan mathematics. *Mathematics in School*, vol. 8, no. 2, pp. 8–9.

A report on five years of teaching in a mathematics area.

41. Faux G. (1979) Two days with top infants. *Mathematics Teaching*, no. 86, pp. ix–xvi.

An account of pupils working in an open plan situation.

42. H.M.S.O. (1980) *Aspects of secondary education in England; supplementary information on mathematics*. Her Majesty's Stationery Office: London.

Detailed information about teachers, pupils, courses and schools.

CHAPTER 7

EXPECTATIONS FROM TEACHING AND LEARNING MATHEMATICS

Introduction

> Mathematics occupies about one-eighth of the secondary schools curriculum, and in primary schools perhaps slightly more. It is widely recognised by pupils, parents and teachers to be an important qualification for employment or for further studies, and it provides a unique type of experience which is an essential component of a complete education.[1]

For any subject to be given such a large proportion of time in school, there must be generally high expectations about the contributions which it can make. The above quotation is from a British government report published in 1977, following a period when there had been a desperate shortage of suitably qualified mathematics teachers which restricted pupils' opportunities for studying mathematics. Some secondary schools had used other subject teachers for mathematics or had timetabled some pupils for perhaps only four instead of five mathematics lessons a week, so that there was a lower quality and reduced quantity of teaching. In primary schools, where mathematics lessons are given by most teachers, only about half had an appropriate mathematics qualification from their own schooldays; this meant that a restriction occurred mainly in the quality of the teaching. Despite the efforts made by these secondary and primary school teachers to foster their pupils' mathematical development, the results in many schools could not and did not match people's expectations.

At the start of the 1980s there is still a shortage of qualified mathematics teachers and it seems that headteachers and senior teachers will need to deploy these staff very carefully for many years. However, this shortage is not likely to reduce the expectations which most people have for pupils already in the schools, so teachers must not ignore the present while planning a better future.

Aims, goals and objectives

Before two or more people discuss expectations, they should make sure that they are talking about the same kind of expectations. Arguments can often arise from a misunderstanding about the level of discussion, and this does nothing to improve the mathematics being learnt or taught. It is often useful to consider three levels, namely, aims, goals and objectives.[2] These levels can be illustrated by reference to the game of football, which most men or women will have watched at some time. When a player kicks the ball, he *aims* it in a certain direction. The ball may go towards the *goal* which comparatively is a fairly large area, erected by the players or by someone else for any of the team to use. During a game played according to set rules, each team gains a number of points, and the *objective* is to score more points than the opposing team. It is absolutely clear whether one score is higher than the other, although some people may not agree that the rules have been correctly applied by the referee.

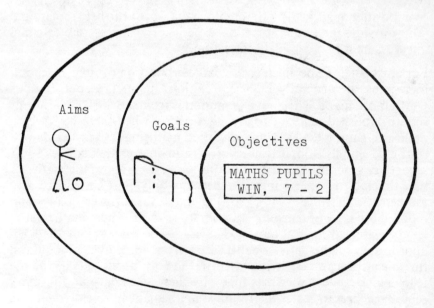

Figure 7.1 A representation of aims, goals and objectives

In education, there is reasonable agreement about the three words having the following meanings:

Aims are declarations of intent, which usually do not indicate any specific action which is to be taken. They may be personally expressed by a teacher (e.g. 'I am going to make my lessons more interesting') or by a pupil (e.g. 'I am going to disrupt Mrs. Brown's lessons.') The aims of mathematics education are considered later in this chapter and in chapter 8.

Goals are more detailed than aims and often result from aims rather in the way that they do in football. These goals are then useful to the teacher in his or her everyday work. Goals are often set so that other people may achieve them (e.g. 'The pupils will understand the four operations with numbers') but no exact rules are laid down to test that achievement. Therefore, two teachers who claim to attain the same goal from a mathematics curriculum may expect different responses from their pupils. This is illustrated by the different kinds of understanding, e.g. instrumental and relational, which have been discussed in chapter 5.

Objectives state what a person should be able to do (e.g. 'A pupil can correctly complete ten written addition sums, using different pairs of whole numbers less than fifty.') Objectives determine a precise end-point whose attainment can be clearly assessed, whereas goals may be differently interpreted. However, a concentration on objectives is not always desirable because it introduces the danger of ignoring such important goals as 'The pupils will be able to think in a mathematical way', merely because these goals cannot be expressed objectively.

Persons who have considered the differences between aims, goals and objectives are more likely to enter into a useful discussion about expectations and are less likely to make such remarks as: 'I don't care about their understanding of number patterns, why can't they multiply 8×6?' This remark compares a goal with an objective, and the members of the discussion group obviously have different expectations about learning. If an argument is to be avoided, they should attempt to reach some agreement about the level of discussion and then concentrate on that one level. It is to be hoped that any such discussion will be helped by the information which follows in this chapter. The information is arranged in sections, where the earlier ones are about the most general expectations.

GENERAL EXPECTATIONS

Equality and individuality

There is an apparent conflict between equality and individuality which has to be resolved. This conflict becomes evident if we examine the aims and organization of a typical comprehensive secondary school. This school was formed by the amalgamation of two very unequal schools, an academic grammar school with predominantly middle-class pupils and a technical/modern school with predominantly lower-class pupils. The existence of two schools had emphasized social and academic differences but the new comprehensive school now aims to start all the pupils on a more equal footing and to give equal chances of their education leading to suitable employment in an unskilled, skilled or professional job. Aims about social and academic equality are part of this school's philosophy and help to determine the school's curriculum and organization. However, looked at in another way the school is a very large number of individuals gathered together in one place. With the possible exception of a pair of identical twins, the pupils and the teachers are all different and the variety of personalities makes it an interesting school in which to work. It is also a typical school because it aims to take account of this variety by encouraging the strengths and correcting the weaknesses (e.g. a lack of numeracy) of each individual; pupils and teachers can therefore expect to have dissimilar treatment. If the two aims of equality and individuality are mutually consistent then this dissimilar treatment cannot clash with equality.[3,4]

Figure 7.2 Is there equality of input or of results?

Looking more deeply at the issues of equality and individuality, the first distinction to consider is that between equality of input and equality of results, as shown in figure 7.2. In the typical comprehensive school which we are considering, the three main inputs which affect the amount that pupils learn are equipment (including books), teachers' experience and teachers' time. The headteacher will not expect to achieve equality between departments by allowing the same amount of equipment money to each, as individual departments have different needs. The next input is the teachers' experience; teachers of differing experience and talent have to be distributed between individual classes in as equal a way as possible. Thirdly, the class sizes have to be determined and this introduces more problems about equality. For example, should the senior mathematics teacher allow the least able and the most able pupils to be taught in smaller classes than the other pupils, when these others might also make relatively better progress if they were given that extra input of teacher's time per pupil?

This leads us on to consider equality of results, because even if an immensely unequal input of teachers' time were allowed it would be impossible to equalize the output so that all pupils reached the same standard.[5] Of course, the pupils' final results are not the only measure of success for a school course. Pupils should benefit throughout the duration of the course, so perhaps we should use some on-going measure of equality. One which is commonly used is equality of opportunity, which recognizes that the results are affected by the individual ability and motivation of pupils, so that the aims of a school may be written as 'equality of opportunity for emotional, intellectual and aesthetic development enabling each pupil to develop his or her individual potential to the full'.

Having related the two issues of individuality and equality in the context of the whole school, we now come to the expectations about mathematics teaching and learning. A fashionable, but sensible, phrase in education is 'to start where the pupils are'. This accepts that no two pupils will be at the same stage of development or have the same abilities, experience, knowledge and potential. However, as in figure 7.3, we could expect all pupils to reach some defined level of numeracy as well as being given the encouragement to reach any higher level which is individually possible. The level of numeracy (see later in this chapter) should be decided by each school in consultation with the representatives of other concerned people. The Secretaries of State for England and Wales have rightly rejected 'tests of basic literacy and numeracy' when considering 'the pupils as individuals'.[6] Such tests already exist in some American state assessment schemes where the unsuitabilities of their 'substance, technical design and use ... have become a central concern for mathematics teachers across the country'.[7]

For both teachers and pupils, another aspect of equality is the realization that any individual has unequal levels of achievement at different times. On different days, a teacher may explain the same mathematical topic well or not so well, and even a pupil's objective test result has a time-limiting value. A familiar example of this is the

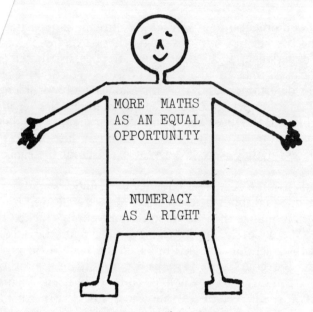

MORE MATHS
AS AN EQUAL
OPPORTUNITY

NUMERACY
AS A RIGHT

Figure 7.3 An expectation from mathematics education

pupil who has 'learnt to do simple equations' at the end of one term but then the teacher has to revise them, or even teach them again, in a later term. Pupils and teachers may also exhibit different temperaments during different lessons, so it is only in general terms that we can even claim that an individual performs at the same consistent level.

The mathematics achievements of boys and girls

Although boys and girls may be expected to have similar levels of achievement when they have been given equal educational opportunities, past evidence shows that teenaged boys frequently perform better than girls[8,9,10] in almost all areas of mathematics except straightforward work with symbols (e.g. manipulating numbers and letters in an equation). This situation is certainly influenced by the different mathematical interests and skills of the two sexes and teachers should provide an education which builds on the existing strengths of each individual, rather than an education which attempts to reduce the differences between the sexes. These differences have already been considered in chapter 5. In countries which have, for many years, provided university education for both men and women, a disappointingly small proportion of women has studied or used higher mathematics after leaving secondary school. This is possibly wasting the talents of some very able people[11] and has serious repercussions resulting in the shortage of qualified and experienced mathematics teachers in schools.

Expectations for pupils with special educational needs

Another important aspect of equality is the provision of *special education* for those children needing it at some time during their school career.[12] The need was estimated in the 1978 Warnock report[13] to extend to perhaps one child in every five at school, only some of whom now receive special or remedial education. A great range of children is obviously included, from those with severe mental and physical handicaps to those of low intelligence or with behavioural or emotional problems. The Warnock report is another step in the changing provision of community services. Earlier this century, severely handicapped children were placed in hospitals to protect them from the problems of normal community life. In effect, this was a policy of segregation by which they were unlikely to ever rejoin the rest of society. During the ensuing years it began to be recognized that their need, and their just entitlement, was to be educated and responsibility for them was transferred to Local Education Authorities. To educate these children with various types and degrees of handicap, the L.E.A.s created, or used, special schools.[14] These schools still segregated children and the next educational stage was to encourage the integration of many handicapped children into normal schools, as when the 1967 Plowden report said that ordinary primary schools should accept handicapped pupils, whenever that was possible.[16]

It is expected that this integration will make it easier for children with special needs to become active participants in, and responsible contributors to, society. While the present segregation does partially cut them off from their peer group it enables specialist teachers to concentrate on what they know to be essential goals of social and academic development, and non-specialist teachers appear to do this less effectively. This specialist teaching is probably most important when the pupil is learning mathematics and English, because low achievements in these two subjects are likely to accentuate difficulties which will anyway occur in adult life.

As sections of the Warnock report are implemented, schools will be expected to provide suitable teachers and equipment for these children. The difficulties which are likely to occur in mathematics teaching may be judged by considering the work of one specialist teacher of blind and partially sighted pupils. His school can only select text books which are available in Braille and he is expected to mark work which is written in Braille. Using special equipment he has to produce diagrams and models for the pupils to use and he is expected to compensate in his teaching for the limitations (e.g. in spatial perception) which are linked with certain medical causes of blindness.

The assessment of physically handicapped boys and girls has shown their average achievement to be two years behind chronological age[17] so that teachers may expect most handicapped pupils to join other pupils who need remedial mathematics lessons. These other under-achievers include an unduly large percentage of pupils from the ethnic minorities in our population, for reasons which have not yet been clearly identified. Teachers must consider this situation in schools[18] to decide whether their teaching of mathematics gives a fair opportunity to all pupils and whether an individual pupil's underachievement in mathematics is due mainly to his or her poor understanding of English.[19,20]

Forms and rôles of verbal communication

Few people would disagree with the statement that one expectation from teaching and learning mathematics is that pupils shall learn to communicate mathematics to others. Schools have traditionally used writing as the most common form of this communication for pupils who are able to read and write, but recent changes such as group work by pupils and less formal teaching mean that more conversation is now being used during mathematics lessons. With both forms of verbal communication, written and spoken, an interesting aspect which is often overlooked is the internal mode of use, i.e. that a person often needs to communicate with himself while learning and performing mathematics. Obvious examples of using this internal mode are counting to oneself and jotting down symbols to help a process of thought. Whether the written form or the spoken form is used, it may perform two rôles. Firstly, there is the rôle of language in mathematics *per se* and secondly, the rôle of communication in the teaching-learning process.

> That mathematics uses a special language, or at least that it uses language in a special way, is completely obvious. The more radical viewpoint, that mathematical activity is simply the construction and application of special languages, has been advanced from two different perspectives: On the one hand, mathematics has been called 'the language of science'; on the other hand, mathematical logicians have developed the concept of a formal language, supplied with a grammar and deductive rules, and have used this to give precision to the notion of a 'mathematical theory.'
>
> Whatever philosophical view one adopts about the relation between mathematics and language, it is evident that the teaching of mathematics involves to some extent the teaching of new linguistic patterns.[21]

In the following sections, these two rôles will be considered separately, although it is accepted that there is some overlap.[23]

The rôle of language in mathematics

Mathematics has its own linguistic structure, which pupils should be able to use with varying degrees of proficiency. For example, nearly everyone uses natural numbers up to one hundred when shopping and travelling by bus, train or car. However, just as there are many people who use the English language without understanding the details of its structure, we must not expect everyone to understand details such as the names of numbers corresponding to nouns, and these nouns being used in mathematical equations (which correspond to sentences).

Words in the English language have associated meanings and children are expected to use nouns to represent objects. These children are not expected to be confused when, for example, the same word 'mother' can refer to different people or different words such as 'father' and 'dad' refer to the same person. Similarly, in mathematics we attach various meanings to symbols; for example, the symbol '3' may represent a concept (such as the idea of 'three-ness') rather than a set of three objects. While in primary school, pupils learn to use alternative symbols like 'three', '3' and 'III' to refer to the same time on the clock, and they are also expected to understand the same symbol '3' when differently used in place values, fractions, powers and various other representations. Realizing these similarities between English and mathematics,[24] it would be interesting to know how our pupils' success with the elementary use of mathematical language compares with their success in the use of the English language.

In order to convey a certain meaning, mathematical language often has to be used more precisely than the English language but I do not think that this should be allowed to restrict the individuality of a pupil or teacher, especially when spoken or written words are for personal use rather than to communicate formally with other people. We expect that the language conveys the correct meaning and this can be done effectively with non-standardized words, as in my own sixth-form days when the teacher referred to $4 \times 3 \times 2 \times 1$ as 'four plonk' instead of using the normal phrase which is 'factorial four'.

The rôle of communication in teaching and learning

Most 5 year old pupils know little more than the simplest nouns of the mathematical language when they start school. This gives teachers the opportunity to start almost from scratch. In these early years everyone expects that there will be verbal communication between pupil and teacher, between pupil and pupil, and between a pupil and himself. (If this last internal mode of use seems unfamiliar then listen to, and watch, a young child who is doing work with numbers or shapes.) Not only is this communication desirable, it is also a necessary operation while learning mathematics although there is not complete agreement about the exact rôle which it plays.[25] Chapter 5 has described the theories of Piaget and Bruner, and the Piagetian view is that language expresses the mathematical structure which has been developed while the Brunerian view is that language is an essential part during the development of the structure.

This need for language exists not only amongst pupils in primary school but also in secondary school;[27] examples are when beginning to study algebra, when solving mathematical problems, and when using imagery and symbolism in the processes of abstraction and generalization.[28,29] Therefore we should expect both forms of verbal communication to be practised throughout the years of primary and secondary schooling. The difficulty of doing this effectively must not be underestimated,[30] as it is often not easy to communicate mathematical ideas by using words, symbols and grammatical forms from the English language.

Figure 7.4 Pupil to teacher: 'I weren't late today cos me mam got me a potato clock.'

As well as talking about mathematics, teachers and pupils have to talk about ancillary matters such as the organization of classroom learning. In these matters, communication difficulty may also occur because of differences in articulation or vocabulary. Figure 7.4 illustrates one difficulty (the English translation is 'I was not late today because my mother got me up at eight-o-clock') and another difficulty occurred when pupils in a London class were told by a Scottish teacher to get out their jotters (the English translation is 'rough work books'). Beyond these two examples of problems experienced by any subject teacher, there are four more specialized aspects of mathematical communication.

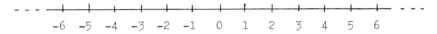

Figure 7.5 The integers represented on a number line

Firstly, we should consider the existence of both apparent and real complexity in mathematical language. Pupils often enjoy using the apparently difficult words like multiplication or tetrahedron but they do not expect to be upset by the thoughtless use of over-sophisticated or confusing language.[31,32,33] For example, most pupils who are beginning to understand the number line (see figure 7.5) which clearly relates the negative numbers to the already familiar numbers 1.2.3. etc., do not expect to be confused by some indiscriminate combination of similar-meaning words like negative, minus, take away, difference, less and subtract, when the teacher is describing operations using that number line.

Secondly, there is a complementary expectation about the permissible use of non-standard language which the pupils have adopted and which does not confuse them. Teachers should encourage their pupils to use exploratory talk[34] when they are searching for a way to fit a new idea into their existing scheme of understanding. This exploratory talk can often be with a fellow pupil but it may be with a teacher.

Thirdly, teachers should expect to discuss mathematics with pupils, (e.g. 'did you expect the graph to be a straight line?') as well as speaking to pupils about learning mathematics (e.g. 'open your books at page 73'). Discussion is needed to assess and encourage pupils, and to assist their mathematical development. Finally, teachers should remember that communication is not an end in itself as it may be in learning a language, but is a means by which mathematical understanding is achieved.

SKILLS, UNDERSTANDING AND INSIGHT

Mathematical skill and understanding

Available evidence suggests that a child can understand without becoming adept in using the particular skill involved (addition of fractions, for example), but if the skill is one in which he ought to become proficient, practice or drill will be needed. On the other hand, if drill is used without understanding, retention does not seem to be as great and, of course, the learning of a skill involving the same understanding but different sorts of symbols will be more difficult if the understanding has not been developed.[35]

This quotation emphasizes that teachers should recognize the interdependence between mathematical skill and mathematical understanding, and then provide a suitable combination of skill and understanding by which pupils will learn. Traditional school mathematics courses were supposed to place too much emphasis on skills, and one of the reasons for introducing the so-called modern mathematics courses and styles of teaching was the expectation that they would give many pupils a better understanding of mathematics but this has not always happened. Mathematical understanding is partly taught, and partly caught through a repeated application of skills.[37] If pupils are not allowed to gain both skill and understanding (i.e. instrumental understanding and relational understanding respectively, which are described in chapter 5), there is little chance of their also gaining mathematical insight.

Mathematical insight

Mathematical insight occurs when all the various elements of a mathematical situation are grasped in their relation to each other and to the whole situation.

Mathematical insight and intuition are well discussed by Professor Brian Griffiths and Dr. Geoffrey Howson, of Southampton University, in their book entitled *Mathematics: society and curricula*.[38,39] They illustrate the mathematicians' knowledge of the power of negation when they do not give examples of insight but of situations which demonstrate lack of insight. Their discussion includes the idea of a developed understanding needing 'the realization that the theory has a model in physics, geometry, or some more familiar or accessible part of mathematics', which emphasizes the importance of the final words 'and to the whole situation' in the above explanation of mathematical insight. It is therefore at a higher level than understanding because it is the ability to connect all the theoretical and real relationships of a whole situation or of its parts. A pupil who is gaining such insight may find that the relationships are intuitively obvious to him although he may not be able to verbally express or logically prove them. This intuitive grasp of a situation is not to be decried, for it can be an important stage in the development of his mathematics education.

THE EXPECTATIONS OF GROUPS OF PEOPLE

Having dealt so far in this chapter with certain aspects of general expectations, the next sections will briefly consider typical expectations of classified groups of people. As these are consensus expectations they will not express the most extreme views and the language of aims and goals will be used.

The expectations of pupils

I make no apology for considering pupils as the first classified group, because failure to meet their expectations can stultify the expectations of other groups of people. The expectations will have to be interpreted for each individual according to his or her need, ability and personality but the aims are virtually common for the whole group. For example, consider one school I know where the pupils expect to successfully study 'real mathematics', i.e. not just to learn arithmetic. An expression of equality was that all 14 year old pupils studied matrices (see figure 7.6) as part of that year's curriculum but this topic was interpreted at suitable levels for the classes of different abilities.

$$\begin{pmatrix} 1 & 3 \\ 7 & 2 \end{pmatrix} + \begin{pmatrix} -1 & 2 \\ 4 & -1 \end{pmatrix} = \begin{pmatrix} 0 & 5 \\ 11 & 1 \end{pmatrix} \qquad \begin{pmatrix} 2 & 5 \\ 1 & -3 \end{pmatrix} \times \begin{pmatrix} 1 \\ 3 \end{pmatrix} = \begin{pmatrix} 17 \\ -8 \end{pmatrix}$$

Figure 7.6 Two examples of matrix calculations

Pupils of all ages expect to recognise, investigate and create patterns[40,41] which help them to see an ordered structure within school mathematics, and thereby develop and display understanding. There are geometric, algebraic and numeric patterns, which have attributes in common with problems, puzzles and games and often provide similar delight and fascination. Another expectation of pupils is that their mathematics should be relevant to their future adult life. This was clearly indicated by the 1968 Schools Council Enquiry no. 1[42] when young school leavers placed 'teaching towards jobs' and 'money management' as the most desirable goals. It was also shown by the study of twelve London secondary schools which reported in 1979 that 'pupils consistently selected 'instrumental' goals such as examination success and preparation for jobs'.[43] There are a few pupils who, in adult life, will become professional mathematicians and for these and others with equal talent[44] opportunities should exist for exceptional stimulation, progress and instruction.

Let us now consider the everyday mathematics lessons. During these lessons the pupils expect to be able to think about the topics and discuss them orally as well as doing written work. They expect the teacher to show them what progress they are making in mathematics and to respect both their attempts and their mathematical skill. To further these aims, the teacher is expected to be knowledgeable about, and competent with, both the subject and the teaching of that subject.[45]

Figure 7.7 'I've got Ma Brown for maths next year, what's she like?'

I think that the above expectations are used subconsciously when pupils assess their teachers (see figure 7.7), as happens in every school. In recent years, more adults have shown an interest in investigating pupils' evaluation of their teachers because this is linked with the effectiveness of teaching. For instance, in 1977 there was a study of learning difficulties in mathematics with special reference to girls, which included the question 'which teacher has been the most help to you?' From interviews with almost 100 boys and girls aged 13 and 14 years, it was concluded that 'Generally the teacher selected was a man, which nullified the hypothesis that girls need women teachers. What both girls and boys need is a good teacher – and they showed that they were well able to spot one. They were also able to spot those who were not maths specialists.'[46] Unluckily, it seems that fewer and fewer pupils can expect to be taught mathematics by graduates; not only are there relatively fewer in schools than for other academic subjects but the percentage actually dropped from 6·9 to 6·3 while the percentage of graduate teachers in schools was increasing from 24·1 to 26·6 during the years 1974 to 1976.[47] (N.B. These are the last years for which published statistics are currently available.)

Secondary school pupils now expect to be given more choice within their mathematics, for example through optional topics and individual projects. This reflects a change in society's attitude. Learning is no longer regarded predominantly as a school activity with academic success bringing its just reward in the future but more as something which is a lifelong process. Learning, therefore, needs to provide intrinsic satisfaction and, at any stage, poor results are neither a disaster nor a social disgrace. 'In several so-called affluent countries young people are already rejecting the ethic of the hard-working man under whose auspices their parents "made it".'[48]

The expectations of parents

If pupils talk about mathematics when they come home from school, they will most likely refer to that day's lessons when 'the teacher was in a good mood' or when 'we had a test and I got seven out of ten'. Such events are highlights for the pupils because they are personal experiences, but parents will probably consider them to be interesting events of relative unimportance. The most important thing for parents is the termly or yearly assurance that their own child is 'getting on well'. Most parents know very little about mathematics itself or about mathematics in school. All parents have memories of the mathematics and teaching in their own schooldays but there are probably very few who use any mathematics beyond handling money, and similar everyday applications of counting or measuring. These memories and applications with, perhaps, the addition of information from an occasional newspaper article or television programme, form the foundation of parents' expectations for their children. It is not surprising that the final unplanned structure is a poor basis for useful discussions with mathematics teachers.

English is the only comparable basic subject in the school curriculum, and it is worrying to find many parents of both primary and post-primary pupils who were noticeably more dissatisfied with mathematics teaching and learning than with English.[49] Although this particular comment is based on nationwide research in Ireland, a similar dissatisfaction might be found if the research were repeated in the United Kingdom or North America.

Almost all parents expect their children to have learnt basic arithmetical skills before they reach 11 years of age or even sooner with the most able pupils. The degree of ability is measured by comparison with other children and even with the parents themselves. A recurring request to teachers is for average and above average pupils to be stretched (mentally) to make them work nearer their potential capacity. This capacity is usually judged by considering numerical rather than spatial achievement (as arithmetic is still commonly thought to be the only basis of school mathematics). Often the capacity is also judged in a rather narrow way; parents invariably expect intellectual skills, sometimes expect understanding and rarely consider any emotional or aesthetic contribution from mathematics lessons. The parents rarely make these requests because they see their child becoming a professional mathematician but because they expect the studies to aid intellectual development and to be of practical application, either in future work or for passing the next examination. Although parents may complain about the 'strange and unfamiliar' mathematics which is in their children's books, they still depend on teachers to select suitable mathematics as an essential part of the school curriculum.

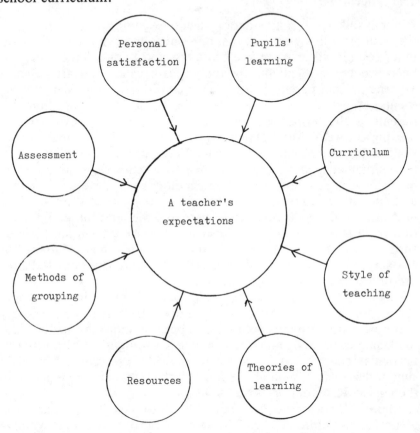

Figure 7.8 Factors which influence a teacher's expectations

The expectations of teachers

An expectation which links teachers with pupils, is that teachers should correctly assess the capability of each individual pupil and then provide suitable work of a high enough standard to encourage all those pupils to achieve their potential.[45] Two recent D.E.S. reports[50,51] have expressed concern about teachers' underestimations of pupils' capabilities, stemming from the teachers' indifference to the outcome or their failure to correctly assess the potential of each pupil.

There are some expectations which link teachers with their school subjects; the following remarks apply equally to the primary school, where a teacher often takes the same class for almost all subjects, and to the secondary school, where a mathematics teacher rarely teaches other subjects (except computer education) although other subject specialists may also teach mathematics. Schools almost invariably segregate mathematics teaching from any other subject teaching,[52] even when the same person also teaches that other subject. There are several school subjects which use mathematical ideas and techniques, for example, art, business studies, economics, general studies, geography and science.[53] Teachers of these subjects expect their pupils to have a form of relational understanding (see chapter 5) in which the techniques are related to concepts and schemes in their own subject rather than in mathematics. Thus a parabolic graph may represent a physical relationship rather than a second degree equation. These teachers also expect the pupils to have certain mathematical skills but may not realize the importance of using the correct stimulus words so that, for instance, a pupil who can successfully calculate the Lowest Common Denominator of two fractions may look blankly at a teacher who is asking about division by the Least Common Multiple.

It must be understood that some mathematicians would not expect to teach mathematics which meets the needs of other subject teachers, unless it was already a part of the actual mathematics courses. We will now consider in more detail the expectations of mathematics teachers.

Firstly, teachers who are members of a school team which is actively involved in teaching mathematics, can expect to be more successful than isolated teachers and to get more satisfaction from working at the school. The team members will give support to each other and are more likely to plan and teach suitable courses for the pupils.[54] Once courses have been planned, teachers expect that suitable text books, work schemes and other equipment shall be available for all pupils in the school. There is evidence[55,56] that these resources are not available in some British schools at present, and it is perhaps time that teachers were more outspoken about the inefficiency of teaching mathematics under such conditions. Teachers should expect their employers to make good use of any resources which are made available, for example, by the falling numbers of pupils in an L.E.A. A good teacher knows that resources are not enough on their own and must also display his own interest and enthusiasm so that the pupils can see mathematics as a powerful human activity and not as a body of stagnant knowledge.[57,58] His efforts will be most effective if he has the support of parents, for it has been shown that their interest and encouragement help pupils to make better progress.[59]

Let us now consider how the teacher's expectations are linked with his choice of contrasting methods of grouping and styles of teaching, all the time realizing the importance of his being allowed to use methods in which he has confidence.[60] Two contrasting methods use similar ability grouping and mixed ability grouping of the pupils. The former supports a general expectation that each pupil has a potential ability which the teacher helps him to fulfil. Some research studies indicate that this method seems to restrict achievement to the expected potential of an average pupil in that group and any restriction of achievement is especially serious for pupils in low ability groups.[59] Mixed ability grouping, on the other hand, often supports an expectation that intelligence can be affected by environmental factors. This means that good teaching and motivation can be expected to produce effective learning to higher levels in some pupils. Either of these methods, used with the mathematics courses, must satisfy the pupils' mathematical needs. It may be that these needs are achieved better now than they were twenty years ago with the majority of children, although this is not true for some of the most gifted children[61,62] whose standards of mathematical achievement and interest are causing national concern.

The expectations of lecturers in higher and further education

Lecturers in colleges of higher education and colleges of further education expect certain academic standards from pupils who have been through primary and secondary school. A good achievement at G.C.E. Advanced-level is required for entrance to higher education, while further education colleges will accept younger students with lower qualifications to begin craft and technical courses.[63] However, educational change has blurred the distinction between the ideas that further education trains people for jobs while higher education provides academic and social benefits. For instance, there are now university engineering courses during which a student works in industry for several months, sandwiched between two periods of academic study. Many tertiary level courses have training, academic and social aims.

College lecturers are often not satisfied with the level of academic achievement of their new students, or with the content of syllabuses which pupils have studied in their final years at school.[64] Each school can only offer a limited number of mathematics courses and it is impossible for these to meet the expectations of lecturers at all colleges to which pupils will go. However, for pupils who will use mathematics at university there is an agreed common-core G.C.E.

A-level syllabus[65] which, with options added, provides a good foundation for undergraduate studies. Most other discussions about suitable syllabuses leading to higher and further education, have been in the context of the proposed changes in public examinations. These examinations are described in chapter 10.

The expectations of employers

There is a quite substantial element of agreement between teachers and employers about mathematics education, but the two groups have certain very different points of view. A story about a teacher named Mr. X may make us more sympathetic towards an employer's point of view. Mr. X's house had a faulty window frame, so he took the damaged strip of wooden beading to the woodyard. When the assistant said 'We stock a slightly different pattern now and, by the way, the new pieces are slightly narrower because they are metric' Mr. X was annoyed because of the extra work needed to make the new piece fit reasonably well. In fact, he was as annoyed as some employers are when they find that school leavers have developed more individualized work patterns (automatically considered worse than the old work patterns) and have been taught to use the metric system for most of their calculations.

Employers are used to specifying the supplies they expect to receive but they cannot specify in the same way for people. As teachers, we have to accept pupils who come into the school, identify their strengths and weaknesses, and plan their education accordingly. This education includes instruction to achieve and maintain simple mathematical skills which employers expect[66] and which some teachers have recently undervalued. However, as well as teaching those skills to pupils, it is important that education prepares them for learning new skills and techniques which may be required by future changes in employment.

The expectations of employers and teachers have been drawn closer together by investigations into the actual mathematical needs in employment and deficiencies in present school achievements.[67,68,69] Better mutual understanding has also come from co-operative linking schemes, sponsored by companies such as British Petroleum, which allow mathematicians from school and industry to work and talk together for several days or weeks. These activities help some teachers to realize how mathematics is used by semi-skilled workers,[70] by craftsmen, by technicians, by administrators and by professional mathematicians.[71] A booklet,[72] sponsored by the Schools Council and the Mathematical Association, illustrates the extent of such co-operation in 1978; it describes thirty-nine projects concerned with basic skills needed by school leavers or with numeracy.

The expectations of society

The previous five sections have considered the expectations of certain groups of people within society. As a summary, the usual educational aim of such groups is not to change society but to effectively retain the *status quo*. Within each group, many people are content to restrict their activities to a personal level and work to bring the actual local achievements nearer to their ideal expectation. This is illustrated by the following passage, which actually refers to primary schools but could be transcribed to refer to other groups of people:

> ...the teacher secures his reward out of what takes place in the classroom, and is not greatly concerned about how the school's curriculum is ordered, what its purpose is in detail or whether change in it should take place, so long as he secures to himself a personally manageable and satisfying set of transactions with his pupils. Given that pupils have little or no conception of how the order of things might be different from what they experience and know, they themselves cannot be a spur towards any specific change. They may actually hinder change, in that they exercise their quite considerable influence over the teacher with the purpose, unconscious perhaps, of remaining within a familiar and understood teaching situation.[73]

For many people, therefore, it is probably true to say that they expect as little change as possible in mathematics education, especially if change individually affects them. There are exceptions, provided by minorities who desire change because they see themselves or others as disadvantaged (and some actually are disadvantaged) by the present system.[74] For example, there are pupils who move house and have to transfer to another secondary school which is using a significantly different examination syllabus. As a second example, there are families[75] whose social culture differs from that consciously or unconsciously nurtured by the school and who feel that the school does not provide a relevant mathematics education.

Dilemmas such as this cannot be resolved without accepting that multi-cultural education is a political and social issue. We can be helped by turning for advice to the sociologists who have considered broadly similar issues, though few people have yet related them directly to mathematics teaching and learning.[76] Professor Bernstein, of the London Institute of Education, has proposed that 'in advanced industrialized societies the social purpose of the school becomes one of educating for diversity in social and economic function'. This requires changes in pupils, schools and family structure whose effect is 'to increase the possibility of innovation within a society and to widen the area of individual choice. At the same time this creates problems of assuring cultural continuity for those transmitting the society's culture, and creates problems . . . of identity in the young.'[78]

NUMERACY

The educational use of the word 'numeracy' seems to have started with the 1959 Crowther sixth form report, where it was described as 'more than the mere ability to manipulate the rule of three'.[79] One has to assume that it was then common knowledge that the 'rule of three' refers to calculating one of the four whole numbers in a:b = c:d when the other three numbers are known. Nowadays numeracy appears to have become a concern of modern society, for both the words 'numeracy' and 'numerate' are in the 1974 revision of the *Oxford Illustrated Dictionary* whereas neither word was in the corresponding 1950 *Concise Oxford Dictionary*. These twenty four years also cover the period of major changes in many school mathematics syllabuses, and major changes in the everyday use of mathematics as shown by the present day metrication of weights and measures, and reliance on electronic devices for numerical calculations.

The low level of numeracy achieved by many pupils is easily attributed to modern mathematics, as a single scapegoat, but it is certain that the blame does not always, or only, lie with modern mathematics. For example, one study showed that pupils from modern ·and traditional G.C.E. Ordinary-level courses did equally well on industrial tests of arithmetic, spatial relationships and mechanical aptitude.[80] Also, although concern for 'numeracy' is new, there have been reports many times throughout the last hundred years about pupils' low standards of achievement in mathematics and the poor teaching of mathematics.[81] There are many adults of all ages who are not numerate. One welcomed result of the present public concern about education is that adult numeracy remediation schemes are now available. One such scheme is 'Make it count', which was started in 1978 by Yorkshire Television and the National Extension College.

Assessing numeracy

Innumeracy of schoolchildren hit the headlines in March 1978 when about eight thousand 16 year old pupils had answered a twenty-three question test set by the Institute of Mathematics and its Applications. The questions ranged from the addition of two-digit numbers to the use of percentages, and only 8·3 per cent of the boys and 4·5 per cent of the girls scored full marks. A school leavers' test of this type, set at a level which all pupils are expected to achieve, is one form of assessment of numeracy which has been considered. An alternative suggestion is that of a progressive sequence of tests (e.g. with questions on multiplication by one digit, by two digit and by three digit numbers) to provide information about the extent of a pupil's capability, which is available for use by teachers and employers.[84]

Defining numeracy

Assessing numeracy is simple when compared with the problem of defining numeracy. One approach, which was first described by Wilson in his 1951 book on *Teaching the new arithmetic*,[85] is to start with the mathematics which a chosen sample of adults actually use in their work and leisure. This mathematics can then be classified to produce a table of applications with their frequencies of use (see figure 7.9) and the definition of numeracy is derived by selecting the most frequently used applications. The main disadvantage of this approach is that the definition of numeracy becomes a list of objective skills without an underlying mathematical structure.

Application	Average frequency of use in a week
MONEY CALCULATIONS UNDER £10	
Multiplication	4.0
Addition	13.3
Checking change	22.5
FRACTIONS, $\frac{1}{2}$, $\frac{1}{3}$, $\frac{1}{4}$, $\frac{1}{8}$.	
Practical application, eg. serving food	2.4
MEASUREMENT	
Accurate metric measurement between 1mm and 3 metres	1.2

Figure 7.9 Typical applications of mathematics which could lead to a definition of numeracy

A second approach is to start with a mathematical goal which can then lead to a more detailed definition. Any prize for the most concisely stated goal must probably go to Mr. Michael Girling's 'Basic numeracy is the ability to use a four-function electronic calculator *sensibly*.'[86] His word 'sensibly' includes the need to check, approximate and perform mental calculations while using the calculator. The ability to use mental calculations is another skill which has been perhaps unwisely neglected by too many teachers, and its reintroduction might easily strengthen the pupils' grasp of other basic skills.[87] This in turn could improve the pupils' confidence in using numbers and so create a more positive attitude when they have to use numbers after leaving school.[88]

All people would agree that pupils need to be able to use numbers but there is not agreement about the means of calculation. Many people deplore an almost total reliance on an electronic calculator and also require pupils to be able to perform accurate arithmetic calculations with pencil and paper. For numeracy, we only need to consider the numbers used in everyday life, so calculation numbers will rarely exceed three significant digits and operations as difficult as long division would be excluded. A full discussion of such an idea of numeracy is provided in *The third R*, a book written by a group of experienced education lecturers.[89] Before leaving the subject of numeracy, it should be said that it is not only an ability to handle numbers. Most teachers would also include everyday geometric and algebraic ideas within a basic school course.

Conclusion

As well as considering the expectations of some major groups of people, this chapter has discussed several issues of a more general nature. When all these expectations and issues are considered, school mathematics has also to be seen as an integral part of the national school system. This system has social intentions and must provide every pupil with at least the minimal standards of literacy and numeracy.

Annotated References for Chapter 7

1. H.M.S.O. (1977) *Mathematics, science and modern languages in maintained schools in England: an appraisal of problems in some key subjects by H.M. Inspectorate.* Her Majesty's Stationery Office: London. See p. 1.

   A review and discussion, touching on many areas of mathematics education. C.S.E. and G.C.E. examination passes for 1964–74 are included.

2. M.A. (1976) *Why, what and how?* Mathematical Association: Leicester.

   A consideration of aims, goals and objectives, with examples of their use in teaching.

3. Silver H. (1973) *Equal opportunity in education*. Methuen: London.

   A discussion of the changing views of equality since 1922.

4. Oxford (1975) Theme for issue: equality and education. *Oxford Review of Education*, vol. 1, no. 1, pp. 1–89.

   Eight articles which explore ideas about equality, expressed in various ways.

5. Cooper D.E. (1980) *Illusions of equality*. Routledge & Kegan Paul: Henley-on-Thames.

   Education is not to promote social equality; the conflict between equality and excellence.

6. H.M.S.O. (1977) *Education in schools, a consultative document*. Her Majesty's Stationery Office: London. See p. 18.

   The Green Paper linked with the Great Debate.

7. N.A.C.O.M.E. (1975) *Overview and analysis of school mathematics, grades K–12*. National Advisory Committee on Mathematical Education, Conference Board of the Mathematical Sciences: Washington D.C. See p. 129.

   A report, with recommendations, on the health of American school mathematics.

8. Fennema E. (1974) Mathematics learning and the sexes: a review. *Journal for Research in Mathematics Education*, vol. 5, no. 3, pp. 126–39.

   The results of 36 research studies of American children from ages 3 to 18.

9. Burton G.M. (1978) Mathematical ability – is it a masculine trait? *School Science & Mathematics*, vol. 78, no. 7, pp. 566–74.

   A survey, with recommendations and a list of forty references.

10. Burton G.M. (1979) Regardless of sex. *The Mathematics Teacher*, vol. 72, no. 4, pp. 261–70.

    An overview of the male/female inbalance in mathematics education, which also includes many references to recent articles.

11. Hopkinson D. (1978) *The education of gifted children*. Woburn Press: London. See chapter 7.

    A book about all gifted children, but also with special reference to mathematics education.

12. Schools Council (1970) *Cross'd with adversity; the education of socially disadvantaged children in secondary schools*; Working paper no. 27. Evans/Methuen: London.

    A study of pupils' problems and the ways that the education service deals with them.

13. H.M.S.O. (1978) *Special educational needs: report of the committee of enquiry into the education of handicapped and young people*. Her Majesty's Stationery Office: London.

    The Warnock report; recommendations on how special education can be integrated into school and society.

14. H.M.S.O. (1976) *The education of children with impaired hearing in England*. Her Majesty's Stationery Office: London.

    A pamphlet with brief details about schools, units, pupils and teachers.

15. D.E.S. (1974) *Integrating handicapped children*. Department of Education and Science: London.

A discussion pamphlet about the policy of integration and its relationship to specific handicaps.

16. H.M.S.O. (1967) Central Advisory Council for Education (England); *Children and their primary schools*, vols. 1 & 2. Her Majesty's Stationery Office: London. See paragraph 545.

This Plowden report is probably the most thorough ever produced in England on every aspect of primary schools.

17. Cope C. & Anderson E. (1977) *Special units in ordinary schools*: University of London Institute Studies in Education 6. National Foundation for Educational Research: Slough.

A study about physically handicapped children who are not in special schools.

18. Gill M. & Gill D. (1977) Multicultural maths. *Mathematics in School*, vol. 6, no. 2, pp. 6–9.

Examples of mathematics from other cultures, and its use in teaching.

19. U.N.E.S.C.O. (1974) *Interactions between linguistics and mathematical education*: report ED-74/CONF. 808. United Nations Educational Scientific and Cultural Organisation: Paris.

The final report and recommendations of a symposium held from 1st. to 11th. September 1974 in Nairobi.

20. Dawe L. (1978) Teaching mathematics in a multi-cultural school. *The Forum of Education*, vol. 37, no. 2, pp. 24–31.

An interesting report on teaching, and analysis of major problems.

21. Henkin L.A. (1972) *Linguistic aspects of mathematical education*. In reference 22, chapter 14.

A discussion of the uses of symbols and quantifiers in school mathematics.

22. Lamon W.E. ed. (1972) *Learning and the nature of mathematics*. Science Research Associates: Chicago.

The development, pedagogy, psychology and communication of mathematics.

23. Austin J.L. & Howson A.G. (1979) Language and mathematical education. *Educational Studies in Mathematics*, vol. 10, no. 2, pp. 161–97. Reprint booklet available from The School Mathematics Project and E.R.I.C.

An overview of the situation, with an extensive bibliography.

24. Love E. & Tahta D. (1977) Language across the curriculum: mathematics. *Mathematics Teaching*, no. 79, pp. 48–9.

A viewpoint on the place of language.

25. Beard R.M. (1972) *The growth of logical thinking*. In reference 26, pp. 164–9.

This chapter is mainly an outline of Piagetian ideas.

26. Chapman L.R. ed. (1972) *The process of learning mathematics*. Pergamon: Oxford.

A book from a course of B.Ed. lectures which includes descriptions of four national projects.

27. Aiken L.R. (1972) Language factors in learning mathematics. *Review of Educational Research*, vol. 42, no. 3, pp. 359–85.

A review of all language factors, with an extensive bibliography.

28. Fischbein E. (1977) Image and concept in learning mathematics. *Educational Studies in Mathematics*, vol. 8, no. 2, pp. 153–65.

A discussion about models being able to initiate and generate learning.

29. Lin C.Y. (1979) Imagery in mathematical thinking and learning. *International Journal of Mathematical Education in Science and Technology*, vol. 10, no. 1, pp. 107–11.

A discussion and examples of diagrams used to help understanding and generate thinking.

30. Johnson P.B. (1972) *Mathematics as human communication*. In reference 22, chapter 13.

An analysis of the components of communication.

31. Harkin J.B. & Rising G.R. (1974) Some psychological and pedagogical aspects of mathematical symbolism. *Educational Studies in Mathematics*, vol. 5, no. 3, pp.255–60.

Difficulties with ambiguous, synonymous, archaic, inappropriate and contradictory symbols.

32. Hanley A. (1978) Verbal mathematics. *Mathematics in School*, vol. 7, no. 4, pp. 27–30.

Examples of mathematical difficulties where words are a contributory factor.

33. Preston M. (1978) The language of early mathematical experience. *Mathematics in School*, vol. 7, no. 4, pp. 31–2.

An inspection of primary mathematics schemes shows problems with vocabulary, readability and perception.

34. Barnes D. (1976) *From communication to curriculum*. Penguin: Harmondsworth. See p. 28.

A book about pupils and teachers, communication and learning, without special reference to mathematics.

35. Willoughby S.S. (1970) *Issues in the teaching of mathematics*. In reference 36, chapter 6. See p. 263.

Twelve issues of mathematics, curriculum, psychology and pedagogy.

36. Begle E.G. (1970) *Mathematics education*: yearbook 69.1 of the National Society for the Study of Education. University of Chicago Press: Chicago.

The new curriculum in mathematics; educational and psychological problems and solutions.

37. Golby M. (1973) 'Drills and skills' and understanding. *Mathematics in School*, vol. 2, no. 2, pp. 23–4.

An argument that older methods were successful and verbal instruction is necessary.

38. Griffiths H.B. & Howson A.G. (1974) *Mathematics: society and curricula*. Cambridge University Press: Cambridge. See p. 215.

An important book about mathematics and education, which gives a broad view of mathematics education.

39. MacDonald I.D. (1978) Insight and intuition in mathematics. *Educational Studies in Mathematics*, vol. 9, no. 4, pp. 411–20.

A discussion and refinement of ideas in reference 38.

40. M.A. (1974) *Mathematics, eleven to sixteen*: Mathematical Association. Bell: London. See chapter 2.

Guidance for the teacher who wishes to present a mathematical course in mathematics.

41. Williams E.M. & Shuard H. (1976) *Primary mathematics today*. Longman: London. See chapters 11, 12, 31.

A detailed teachers' guide to the development of mathematics in primary and middle school.

42. Schools Council (1968) *Enquiry 1: young school leavers*. Her Majesty's Stationery Office: London.

An enquiry into facts about schools and jobs in preparation for raising the school leaving age to 16.

43. Rutter M. et al. (1979) *Fifteen thousand hours: secondary schools and their effects on children*. Open Books: London. See p. 14.

A very interesting report on 1487 children as they progressed through 12 schools.

44. Kent D. (1978) Isobel. *Mathematics Teaching*, no. 85, pp. 12–14.

An account of recognizing a future mathematician.

45. Nash R. (1976) *Teacher expectations and pupil learning*. Routledge & Kegan Paul: London, Boston. See chapter 6.

A discussion of the inter-related opinions, attitudes, feelings and actions of teachers and pupils.

46. Sturgeon S.B. (1979) *Interviews to investigate learning difficulties in mathematics with particular reference to girls*. Department of Mathematics and Statistics, City Polytechnic: Sheffield.

Follow-up interviews, by the B.P. Fellow, with pupils in four comprehensive schools.

47. H.M.S.O. (1976) *Statistics of education, vol. 4, teachers*. Her Majesty's Stationery Office: London. See table 36.

One volume of the annual comprehensive statistics.

48. Husen T. (1972) The 'learning society' and tomorrow's schools. *London Educational Review*, vol. 1, no. 2, pp. 53–9. See p. 58.

Lifelong education is likely to be the normal thing, brought on by an accelerating rate of change.

49. Kellaghan T. et al. (1976) The mathematical attainments of post-primary school entrants. *Irish Journal of Education*, vol. 10, no. 1, pp. 3–17.

The results of objective tests based on the content of the primary curriculum.

50. H.M.S.O. (1977) *Gifted children in middle and comprehensive secondary schools*: Matters for discussion 4. Her Majesty's Stationery Office: London.

Giftedness is defined and its place in school and subject is considered.

51. H.M.S.O. (1978) *Primary education in England: a survey by H.M. Inspectors*. Her Majesty's Stationery Office: London.

An appraisal of mathematics and other subjects in 542 schools.

52. H.M.S.O. (1978) *Aspects of secondary education in England*: supplementary information on mathematics. Her Majesty's Stationery Office: London.

Detailed information about teachers, pupils, courses and schools.

53. Ling J.F. (1977) *The mathematics curriculum: mathematics across the curriculum*. Schools Council, Blackie: Glasgow.

A book from the series of constructive and critical discussions.

54. See reference 43, pp. 112–13.

55. Guardian The (1979) The scandal of schools without books. *Education Guardian*, 6 March, p. 11.

Observer The (1979) How pupils pay the price for economy. *The Observer*, 10 June, p. 3.

Two reports on shortages of books and equipment in British schools.

56. H.M.S.O. (1979) *Aspects of secondary education in England*; a survey by H.M. Inspectors of Schools. Her Majesty's Stationery Office: London. See paragraph 12.9.

The report of a thorough investigation of the final two years of education in 384 schools (10% sample).

57. Wheeler D. (1975) Humanising mathematical activity. *Mathematics Teaching*, no. 71, pp. 4–9.

Why humanising is needed, how to do it, and the quality of awareness.

58. Watson F.R. (1978) $M = C + P$: some thought on attainment in mathematics. *Mathematics in School*, vol. 7, no. 4, pp. 33–4.

Mathematics equals conjecture plus proof, and is not arid basic facts.

59. Pidgeon D.A. (1970) *Expectation and pupil performance*. National Foundation for Educational Research: Slough.

Some studies of the influence of environmental factors on motivation and performance.

60. Brissenden T.H.F. (1980) *Mathematics teaching; theory in practice*. Harper & Row: London, New York.

A programme to help teachers become more effective in the classroom.

61. See references 50 and 51.

62. Trown A. (1978) What shall we do about the gifted? *Mathematics in School*, vol. 7, no. 2, pp. 6–8.

Recognition of the mathematically gifted and appropriate action to take.

63. Appleton T. (1978) Mathematics in further education. *Mathematics in School*, vol. 7, no. 5, pp. 24–5.

An introduction to work of the Mathematical Association sub-committee on industry and business mathematics.

64. Farnsworth L.H. & Pike D.F. (1976) Modern mathematics and further education. *Mathematics in School*, vol. 5, no. 5, pp. 26–8.

A double article about the difficulties of students and the views of lecturers.

65. S.C.U.E. & C.N.A.A. (1978) *A minimal core syllabus for A level mathematics.* Conference on University Entrance & Council for National Academic Awards: London.

Suggestions for a syllabus of core and options, compiled by considering present syllabuses and the needs of university departments.

66. Fitzgerald A. (1976) Mathematical knowledge and skills required by pupils entering industry at the 16 + level. *Mathematics in School*, vol. 5, no. 3, pp. 22–3.

Fitzgerald A. (1976) School mathematics and the requirements of industry. *The Vocational Aspect of Education*, vol. 28, no. 70, pp. 43–9.

Two articles discussing a competency list which could lead to graded tests.

67. U.B.I. (1978) *Literacy numeracy attitudes.* Understanding British Industry resource centre, Sun Alliance House, New Inn Hall Street, Oxford OX1 2Q3.

A statement on school-industry problems, with comments on relevant reports.

68. I.M.A. (1975, 1976, 1977) *Mathematical needs of school leavers entering employment, I, II, & III*: Symposium proceedings series 6, 11, 14. Institute of Mathematics and its Applications: Southend.

Three titles selected from several which deal with the school-employment interface.

69. H.M.S.O. (1979) *Local authority arrangements for the school curriculum*; Report on the circular 14/77 review. Her Majesty's Stationery Office: London. See section C5.

L.E.A. replies on many aspects of the curriculum; it contains comments and bar graphs about four questions on school mathematics.

70. Fitzgerald A. (1980) School mathematics and employment at 16 + with particular reference to commercial work. *Mathematics in School*, vol. 9, no. 3, pp. 26–31.

The mathematical needs of junior clerks and business technicians.

71. Pollack H.O. (1976) What industry wants a mathematician to know and how we want them to know it. *Educational Studies in Mathematics*, vol. 7, nos. 1/2. pp. 109–12.

An industrial mathematician gives his opinion on the mathematics education needed to do his kind of work.

72. Bailey D.E. (1978) *A survey of mathematics projects involving education and employment*. School of Mathematics: University of Bath.

This booklet is a starting point for a more intensive investigation.

73. Taylor P.H. et al. (1974) *Purpose, power and constraint in the primary school curriculum*. Macmillan: London. See p. 62.

A Schools Council study of influences of society on the existing curriculum.

74. See reference 6, pp. 21–3.

75. Douglas J.W.B. (1964) *The home and the school; a study of ability and attainment in the primary school*. Macgibbon & Kee: London.

A longitudinal study, which suggests that streaming reinforces the process of social selection.

76. Williams R.P. (1978) *The sociologist and mathematical education.* In reference 77, chapter 3.

The reasons given for mathematics education, and the consequences, may be at variance with the intentions.

77. Wain G.T. ed. (1978) *Mathematical education.* Van Nostrand Reinhold: Wokingham.

A collection of chapters on mathematics and mathematics education, by respected contributors.

78. Bernstein B. (1975) *Class, codes and control, volume 3: Towards a theory of educational transmissions.* Routledge & Kegan Paul: London, Boston. See pp. 58–9.

A sequence of essays which investigate the effect of class relationships upon institutionalizing codes in the school.

79. H.M.S.O. (1959) *15 to 18: a report of the Central Advisory Council for Education (England).* Her Majesty's Stationery Office: London. See Paragraph 401.

The Crowther report, covering many aspects of concern about school leavers.

80. Fitzgerald A. (1978) Pupils' performances on industrial selection tests in relation to their mathematical background. *Educational Research.* vol. 20, no. 2, pp. 122–9.

This study of higher ability pupils answers, and raises, some interesting questions.

81. McIntosh A. (1977) When will they ever learn? *Forum,* vol. 19, no. 3, pp. 92–95. Reprinted in *Mathematics Teaching,* no. 86, pp. i–iv (1979).

A collection of quotations about school mathematics teaching and standards during the last 100 years.

82. Guardian The (1978) Multiplying problems of the fifth. *The Guardian,* 9 March, p. 4.

A news item about fifth-year secondary pupils taking the I.M.A. numeracy test.

83. I.M.A. (1979) *Numeracy:* occasional publications no. 1. Institute of Mathematics and its Applications: Southend.

This booklet follows others which report various discussions on numeracy.

84. J.M.C. (1977) *Basic mathematical skills – curricula and assessment:* paper J.M.C. 77/3. Joint Mathematical Council: London.

A discussion document which considers various issues about numeracy.

85. Wilson G.M. (1951) *Teaching the new arithmetic.* McGraw Hill: New York.

Originally published in 1939, this book considers arithmetic to be a tool used by children and adults.

86. Girling M. (1977) Towards a definition of basic numeracy. *Mathematics Teaching,* no. 81, pp. 4–5.

A discussion of the mathematical understanding needed to use an electronic calculator sensibly.

87. Ewbank W.A. (1977) Mental arithmetic – a neglected topic? *Mathematics in School,* vol. 6, no. 5, pp. 28–31.

Reasons for using mental arithmetic and examples of its use.

88. Sturgess D. (1978) What should they know at 16? *Mathematics Teaching*, no. 85, pp. 22-4.

An article which emphasizes the importance of confident handling of a short list of abilities.

89. Glenn J. A. ed. (1978) *The third R: towards a numerate society.* Harper & Row: London, New York.

A clear and simple analysis of basic concepts and processes.

CHAPTER 8

THE MATHEMATICS CURRICULUM FOR THE 1980s: SPECIFICATION AND AIMS

Introduction

The previous chapters have explained the context into which the school curriculum fits. The British education system does not start with a definition of the curriculum and neither does this book. To start with a definition would be equivalent to starting a mathematics lesson with the instruction 'Learn that area equals length times breadth' although some of the pupils had no prior understanding of the concept of area. Our education system allows mathematics teachers in individual schools to be responsible for choosing their curriculum, within certain implied limits. The choice has always been based very much on what teachers had managed to do in the classroom and what they wished to do. This practical basis is now combined with curriculum theory and the combination will be described in the following pages.

Four stages of curriculum reform

Before any new or revised mathematics curriculum is successfully introduced into a school or group of schools, the teachers concerned should discuss it thoroughly. There should also be as much experimentation as possible to allow these teachers and their pupils to test any new ideas. The whole process of curriculum reform has four stages, namely, specification, development, dissemination and implementation, and these stages will now be explained.

Specification of the curriculum is the first stage; it will be discussed in the following pages and its elements are shown in figure 8.1. This figure shows that feedback from later stages is one input to the

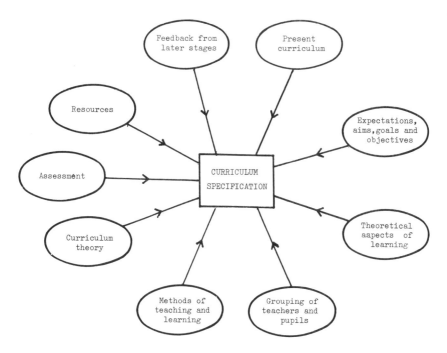

Figure 8.1 Curriculum specification: the first stage of introducing a new or reversed curriculum

specification, so that the four stages are not completely sequential. The *development* from this specification is often made with the help of a small group of enthusiastic teachers who develop the content and method of use of the new curriculum materials until they are considered suitable for use by other teachers and classes. The third stage is the *dissemination* of materials to other people and this will often be organized by the staff at L.E.A. teachers' centres.[1,2,3] Dissemination is a process of first explaining why and how the materials can be used and then making them available. It must be realized that this, by itself, will not necessarily lead to them being used in a uniform way. For example, after an investigation of the use of the Scottish Education Department Common Mathematics Course, the researcher wrote: 'I found that the only commonality between schools lay in the employment of red sheets and red cards. All children used the red sheets and red cards of the modular system. Their format was constant, but not their system of use.'[4] Similarly, teachers in the same school may use curriculum materials in widely different ways so that there must always be an *implementation* stage. This is when teachers, other than the enthusiastic developers, are helped to make the most effective use of the materials with their own classes. It is only in individual classrooms that materials, teachers and

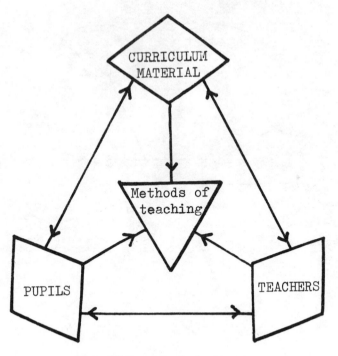

Figure 8.2 Interaction in the classroom

pupils interact (see figure 8.2) and it is there that help from more experienced teachers should be available. If this help is not provided, the material is likely to be wastefully misapplied in some classrooms and consigned to the back of a store cupboard in others.

SPECIFICATION

Inspectors' views on the curriculum

> There is no centralised control of the curriculum or of teaching methods in England and improvement is, perhaps more than in any other country, a matter of improvement in individual schools. There are no universal remedies since all do not suffer the same disease.[5]

The above passage comes from an appraisal of problems in primary and secondary school mathematics, which was published by the Department of Education and Science (D.E.S.) in 1977. It emphasizes that it is important for teachers to improve the education in their own school. This will help to meet the expectations of that school's pupils and parents. Indirectly it may also help pupils in other schools, as the successes of a few people can be transmitted to others through local or regional groups of teachers.

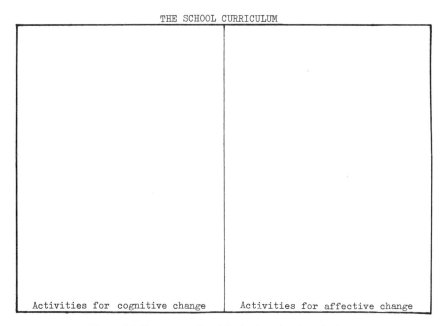

Figure 8.3 Two types of activity in the school curriculum

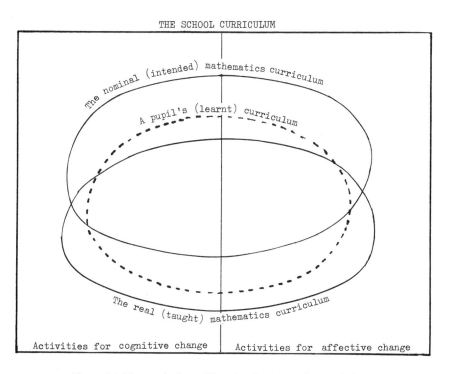

Figure 8.4 The nominal, pupil's and real mathematics curriculum

Of course, there is room for improvement in most school mathematics teaching,[6,7] and the above quotation implies that correct diagnosis of the disease is needed before we can discover the remedies. Some D.E.S. Inspectors gave one diagnosis in a curriculum paper published in the following year, where they wrote ' ... in matters of the curriculum ... variety can reflect a healthy environment and vigorous and purposeful development in response to local need and opportunity; but equally it can be associated with an inadequate sense of direction and of priorities, with too little coordination both within and between schools, and with a reluctance to evaluate the curriculum offered as a whole.'[8] I am delighted that the inspectors applauded a wisely chosen variety of methods and content in a school curriculum, as this should lead to purposeful and interesting learning of mathematics.

The school curriculum

A useful definition of the curriculum is that offered by the philosophers Paul Hirst and Richard Peters in 1970: 'the label for a programme or course of activities which is explicitly organized as the means whereby pupils may attain the desired objectives, whatever these may be.'[9] (Note that this word 'objectives' embraces all the aims, goals and objectives which I have defined in chapter 7.) Thus the school curriculum is the course of educational activities explicitly organized by the teachers and pupils in the school over some period of time. The length of this period of time varies; it could be from three to seven years if we are considering an individual pupil.

Because most schools have cultural, intellectual and social aims[10,11] this curriculum will be broad and designed to include activities which bring about both cognitive change and affective change (see figure 8.3). A distinction used to be made between lessons within the curriculum (which promoted mainly cognitive change) and extra-curricular activities (which promoted mainly affective change) but the above definition takes a more integrated view by stressing that mental or physical activity is needed for any change. (See 'progress and activity methods' in chapter 4.)

Being part of the school curriculum, the mathematics curriculum[12,13] includes not only the syllabus content but also the methods of teaching and less central activities such as mathematics clubs and visits to places where mathematics is used. This mathematics curriculum can be represented by drawing three closed curves on figure 8.3 to make figure 8.4, as explained in the following paragraphs.

There are three closed curves because there are three slightly different curricula to be represented; namely the nominal, the real and the one learnt by a pupil. Some differences between these will be shown by considering a teacher's use of a mathematics work card scheme. The *nominal curriculum* is expressed by a set of work cards which present the topics on a syllabus, and by explanatory notes for the teacher. Then the *real curriculum* is the interpretation which the teacher makes, and presents to the group of pupils. Finally the *pupil's curriculum* is what he or she actually learns.[14] (This is shown by a dotted curve because it is for just one member of the class.) Of course, despite the individuality of teachers and pupils, there is a large common area between the three different curricula, for those school classes which are using the same work card scheme.

Curriculum change and curriculum theory

Most of the changes in mathematics education which have been outlined in chapter 2 were brought about by practising teachers who had no theoretical knowledge of how a curriculum changes. They did a good job, mainly correcting the wrongs that existed rather than planning for the future, but such an approach would probably be less successful in meeting the needs of present day pupils who attend all purpose schools which have to serve a more complex and faster changing society.

Since 1950, curriculum theory has grown into that important area of educational studies which gives guidance to those people who are developing a curriculum.[15,16] This guidance does not ignore the importance of 'foundation' studies such as history, philosophy and sociology of education, because the starting point for any curriculum change must include a consideration of the educational aims and goals of the school or schools. This consideration was emphasized in Ralph Tyler's book[17] with its so-called 'objectives model' of curriculum change, which was influential in America from 1949 but is now outdated in many ways. That model has four key questions which are:

1. What educational purposes should the school seek to attain?
2. What educational experiences can be provided that are likely to attain these purposes?
3. How can these educational experiences be effectively organized?
4. How can we determine whether these purposes are being attained?

Tyler's model, like any other, is only a convenient representation of what actually happens; the model is expressed simply, and it can be applied generally because it ignores trivial elements and concentrates on the major educational factors. These factors also occur in other models and it is not surprising therefore to find that their special relevance to mathematics education is discussed in other parts of this book.

In figure 8.3, the school curriculum was divided into activities for affective and cognitive change, and this division is emphasized by two other early books which deal with objectives. These books are Krathwohl's 1964 *Taxonomy of educational objectives in the affective domain* and Bloom's 1956 *Taxonomy of educational objectives in the cognitive domain*.[18] This latter book considers knowledge, comprehension, applications, analysis, synthesis and evaluation (in that order) to be the possible outcomes from any topic in a well constructed curriculum. Bloom's theoretical approach to considering the curriculum is easily applied to mathematics in schools[19] and this was done in a 1972 series of 'educational technology' articles.[20] These began with a consensus of educational aims to form 'the framework on which the whole of . . . mathematics teaching should hang'. These aims were then translated into specific objectives, many of which could be achieved by teaching familiar topics in the classroom. The whole process is shown in figure 8.5.

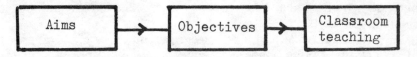

Figure 8.5 An application of educational technology to curriculum design

This use of three stages, aims to objectives to teaching, demonstrates one application of a theoretical method, but some teachers would not consider it a desirable application.[21,22] One reason is that teaching can be rather sterile if its only purpose is to satisfy objectives and another reason is that some aims, such as the pupils' developing a liking for mathematics, probably cannot be translated into specific objectives.[23] Both these reasons mean that figure 8.5 needs the addition of another route from aims to classroom teaching, which does not pass through objectives. However, the route through behavioural objectives[24] must not be erased as it is still important; it is often applied during teaching, and used during the assessment of pupils, in many schools.

There are other theoretical approaches which have been proposed and which (1) would be approved by some teachers but not by all teachers and (2) could be applied to the mathematics curriculum. The details of these approaches are described elsewhere[25,26] but it is of general interest to think about the two contrasting views of the curriculum, proposed by Professor Denis Lawton of the London Institute of Education:

The Classical view of curriculum stresses knowledge in terms of disciplines and ultimately of school subjects and sees the curriculum as the induction of young members of society into the established forms of thought and understanding; the Romantic view of curriculum, on the other hand, sees education as an integral part of life rather than preparation for the adult world.[27]

Whichever view is held by a mathematics teacher, he or she can consider the general curriculum theory which has already been explained and then apply it to mathematics in particular.

Mathematics in curriculum practice and theory

Looking back at the development of school mathematics which was outlined in chapter 2 we see that the two threads which first occurred were Euclidean geometry which represents axioms and logical propositions, and arithmetic which grew from real-life experiences and was valuable for tasks like book-keeping. Pure mathematicians and mathematics teachers have shown that these threads can be intertwined, for instance by applying geometry to everyday objects and by providing a formalized structure for the real numbers. This intertwining has formed one school subject, and most people are in no doubt that mathematics is a unique and vital part of the school curriculum. Because primary and secondary schools treat mathematics in this way, then it seems logical that any realistic curriculum theory should support this practice.

A curriculum theory can be used to look at all the knowledge which pupils assimilate in school and analyse how the pupils can most effectively learn from it. This analysis may support the traditional division of teaching time into separate subject lessons or it may recommend the amalgamation of some subjects, because they are very similar or because they complement each other in some desirable way. One such analysis occurs in the *disciplines thesis* which postulates firstly that knowledge can be separated into distinct disciplines or forms, and secondly that mathematics is one of these disciplines.

The two main proponents of this thesis are Philip Phenix,[28] Professor of Philosophy and Education at Teachers College, Columbia and Paul Hirst,[29] the Cambridge philosopher and epistemologist. If this thesis is taken to be true, then the argument follows that a school curriculum based on units in each discipline will be the most effective way of learning about the different forms of knowledge, whereas cross-disciplinary studies are more likely to offer shallow and undisciplined thinking. Phenix and Hirst's grounds for determining a discipline include a distinctive structure which connects certain representative concepts or ideas, and distinctive methods of enquiry and testing. From these grounds they have tried to justify their conclusions, which include mathematics being a separate discipline.

This justification has been challenged in an article by Kenneth Ruthven who was then at Stirling University. He does not dispute that mathematics is separate but he challenges the form of the arguments which 'seem to conflate logical, social and commonsense definitions'.[30] Ruthven, in his article, uses a technique which is akin to mathematical problem solving and which demonstrates the power of curriculum theory. He develops his theoretical arguments, using mathematical processes where necessary, to reach a conclusion which has then to be applied in a school. He concludes that, reconciled with a traditional technical content of basic, vocational and specialist education in mathematics there should be a general cultural content which shows:

1. What are mathematicians trying to do?
2. What is the point in doing it?
3. How do they go about doing it?
4. Why do they do it that way?
5. How does what they do affect or relate to the rest of social activity?

In primary and secondary schools where the teachers have consciously or unconsciously adopted this combined technical and cultural approach, there are pupils who could answer some of those questions. If this general cultural content were to become an explicit part of a school course, it would have a similar purpose to the 'social context' part of computer education courses (see chapter 9). Computer education teachers have usually found the 'social context' part much more difficult to present than the technical parts and they have developed two methods of presentation, case studies and projects, which teachers might also find useful when presenting cultural mathematics.

The suggested introduction into school mathematics of a general cultural content which has to be reconciled with the traditional content, may not seem to be a new method of curriculum development. However, it is not the same as the old method of curriculum development, where some teachers intuitively decide to introduce extra (e.g. cultural) mathematics and then have to decide what must be omitted to make room for it. The difference is in the way the decision has been reached, and it is not known whether the new method is going to be more successful because of its theoretical base. It ought to be so because, unlike the old method, it considers previous experiences of development and is concerned with contributions to the whole school curriculum.

The contribution of mathematics to the curriculum

Since the Second World War the developing school curriculum has included a *greater* and more *widespread* contribution from the mathematics curriculum.[31] We know, from chapter 2, that when pupils attended separate grammar, modern or technical schools the three types of school had rather different mathematics curricula. It follows, therefore, that when these secondary schools were combined their individual curricula had to be similarly combined into one with a greater content, much of which formed a common curriculum for all pupils. This content was often further increased by the change to modern mathematics, which also had a similar effect in primary schools. Over the same period, mathematics has become more widely applied in industry, commerce and government; it now affects the lives of most people and this wider application has moved over into schools.[32] This is most obvious in the upper secondary school, where the old sixth form choice of mathematics only with physics or chemistry probably left many adults with the impression that mathematics has a natural affinity only with experimental sciences. Its educational links with other sciences and non-sciences, such as geography and art,[33] might have been realized sooner by looking at the activities of mathematicians. There are probably as many mathematicians with an interest in music as with an interest in science, and examples such as this suggest that today's school mathematics courses with their more widespread applications may be a truer representation of the discipline.

The contribution expected in 1978 from the mathematics curriculum may be judged by the following excerpt which lists some suggestions for a common curriculum for pupils from 11 to 16 years.

> Mathematical education should not be seen as concentrating only on its own curricular area; on the contrary, it can have an influence on several, if not all, of the areas of experience. It contributes to the aesthetic area by developing a sense of order through an emphasis on patterns in number and shape, by fostering an appreciation of symmetry in shape and form, and by searching for the elegant solution to a problem. Pupils are encouraged to be creative when, for example, they are asked to make up their own problems and provide their own solutions and not simply imitate the work of others.
>
> Mathematics cannot progress without the help of language, and in return, the subject helps linguistic development through the need to refine and make precise the language used. It has a similar reciprocal relationship with the scientific area, for scientific

methods are used in the learning of the subject and mathematics is frequently applied in science. Social, political and ethical issues can be clarified by the use of statistical and other forms of mathematical argument.

Apart from the development of strictly mathematical skills, mathematics requires neatness and accuracy, clear logical thinking, and precise and concise expression and communication. These are valuable personal skills which help to prepare pupils for the world of work and to take up their place in society. Many children find mathematics difficult and think it is harder to learn than other school subjects, probably because they can recognise 'failure' in it more readily; at the same time the subject is important for them and their response to this challenge has implications for their own personal development.[34]

It will be seen that these paragraphs are all concerned with the widespread application of mathematics and I hope that only scant mention is made of the 'own curricular area' of mathematics education because teachers are expected to already be familiar with this and to realize its importance. Another possible downgrading of specialist mathematics occurs in the 1965 Scottish Education Department report on primary education,[35] which places mathematics as a subset of environmental studies.

Aim for dynamic progress by mathematically able pupils

The fear of downgrading specialist mathematics, which was mentioned in the last section, seems perhaps justified as far as some of the most mathematically able pupils are concerned. A 1977 appraisal by some of Her Majesty's Inspectors said:

> A further cause for concern is the quality of mathematical education available to those children ablest in the subject. Too often schools provide insufficient challenge to the highly gifted. In primary schools the problem is every bit as important as it is at the secondary stage. The difficulties are frequently associated with comprehensive reorganization, but grammar schools do not automatically provide the challenge needed by children of this level of ability.[36]

Because these gifted pupils[37,38] quickly assimilate ideas, they can easily make average progress through school with hardly any intellectual effort. Their exceptional abilities may not be noticed by their teachers, who therefore allow pupils who could make dynamic progress to live an intellectually inert existence. Every able pupil, and indeed every pupil, must be encouraged to make as much progress as possible in mathematics; this progress should be an overall aim when teachers are designing a mathematics curriculum.

Balanced aims for the mathematics curriculum

> *Double, double toil and trouble;*
> *Fire burn and cauldron bubble.*
> *Curriculum balance we must make*
> *So in the cauldron boil and bake*
> *Knowledge, fact; traditional fare*
> *Then liking, feeling add their share.*
> *Include a modicum of skill*
> *Add understanding in, until*
> *With spicy pleasure quelling moans*
> *And purest maths. from experts' bones*
> *And profitable potion names*
> *We mix a brew which meets our aims.*

Figure 8.6 The curriculum cauldron (with acknowledgement to the witches of Macbeth)

In chapter 5 we have already considered the theory behind two areas where today's schools are producing a more balanced mathematics curriculum. The first area consists of the aims for cognitive and affective development in pupils. Most movement away from the predominance of cognitive aims appears to have been made during the 1970s in primary schools,[39] with the result that many pupils and teachers are now believed to have a greater liking for mathematics. It is to be hoped that the next annual surveys of the Assessment of Performance Unit[40] will prove that attitudes to mathematics are improving in many schools. Even if primary school pupils know fewer facts than corresponding pupils knew in 1960, as some people believe, this change of balance should help teachers in secondary schools where most new pupils will be favourably motivated for studying mathematics. In the 1979 national survey, there is no evidence about secondary school pupils' attitudes to mathematics but there is a critical comment[41] that few secondary teachers try to make the school curriculum foster the pupils' personal development.

The second area is concerned with different kinds of understanding. In the 1970s there were parents, employers and even other teachers who did not realize that mathematics teachers were aiming to give their pupils a new balance between mastery of skills and gaining relational understanding. When these people realized that less emphasis was being put on traditional skills they saw it as a sin of omission and hurled a barrage of criticism at the teachers. This crisis would not have occurred if mathematics teachers had effectively communicated their aims to parents and employers.

A third area of balance is the more alliterative combination of pleasure, profit and purity,[42] with all three being short-term and long-term aims. Teachers and pupils can gain pleasure from successfully doing mathematics, which then provides motivation for future occasions. However, no good teacher and not many pupils could be satisfied with mere pleasure so a consideration of profit enters in. Profit comes from being able to use one's mathematics in different ways, such as in school, in employment or in gaining further qualifications. The third 'p' is purity, which is to do with the often unique characteristics of mathematics. Mathematicians are responsible for a discipline with relationships between concepts about number and space, with methods of proof and rules of logic, and with numerous other special characteristics. All of these make it worth studying at some depth by all pupils and at great depth by those who are mathematically gifted.

Representation of the mathematics curriculum

It was suggested in chapter 1 that different representations of a topic help to promote intelligent discussion of that topic. Suitable diagrams which will represent the most important parts of the mathematics curriculum are therefore needed. One very important part is numeracy, i.e. the mathematics which almost every pupil needs to learn and beyond which many pupils will progress. As numeracy is a minimal aim, we must be careful not to overemphasize it in any diagram. A common analogy is with fruit (see figure 8.7) which could depict the core, i.e. the minimal aim, as containing seeds from which new growth occurs. Unfortunately, this analogy is not a wholly suitable one as most people do not grow fruit; they eat the outside and then throw away the core.

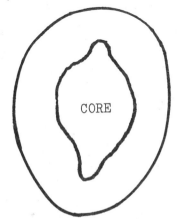

Figure 8.7 Minimal aims represented by a core

A sub-committee of the Mathematical Association has suggested[43] another representation of the whole mathematics curriculum, as shown in figure 8.8. The dotted line encloses the real curriculum of one school. Every pupil would be taught all the mathematics in the kernel and a suitable amount of that in the core and flesh, depending on the pupil's interest and ability.

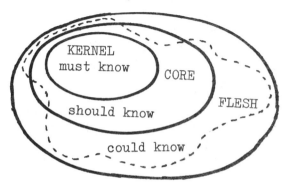

Figure 8.8 A representation of the Mathematical Association Everyman syllabus

The alternative image of a corridor which was introduced by a mathematics education lecturer, Tony Fitzgerald,[44,45] is perhaps a more dynamic and open ended analogy of a school mathematics curriculum (see figure 8.9). The corridor does not have a pre-determined finish, which suggests that each pupil can go as far as individually possible along that corridor. While doing so, the pupil may visit any of the rooms which interest him, and these rooms represent mathematics topics which extend the minimal mathematics of the main corridor.

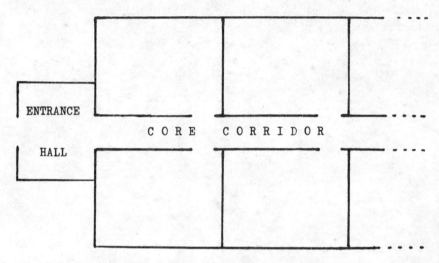

Figure 8.9 The mathematics curriculum represented by a core corridor and mathematics topic rooms

Continuity

A complete mathematics education for any pupil[46] is perforce broken up into parts by his or her movement from class to class and school to school, and some pupils or parents criticize the resulting gaps or repetitions in the curriculum. (Note that undesirable repetition should not be confused with an intentional return to a topic for reasons of reinforcement or development as in the spiral curriculum model shown in figure 4.2.) In really efficient education these parts of the curriculum need to fit neatly together, and some groups of teachers have tried to achieve this.[47] They have decided that such co-ordination needs three things; firstly, a teacher or adviser who is concerned about continuity and will initiate action, secondly, an assessment of the existing situation within a school or between a group of schools and thirdly, appropriate resultant action on the curriculum content and methods of teaching used by the teachers.[48]

The existing situation for a few pupils who moved to new schools was investigated during an enquiry into mathematics teaching in middle schools and the conclusions were rather discouraging:

> ...close liaison between the teachers concerned, at all levels, is vital; its importance cannot be over-emphasized. Unfortunately, the majority of replies show a very different picture, in which liaison between successive schools is often haphazard, if it exists at all. Between first and middle schools there was sometimes quite frankly no attempt at co-ordination; sample comments:

> 'No co-ordination.'
> 'Little that I know of.'
> 'Not tried – we have time to correct their mistakes.'

Fortunately some schools show a more constructive outlook:

> 'Staff visits in both directions; interchange schemes of work; subsequent discussions.' 'Special post for liaison with first school; most of staff familiar with content and method in first school and carry them forward in our first year.'[49]

If the results of this small enquiry are typical, then there are many pupils in the country who experience an undesirable lack of continuity between schools. This is not necessarily the fault of the teachers because there are some who do not have the time or encouragement to plan and use sequential curricula; often there are more immediate problems such as providing efficient mathematics teaching in a school which does not have enough suitably qualified teachers.

Continuity of the curriculum within one school is easier to achieve as there will be one person who has the authority and responsibility to take suitable action. Examples have already been given in chapter 3 of groups of teachers who agree to use courses and teaching methods which they have decided are correct for a certain stage in their pupils' development. At other stages, it could be agreed to use different courses and methods so that the parts could be combined to form a continuous and progressive course for every pupil.

Aims and goals for the mathematics curriculum

Let us now try to summarize the aims and goals for the mathematics curriculum. We have just been dealing with the minimal aim of numeracy, which was discussed in chapter 7 where we also considered the expectations leading to other aims. Because some extra higher level of mathematics is often desirable or needed, both in school and in later life, a second aim must be to provide the opportunities for pupils to attain these levels of *specialist and vocational* mathematics. Thirdly, there are certain *cultural* aims which reflect the activities and influence of mathematicians (see figure 8.10).

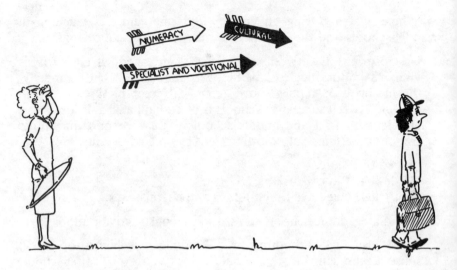

Figure 8.10 Aims for the mathematics curriculum

When converting all these aims into goals, there are three important factors to consider, namely (1) content, (2) attainability and (3) continuity. These factors can be summarized in simple terms; firstly the goals must accurately represent relevant parts of theoretical and everyday mathematics, secondly, the standard set must be the highest attainable by pupils and teachers in the relevant schools and thirdly, there must be enough continuity in the curriculum to enable pupils to successfully follow it throughout one school or even from one school to another when pupils are transferred.

Commensurate goals can be achieved within the education system of England and Wales, despite its decentralized structure which often allows L.E.A.s and schools to make curricular decisions and parents to choose the schools for their children. The system is not ideal of course (and no other system would be perfect either) but it does encourage consultation within and between many groups of people. Information about goals at different stages of education comes from these consultations. This information is available to other teachers and various selected publications are listed at the end of this chapter. For each educational stage, these books provide well considered advice which must be combined with local information about internally determined factors (e.g. school staff, pupils and equipment) and externally determined end points (e.g. C.S.E. examinations). It would not be helpful if goals and objectives were listed in more detail here since it is essential that each school has its own list compiled by the senior mathematics teacher.[50]

SPECIAL AREAS OF THE MATHEMATICS CURRICULUM

During recent years, new areas of the mathematics curriculum have been developed and the following deserve special mention.

Early mathematical experiences

The phrase 'early mathematical experiences' emphasizes the importance of the personal experiences of a young child. For example, when an infant investigates the shapes of everyday objects[51,52] it is building a foundation for future mathematical learning.[53] The phrase is also the title of a Schools Council project which was started by Professor and Mrs. Matthews at Chelsea College, London, in 1974. This project included an investigation of the relationship of language to objects, and has led to the publication of descriptive booklets[54] about mathematics for the 3 to 7 year old child. This was the first methodical study of actions and words through which children developed mathematical concepts, and the results will interest many teachers and students.

Probability and statistics

Probability and statistics have come into the mathematics curriculum[55] both through the use of mathematical techniques in statistical applied mathematics in the upper secondary school[56] and through the increased use and quotation of statistics on television and in newspapers. Most adults have probably seen many figures like 8.11 without being aware that they are called pie charts. They are simple pictorial representations of statistical data and there can be few junior school pupils who have not drawn and coloured some of them. Statistics appears in popular primary school texts such as *Mathematics for schools*[57] and in secondary school texts for courses through to Advanced-level of the General Certificate of Education.[58] In common with courses in other branches of mathematics, statistics courses have changed their format. Instead of pupils merely substituting numbers into standard formulae to obtain the correct numerical results, they are now concentrating on empirical studies;[59,60] this experimental work has led to their having a better understanding of the purpose of statistics. In adult life, statistics is applicable to many subjects besides mathematics, and this is emphasized by the 1975 Schools Council Project on Statistical Education (P.O.S.E.)[61] and its journal *Teaching Statistics* which deals with many subjects in the school curriculum.

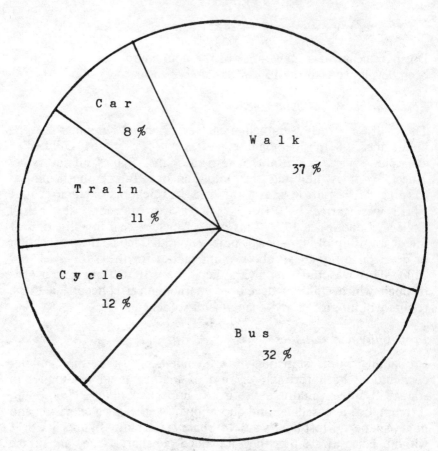

Figure 8.11 A pie chart showing the ways pupils travel to school

Applied mathematics

The only 'applied mathematics' taught in schools used to be the traditional sixth form mechanics courses. After the Second World War, mathematics became widely used by the government, commerce and industry, and schools responded by introducing relevant applied mathematics into the curriculum. Changes began in the 1960s with the introduction of mathematical statistics and probability into a sixth form course for the G.C.E. Advanced-level syllabus of the Mathematics in Education and Industry (M.E.I.) project.[62] Other applications, often concentrating on specific topics,[63,64,65,66,67,68] have been introduced since then at many places in the curriculum. The latest interest has been to emphasize the complete process of mathematical modelling;[69] namely, perception of the problem, application of suitable formulae and a final assessment of the solution. It was only the middle third of this process which used to be included in the traditional applied mathematics curriculum.

Recreational mathematics

Recreational mathematics is the agreeable occupation of time with games, problems or puzzles which have a mathematical content. This activity is in accord with Professor Geoffrey Matthews' remark in his 1978 Presidential address to the Mathematical Association[71] that within a curriculum 'it is forbidden not to waste time'. This means that young mathematicians must not be so busy that they have no time for mathematical contemplation and reflection.

This recreational mathematics will be most effective if it is integrated into the curriculum for most pupils. Then it will not be undervalued by pupils and teachers, and regarded just as enrichment material. This does not mean that it must play a major rôle but that it must take its place alongside other areas of the curriculum. Examples of the use of recreational mathematics are in class teaching,[72] in mathematics clubs,[73] in remedial teaching,[74] in projects or optional courses[76,38] and in the annual mathematics contests (jointly organized by the Mathematical Association and the School Mathematics Project) by which teams are chosen to compete in the British and International Mathematical Olympiads (the B.M.O. and I.M.O.).

Previously all pupils will have played and enjoyed games outside school, without realizing that these games were teaching them to follow rules, to devise gambits, to create patterns of moves, to work with other children, etc. The fact that they will now occasionally play educational games at school must not be allowed to spoil their natural enjoyment of games played for fun.

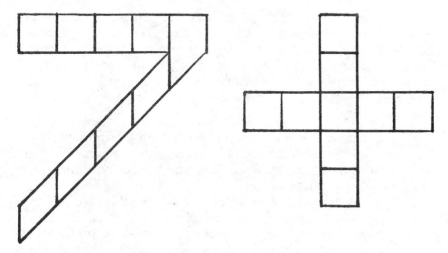

Figure 8.12 Two simple crossword puzzles; the solutions give names of angles
HORIZONTAL CLUE   To Fish with line and bait
VERTICAL CLUE   The opposite of left
DIAGONAL CLUE   Sharp

The history of mathematics

In the 1950s the history of mathematics was included in two G.C.E. Ordinary-level syllabuses,[77] but this only lasted a few years for it was not a generally popular topic with pupils or teachers. History probably disappeared then because of the teachers' lack of knowledge about historical mathematics and the pupils' resistance to this 'non-mathematical' topic for which they had to write essays instead of the usual proofs and solutions. Recently, however, the steady publication of historical articles, for example in *Mathematics in School* since the early 1970s, indicates that a few mathematicians are keenly interested and the history of mathematics might become a popular school topic, especially with 'non-mathematical' pupils who are uninspired by the present work with shapes and numbers. The topic should not be allowed to become a soft option in the mathematics curriculum and an effective way of using it must be found if it is to gain popularity. This might initially be done through the preparation and presentation of pupils' projects,[78] which the teachers might use to demonstrate that their pupils have done worthwhile work which should be classified as historical mathematics rather than as mathematical history.

Some teachers already use historical facts about people and events to generate interest in relevant topics from the curriculum[79,80] and this use should probably become more widespread.

Conclusion

We must assume that, during the 1980s, the mathematics curriculum will continue to change. This is because it is part of a slowly changing system which is influenced by many variables. To take an example from secondary education, the following factors are some which influenced the British Government's 1978 case for a common curriculum for pupils of ages 11 to 16 years:[8]

1. The aims of a mathematics curriculum have changed so that, for instance, it now concentrates less on the transmission of factual knowledge and increasingly emphasizes the development of relational understanding; a new curriculum could reflect this change.
2. Two separate curricula were natural when there were G.C.E. courses in grammar schools and C.S.E. courses in modern schools, but many of today's comprehensive schools find it unsatisfactory to separately group pupils for these two different curricula.
3. The expectations of non-educationalists used to have very little influence on the curriculum. Education is becoming

increasingly accountable to society[12] and a common curriculum would help to ensure that every pupil is prepared for adult life.

4. To allow for a decreased stability of family life and an increased likelihood of changes in parental employment, pupils need to be able to move fairly easily from school to school across the country.

5. Class and blackboard teaching is now less frequently used and teachers are encouraged to use a greater variety of methods of teaching and learning, which may make more use of television and computers.

The next chapter will discuss 'computers in education'. It will outline the development of educational computing and describe current computer applications in schools.

RECOMMENDED BOOKS ON THE MATHEMATICS CURRICULUM

N.B. The following books are listed in the sequence of the pupils' ages.

N.C.T.M. (1975) Payne J.N. ed. *Mathematics learning in early childhood*: yearbook 37. National Council of Teachers of Mathematics: Reston.

A guidebook of theoretical and practical aspects of teaching 3 to 8 year old pupils.

A.T.M. (1967) *Notes on mathematics in primary schools*: Association of Teachers of Mathematics. Cambridge University Press: Cambridge.

A discussion of the possible breadth of mathematical experiences.

Glenn J.A. ed. (1977) *Teaching primary mathematics: strategy and evaluation*. Harper & Row: London, New York.

Recommendations for producing successful teaching and learning.

H.M.S.O. (1979) *Mathematics 5-11: a handbook of suggestions*. Her Majesty's Stationery Office: London.

This book provides a checklist for pupils' achievement and detailed guidance on teaching.

Williams E.M. & Shuard H. (1976) *Primary mathematics today*. Longman: London.

A detailed teachers' guide to the development of mathematics in primary and middle schools.

A.T.M. (1977) *Notes on mathematics for children*: Association of Teachers of Mathematics. Cambridge University Press: Cambridge.

A team of writers considers learners' experiences with numbers.

M.A. (1976) *Why, what and how?* Mathematical Association: Leicester.

A consideration of aims, goals and objectives, with examples of their use in teaching.

M.A. (1974) *Mathematics eleven to sixteen*: Mathematical Association. Bell: London.

Guidance for the teacher who wishes to present a mathematical course in mathematics.

Schools Council (1977-79) *The mathematics curriculum*. Blackie: Glasgow.

A series of surveys of most mathematical topics for pupils from 11 to 16 years old.

U.N.E.S.C.O. (1973) *New trends in mathematics teaching*, volume 3, 1972. United Nations Educational, Scientific and Cultural Organization: Paris.

Goals and objectives are included for most topics studied by pupils from 5 to 18 years old.

Annotated References for Chapter 8

1. Pinfield B. (1975) Manchester teachers' centre. *Mathematics in School*, vol. 4, no. 1, pp. 2-3.

   An account of mathematical activity in this general teachers' centre.

2. Wright D.E. (1975) Progression in primary mathematics. *Mathematics in School*, vol. 4, no. 2, pp. 30-3.

   An account of curriculum development by practising teachers.

3. M.T. (1975) In service education; Topic for whole issue. *Mathematics Teaching*, no. 72.

   An interesting series of articles about in service courses.

4. Morgan J. (1977) *School mathematics under examination: 1, Affective consequences of an individualized learning programme.* Dime Projects, Education Department, University of Stirling: Stirling. See p. 28.

   A report on the development of a suitable reporting system and its use to assess Scottish project materials.

5. H.M.S.O. (1977) *Mathematics, science and modern languages in maintained schools in England: an appraisal of problems in some key subjects by H.M. Inspectorate.* Her Majesty's Stationery Office: London. See paragraph 18.

   A review and discussion touching on many areas of mathematics education. C.S.E. and G.C.E. examination passes for 1964-74 are included.

6. H.M.S.O. (1979) *Aspects of secondary education in England; a survey by H.M. Inspectors of schools.* Her Majesty's Stationery Office: London.

   The report of a thorough investigation of the final two years of education in 384 schools (10% sample).

7. H.M.S.O. (1980) *Aspects of secondary education in England; supplementary information on mathematics.* Her Majesty's Stationery Office: London.

   Detailed information about teachers, pupils, courses and schools.

8. H.M.S.O. (1978) *Curriculum 11-16.* Her Majesty's Stationery Office: London. See p. 3.

   How a curriculum which is tied to examinations can meet the needs of pupils and society.

9. Hirst P.H. & Peters R. (1970) *The logic of education.* Routledge & Kegan Paul: London, Boston. See p. 60.

   A thesis about the nature of education and an exemplification of modern educational philosophy.

10. Dunn J.A. (1977) 'Social' mathematics. *Mathematics Teaching*, no. 79, pp. 25-6.

    There are two forms of social learning, micro relating to school and macro relating to society.

11. H.M.S.O. (1977) *Education in schools, a consultative document*. Her Majesty's Stationery Office: London. See pp. 6–7.

    The Green Paper linked with the Great Debate.

12. H.M.S.O. (1980) *A framework for the school curriculum*. Her Majesty's Stationery Office: London.

    How legal responsibilities should be exercised. This includes a proposal that not less than 10% of compulsory school time should be given to mathematics.

13. H.M.S.O. (1980) *A view of the curriculum*; Matters for discussion no. 11. Her Majesty's Stationery Office: London.

    An H.M.I. discussion booklet which includes an appendix on suitable school mathematics from 5 to 16 years.

14. Goodlad J. (1966) *School, curriculum and the individual*. Blaisdell: London.

    This book, on p. 42, proposes five levels of curriculum; namely, ideal, formal, perceived, operational and experiential.

15. Holt M. (1978) *The common curriculum*. Routledge & Kegan Paul: London, Boston.

    An easily read book on its structure and style in the comprehensive school.

16. Lawton D. et al. (1978) *Theory and practice of curriculum studies*. Routledge & Kegan Paul: London, Boston.

    An introductory textbook written by London Institute of Education lecturers.

17. Tyler R.W. (1949) *Basic principles of curriculum and instruction*. University of Chicago Press: Chicago.

    An early attempt to provide good curriculum development.

18. Kratwohl D.R. et al. (1964) *Taxonomy of educational objectives; Handbook II; Affective domain*. D. McKay: New York.

    Bloom B.S. et al. (1956) *Taxonomy of educational objectives; Handbook I; Cognitive domain*. D. McKay: New York.

    Two books for teachers and curriculum planners, based on pupils' behavioural outcomes.

19. Wood R. (1968) Objectives in the teaching of mathematics. *Educational Research*, vol. 10, no. 2, pp. 83–98.

    Behavioural psychology has led to objective testing, with examples of its use in projects.

20. Hollands R. (1972) Educational technology: aims and objectives in teaching mathematics. *Mathematics in School*, vol. 1, nos. 2,3,5,6, various pages.

    The use of educational technology to systematically produce a simple practical plan.

21. Backhouse J.K. (1977) Categories for the A.P.U. 1978 mathematics survey. *Mathematics Teaching*, no. 81, pp. 16–17.

    Different ways of thinking about the learning of mathematics.

22. Freudenthal H. (1978) *Weeding and sowing*. Reidel: Dordrecht. See section III 2.

    An attempt to found a theory of teaching mathematics by observing and analysing learning processes.

23. *London Educational Review* (1973) Aims of education: an interdisciplinary inquiry. vol. 2, no. 3, whole issue.

Ten contributions which focus on foundation and teaching subjects.

24. Ausubel D.P. and Robinson F.G. (1971) *School learning: an introduction to educational psychology*. Holt, Rinehart & Winston: New York. See chapter 2.

A presentation of Ausubel's theory which focusses on classroom learning and teaching.

25. Whitfield R. ed. (1971) *Disciplines of the curriculum*. McGraw Hill: London.

Subject specialists have contributed chapters about the curriculum for pupils from 9 to 16 years old.

26. Barrow R. (1976) *Common sense and the curriculum*. George Allen & Unwin: London.

This book discusses the different approaches to the curriculum before considering details about primary and secondary school subjects.

27. Lawton D. (1973) *Social change, educational theory and curriculum planning*. University of London Press: London. See p. 22.

Curriculum principles, traditions and practice.

28. Phenix P.H. (1964) *Realms of meaning*. McGraw Hill: London, New York.

In considering the curriculum for general education, Phenix classifies mathematics with the languages.

29. Hirst P.H. (1974) *Knowledge and the curriculum*. Routledge & Kegan Paul: London, Boston.

A collection of interrelated papers on the theme of liberal education and the nature of knowledge.

30. Ruthven K. (1978) The disciplines thesis and the curriculum: a case study. *British Journal of Educational Studies*, vol. 26, no. 2, pp. 163–76. See p. 165.

The thesis applied to mathematics and its implication for the curriculum.

31. Griffiths H.B. & Howson A.G. (1974) *Mathematics: society and curricula*. Cambridge University Press: Cambridge.

An important book about mathematics and education, which gives a broad view of mathematics education.

32. U.N.E.S.C.O. (1973) *New trends in mathematics teaching: volume 3, 1972*. United Nations Educational, Scientific and Cultural Organization: Paris. See chapter 7.

The first volume in an improved format which is informative and scholarly.

33. Ling J.F. (1977) *The mathematics curriculum: mathematics across the curriculum*. Schools Council; Blackie: Glasgow.

A book from the series of constructive and critical discussions.

34. See reference 8, p. 24.

35. H.M.S.O. (1965) *Primary education in Scotland*. Her Majesty's Stationery Office: Edinburgh.

The first report on post war Scottish primary schools.

36. See reference 5, p. 5.

37. Hoare G. & Wood A. (1980) Mathematically gifted children. *Mathematics in School*, vol. 9, no. 3, pp. 33-4.

    An introductory article about the work of an M.A. committee.

38. I.M.A. (1980) Six articles about mathematically gifted children. *Bulletin of the Institute of Mathematics and its Applications*, vol. 16, nos. 2/3, pp. 38-53.

    One article about L.E.A. work in Essex and other articles about voluntary work.

39. H.M.S.O. (1978) *Primary education in England: a survey by H.M. Inspectors.* Her Majesty's Stationery Office: London.

    An appraisal of mathematics and other subjects in 542 schools.

40. D.E.S. (1980) *Mathematical development: primary survey report no. 1, A.P.U.* Department of Education and Science: London.

    The results of the 1978 assessment of 11 year old pupils.

41. See reference 6, section 2.2.

42. e.g. see Marjoram D.T.E. (1974) *Teaching mathematics.* Heinemann: London. (chapter 2).

    Good advice, with many examples from classroom topics. There is an extensive classified bibliography for library and teacher.

43. M.A. (1979) *Prior objectives in mathematics modelled for the everyman syllabus (11-16).* Mathematical Association: Leicester.

    An interim report about curriculum design and core content.

44. M.A. (1977) *The bunny book of numeracy: a green paper for discussion.* Mathematical Association: Leicester.

    A collection of seven short essays.

45. Fitzgerald A. (1978) Corridor of power. *Mathematics in School*, vol. 7, no. 1, pp. 23-5.

    Pupils should progress as far as possible along the mathematical corridor.

46. Williams D. (1978) *Learning and applying mathematics.* Australian Association of Mathematics Teachers, M.A.V. Services, Box 35, Rosanna, Victoria 3084.

    A collection of sixty articles about primary, secondary and tertiary education.

47. H.M.S.O. (1979) *Local Authority arrangements for the school curriculum*: Report on the Circular 14/77 review. Her Majesty's Stationery Office: London. See sections C4-C7 & D.

    A summary of L.E.A. replies on many aspects of the curriculum; it includes comments and bar graphs about four questions on school mathematics.

48. Sturgess D. (1979) Primary – secondary school liaison on mathematics teaching. *Mathematics in School*, vol. 8, no. 1, pp. 26-7.

    A report on the action taken by one group of schools.

49. M.A. (1976) *Mathematics in middle schools*. Mathematical Association: Leicester. See p. 3.

A report from the 5–13 sub-committee, with reprinted articles from Mathematics in School.

50. Manchester College of Education (1970) *Notes on guidelines in school mathematics*. Rupert Hart Davis: London.

Advice on devising, or checking, a primary school curriculum.

51. Glenn J.A. ed. (1979) *Children learning geometry*. Harper & Row: London, New York.

How young children gain spatial awareness, and activities which promote this learning.

52. N.C.T.M. (1975) Steffe L.P. ed. *Research on mathematical thinking of young children*. National Council of Teachers of Mathematics: Reston.

A presentation and discussion of six empirical Piagetian based studies related to primary school aged children.

53. Choat E. (1979) *Children's acquisition of mathematics*. National Foundation for Educational Research: Slough.

A discussion on the awakening of mathematics in children from two to eight years old.

54. E.M.E. (1977) *Early Mathematical Experiences*: six double-topic booklets and supporting materials. Addison Wesley: London.

Ideas on how to use young children's activities so that they lead to mathematics.

55. Rade L. ed. (1975) *Statistics at the school level*. Wiley: London.

Information about its teaching and syllabuses in many countries.

56. M.A. (1975) *An approach to A level probability and statistics*; Mathematical Association. Bell: London.

A handbook for teachers, which relates the statistical situation to the mathematical model.

57. *Mathematics for Schools*. Text book series published by Addison Wesley: London.

The Harold Fletcher modern mathematics course which is used in many primary schools.

58. Parsonson S.L. (1970) *Pure mathematics*: volume 1. Cambridge University Press: London.

An advanced level G.C.E. textbook for use with the 'Mathematics in Education and Industry' syllabus and similar courses.

59. Sherwood P. (1978) Probability in the junior school. *Mathematics in School,* vol. 7, no. 3, pp. 6–7.

The use of some of Dr. Varga's ideas in worksheets which start from intuition and experiment.

60. Dolan O. (1978) Project work in statistics. *Mathematics in School*, vol. 7, no. 1, pp. 10–11.

A report on a mode 3 statistical option in C.S.E. mathematics.

61. Kapadia R. (1979) Statistical education 11 to 16: the Schools Council project. *Teaching Statistics*, vol. 1, no. 1, pp. 11–14.

A report on the project and the teaching methods developed.

62. For details of this project see: Mathematical Association (1976) *A revised guide to mathematics projects in British secondary schools.* Bell: London.

This booklet gives brief factual details about sixteen current projects.

63. M.A. (1964) *Applications of elementary mathematics*: Mathematical Association. Bell: London.

Examples which use algebra, geometry and trigonometry learnt in the lower and middle secondary school.

64. M.A. (1967) *Applications of sixth form mathematics*: Mathematical Association: Bell: London.

Examples which use algebra, trigonometry and calculus learnt in the upper secondary school.

65. Pass N. (1975) Using the M.M.C.P. packs. *Mathematics in School*, vol. 4, no. 6, pp. 5–6. Pass N. (1976) Using the communications pack. *Mathematics in School*, vol. 5, no. 1, pp. 12–14.

Two articles about the use of 'Mathematics for the Majority Continuation Project' materials for the less able 13 to 16 year old pupils.

66. Flemming W. (1977) Mathematics applicable. *Mathematics in School*, vol. 6, no. 3, pp. 14–16.

A report about a well developed applications project for secondary school pupils.

67. Kirk R.J. (1978) The role of applications of mathematics in secondary schools. *Mathematics in School,* vol. 7, no. 3, pp. 31–3.

Mathematics applied to telephone kiosks and slug control.

68. N.C.T.M. (1979) Sharron S. & Reys R.E. eds. *Applications in school mathematics*: yearbook. National Council of Teachers of Mathematics: Reston.

A set of creative applications to biology, economics, sociology, etc.

69. Hall G.G. (1978) *Applied mathematics*. In reference 70, chapter 2.

The scope of modern applied mathematics and the importance of the modelling process.

70. Wain G.T. ed. (1978) *Mathematical education*. Von Nostrand Reinhold: Wokingham.

A collection of chapters on mathematics and mathematics education by respected contributors.

71. Matthews G. (1978) Sausages and bananas. *Mathematical Gazette*, vol. 62, no. 241, pp. 145–56. See p. 147.

A discussion of importance, unimportance and the banana principle.

72. Smith S.E. and Backman, C.A. eds. (1976) *Games and puzzles for elementary and middle school mathematics*. National Council of Teachers of Mathematics: Washington.

A very useful set of articles, reprinted from the *Arithmetic Teacher*.

73. Todd A. (1968) *The maths club*. Hamish Hamilton: London.

A handbook of activities which pupils will probably enjoy and find valuable.

74. Dean P.G. (1978) *A study of the use of mathematical games in a primary school*. In reference 75, chapter 9.

How commercially available games were used to help a group of low-achieving pupils.

75. Megarry J. ed. (1978) *Perspectives on academic gaming and simultation 1 & 2*. Kogan Page: London.

The proceedings of the 1975 and 1976 annual S.A.G.S.E.T. conferences.

76. Eyre R. & Dean P.G. (1978) The development of draughts by sixth form students. *Mathematics Teaching*, no. 84, pp. 39–42.

An account of an entertaining, instructive, investigative course where students do mathematics.

77. Green D.R. (1976) History in mathematics teaching. *Mathematics in School*, vol. 5, nos. 3 & 4, pp. 15–17 & 5–9.

Two articles about texts and syllabuses in the nineteenth and twentieth centuries.

78. M.A. (1980) *The use of pupil's projects in secondary school mathematics*. Mathematical Association: Leicester.

A booklet about the content, supervision and assessment of projects.

79. N.C.T.M. (1969) Hallerberg A.E. et al. eds. *Historical topics for the mathematics classroom*: yearbook 31. National Council of Teachers of Mathematics: Washington.

Brief historical information about many topics, eg. prime numbers and vectors.

80. M.A. (1974) *Mathematics, eleven to sixteen*; Mathematical Association. Bell: London. See section 7.5.

Guidance for the teacher who wishes to present a mathematical course in mathematics.

CHAPTER 9

EDUCATIONAL COMPUTING

Introduction

Educational computing has only recently been introduced into schools, where it is usually the responsibility of the mathematics teachers. These teachers have been studying mathematics since they started school but they have probably had few opportunities to study computing which they often have to teach at various levels. This chapter aims to provide material by which teachers can broaden their experience of computing. The first part describes the present position of computing in schools and explains how it reached that position. The chapter then analyses the different rôles of computing in schools and finally provides information about the various ways in which a teacher can obtain support.

Why computing is in the curriculum

The first thing to realize is that computing is not considered to be a necessary part of the school curriculum in England and Wales. The evidence for this is that there are pupils who do not receive a single lesson about computing during their school careers. If mathematics were similarly ignored there would be considerable protest but the omission of computing causes no general outcry. Computing must therefore be seen merely as an optional subject on the curriculum.

As will be described later, the piecemeal development of educational computing was produced by groups of enthusiasts, mainly mathematicians, who thought that it was desirable. They could only introduce it into the curriculum because they had the support of some senior staff and pupils. This means that it has an almost unique aura,

195

and telling motivation, for such cooperative acceptance is unknown with any other present day subject. This introduction of computing is an example of 'unplanned drift' in the whole curriculum, with the immediate result that time given to computing often reduces the time available for mathematics. The 1979 national secondary school survey[9] has expressed H.M.I.s' concern about the growth of optional subjects in the fourth and fifth years and, in this context, teachers must justify their inclusion of computing in the curriculum.

Teachers in England and Wales may look enviously at the more centralized education system in Scotland, where there is no doubt that computing is in the curriculum. In 1969, a committee report of the Scottish Education Department (S.E.D.) instigated a national policy for computing in schools. Within a few years, the schools had special textbooks and regional computer centres had been established.[10] The S.E.D. committee, under the chairmanship of Mr. B. T. Bellis, offered this justification:

> The computer has become, indeed, an integral feature of everyday experience in government, business, industry, science, medicine, and so on . . . Some school pupils will eventually find satisfying careers in developing computers or in working with them in some field of application; others, less directly involved, will nevertheless require to be sufficiently well-informed to be able to make use of computers. . . . School pupils must not grow up in ignorance of this new social and industrial revolution.[11]

This justification is based on the educational needs of individual pupils, and is in agreement with other stated educational aims. For example, 'Broadly speaking the aims of education are to develop the body, mind and personality so that one may have a broad and clear view of the world around, may be able to live a full and satisfying life and can make as valuable a personal contribution to the world as possible.'[12] The 'broad and clear view' about computing should dispel any fear of the machine, and give each pupil a suitable understanding of the capabilities of a computer and its rôle in society. This is necessary because pupils do not yet experience computers in their everyday life, in the same way that they experience similar machines, such as motor cars and television sets. As well as aiding the development of the individual, this understanding can be of local or national importance. Computers contribute to the economic success of a country, and well qualified people must be available to control them and to control their beneficial use.

In schools where mathematics lesson time is used for computing, teachers should consider how it can contribute to the teaching and learning of mathematics itself.[13] Problem solving is a characteristic mathematical process where the computer is a valuable teaching aid.

Professor George Polya, of Stanford University, has encouraged the structuring of problems and problem solving,[14] by which computer programs can be used to solve mathematical problems. Not only can a pupil solve problems but he can start with a program for a specific problem and then develop it to solve an associated general problem. This progress from the specific to the general is a characteristic which many mathematics teachers encourage in their pupils.

The actual writing of a program provides mathematical-type training[15] because the writer has to begin with a clear understanding of the situation and then devise a logical representation of it. When solving a problem, the program writer has to develop a so-called *algorithm*, that is, a finite sequence of steps which, when followed, will lead to the solution. After the program is first written, it is tested in the computer which becomes a valuable tutor. Either the pupil is rewarded by the program working correctly or the computer identifies places where the program is wrong, for logical or other reasons. It is interesting to realize that some pupils prefer this impersonal program correction from the computer rather than similar personal correction from the teacher.

A second school application,[16,17] which has come from university research on artificial intelligence,[18] is for pupils to gain understanding by exploring a computer based mathematical situation, instead of by learning mathematical facts. This is an example of the educational change from a concentration on the pupils' knowledge to an equal concern for the pupils' investigation of mathematics.

Beyond secondary school, computing has influenced mathematical thinking and has changed the nature of mathematical activity. One common application is the extensive use of mathematical models, for example, within a simulation. The computer program contains the model which may be used with current data to influence decisions about the future. Simulations used in school enable the pupil to study, as a mathematician, the relationship between the input and the output without the distraction of intermediate arithmetical calculations.

Computing and its area of knowledge

In chapters 5 and 8 it has already been shown that mathematics is a well established subject with distinctive content (e.g. number, mathematical logic, proof). However, it is debatable whether computing is a subject in its own right. Computing has grown from the subject of mathematics, from information processing and also from the existence of a machine, the computer. The machine has attracted a group of people, the computing professionals, who have collected knowledge from already existing subjects. Part of this collection is offered for pupils and students to learn and use on courses which, according to their depth and emphasis, may have any one of a variety of titles. Titles commonly used for school courses include Computer Studies, Computer Science, Data Processing and Information Processing.[19,20,21] The only claim for such a course to represent a subject, as it is classified in many secondary schools, may be the organizational structure of the school into subject departments which use subject teachers. This structure leads to the assumption that teachers must teach subjects.

The organization of computing in schools

This section explains the typical ways in which computing is organized in schools. Computing staff, pupils and the organization of computing courses are first considered. Then, the use of computing by other departments and the organization of equipment are discussed.

In most schools, the senior mathematics teacher is responsible for computing and, although this arrangement brings more work to the already busy mathematics teachers, that senior teacher should carefully consider the implications (for example, a limitation of the use of a computer) of any suggested change in this responsibility. One reason why such a change might arise is because of a re-structured school organization, e.g. amalgamating the separate departments into perhaps four faculties, namely, creative arts, humanities, languages and sciences. In the sciences faculty, teachers could justifiably claim responsibility for computing as it involves electronics and is used in scientific work and investigation. Teachers in the humanities faculty could likewise claim responsibility, as computing is widely used for collecting and sorting information in our society. If a choice had to be made between such conflicting claims, it would probably be decided by considering the staff available, and the courses which the school expected to provide in the coming years. When the senior mathematics teacher is not responsible for computing, it is probably in one of these two situations:

1. Computing, including data processing, has a significant place on the school curriculum. This is acknowledged by appointing a head of computer studies.
2. Another member of the staff has a special interest in computing but he organizes it alongside his other subject teaching commitments. This teacher's other subject is often mathematics, although he or she can be from any other department.

This latter situation, where a member of the staff has a special interest in computing, is generally the only reason why computing is organized for pupils in a primary school.

It is advisable for the teacher who is responsible for computing to be supported by other teachers. These supporting members of staff are also usually mathematics teachers but, for more general courses, should ideally include non-mathematicians who will emphasize the non-mathematical aspects of computing. Supporting members of staff can be selected in two ways:

Self selection, where a teacher has become interested in computing and seeks experience and training. The teacher responsible for computing should try to promote such self selection, but must otherwise depend on –

Directed selection, where a teacher is told that computing is part of his or her duties. This second type of selection may be necessary because computing is a part of a syllabus, e.g. integrated into a mathematics course. It may also be necessary because, as happens too often, a school has only one person able to teach a computing course and the head teacher wishes to ensure continuity. Then, if the original person leaves, or becomes ill, there is a guarantee that pupils will be able to complete a course they have already begun.

Whatever types of courses are offered, and those will be considered later in this chapter, they may be compulsory for all pupils, or optional for some pupils. The duration of each course will be controlled by restrictions of the pupils' time, or the total teaching time available, as well as by external examination requirements. Many courses can be made suitable for pupils from 9 to 18 years of age. Compulsory courses for all pupils need use only two mathematics or general studies lessons a week. These courses are usually organized for a part or the whole of a year before pupils reach the age of 14 years. This has two advantages, firstly, the course comes while the pupils are still having a broad general education and, secondly, it serves as an introduction by which pupils can knowledgeably choose a following optional course. This may be an assessed course for a public examination or may be one option in general studies.

Especially since the advent of microcomputers, many schools have a computer club which meets before, during or after normal school hours. This club should be organized so that enthusiastic pupil members, after gaining suitable experience, are encouraged to take some responsibility for running the club. This provides a valuable educational resource which does not require too much of the teachers' time. Through such a club, courses might also be organized where teachers and pupils together could investigate new uses of the computer; enthusiastic pupils can be a good catalyst for encouraging other teachers to appreciate the value of educational computing. This approach has been used to develop courses in France[22] in a more structured way than we have used the approach in Britain.

If several people are using computing in their teaching, the positioning of any computer equipment has to suit their teaching requirements and many schools use an adjoining office and classroom. The equipment may be used in the office by a small group of people but, for other lessons, it is moved or linked into the classroom. Ideally, this office and classroom combination should be regarded as a computing laboratory, to which any teacher may bring a class for regular or occasional lessons. For regular lessons it is also possible to wire extension sockets to several teaching rooms if the computer equipment is not portable, or to transport a microcomputer from room to room on a light trolley.

The development of educational computing

In 1957, computers were just beginning to be recognized as viable resources for mathematicians and it was then stirring news that 'By the end of next year, there will be well over 100 digital computers operating in the country. [Britain]'[23] Luckily, Mr. Hammersley of Trinity College, Oxford, organized a conference that year to which industrialists and school teachers were invited.[24] Computers were beginning to make their great impact in industry, with mathematicians tackling problems which a few years earlier would have been rejected as being impossible to solve. Members of that conference hoped that, before long, computers would begin to make as great an impact in schools.[25]

Some contact was already being made between a few enthusiastic school teachers and a relatively small number of computer experts. A two-way communication between these groups was successful because the computer experts needed to encourage interest in, and recruits to work with, their machines while the teachers wanted to understand the computers and to have the opportunity of using them. These teachers talked to their pupils, some of whom then also wanted to use computers. To encourage this, some schools made private arrangements with computer departments in universities and industries and a typical early arrangement was that between Dover Grammar School and Leeds University in 1961.[26] At that time, the content of school computing was almost exclusively the programming of mathematical problems, and the only resource books were manufacturers' technical manuals.

From the early 1960s, more suitable literature began to be available from both computer manufacturers and professional workers, either independently or through the British Computer Society (B.C.S.) and then through the National Computing Centre (N.C.C.). These two bodies also took a lead in co-ordinating, and advising about the rôle of, computing in schools. The most effective national non-commercial group was, and is, the B.C.S. Schools Committee[27] which was started in 1964. This committee, in 1966, founded the Computer Education Group (C.E.G.); in 1969, started publishing the printed journal *Computer Education*; and also promoted many valuable meetings and reports: Of these, one outstanding report was *Computer Education for All* [28] which set out the framework of many courses still being taught in British schools.[29]

Some teachers have made, and still do make, two major criticisms of British courses in computing. The first is that they are too examination orientated and the second is that they are too mathematical. Both these criticisms arise because the organization of education into subjects has controlled the growth of these courses, many of which lead to public examinations. (The public examination system is explained in chapter 10.) The earliest nationally recognized school computing examination was based on the Oxford G.C.E. Board Advanced-level syllabus devised in 1966.[30] As G.C.E. Boards did not then have computing examiners, proposed syllabuses had to be considered by mathematics examiners. Within schools, as explained earlier in this chapter, computing was integrated into mathematics courses unless separate time was available. With either alternative, computing courses had to reflect the expertise of the staff, as well as often providing status for both the teacher and the course. Therefore, there were again pressures for computing courses to be mathematical and examinable.

In the early 1970s, computing courses really began to flourish when this relatively unknown, semi-practical, subject provided a boost for the new Certificate of Secondary Education (C.S.E.). The C.S.E. board members were looking for examinable subjects which were both less academic than, and different from, those already examined by the G.C.E. boards. In 1970, nine out of thirteen C.S.E. boards were examining pupils in computing and further development was encouraged by a B.C.S. Schools Committee report[31] giving details of seven Mode III syllabuses which had been accepted. Soon all C.S.E. boards examined computing and the number of candidates grew to 5487 in 1974, and to 16210 in 1979 (see figure 9.1). This growth was certainly influenced by the raising of the school leaving age in 1972 because computing was considered to be a suitable course for the extra year, either as a non-examinable option or as an examinable C.S.E. course.

Courses for this rapidly increasing number of pupils would have been impossible if courses had not been organized for teachers. Such teachers' courses were first offered by universities, colleges and

Year	CSE	GCE O-level	GCE AO-level	GCE A-level	CEE	Total
1974	5487	400		1000		6887
1975	8785	1335		1340		11460
1976	13181	3217	116	1512		18026
1977	15218	6091	109	1764		23182
1978	15489	8417	511	1769	233	26419
1979	16210	11635	765	2323	591	31524

Figure 9.1 Public examination entries which show the growth of computer education courses (From reference 32)

computer manufacturers.[33] Local Education Authorities (L.E.A.s) began to take responsibility for running courses from the early 1970s and also began to provide computer facilities especially for school use. This provision of courses and facilities was nationally developed both in Scotland[34] and in Northern Ireland.[35] In England and Wales the development was more piecemeal but it has generally passed through the same phases everywhere. During the first phase, schools were allowed to run programs at, perhaps, a technical college or town hall where one lecturer or programmer was given an added responsibility for school liaison. This person started by giving advice on languages and programs, but was soon also organizing teachers' courses about syllabus content. Someone in school education (as contrasted with tertiary education) had to be responsible for these developments, so a school mathematics adviser would be given an added responsibility for computing, or a special computer education appointment would be made at a fairly senior level. Not only did such a person organize courses and give advice, he would often also upgrade the computing facilities available (see details later in this chapter) and be supported by newly appointed full time staff to liaise with schools and perhaps run an educational computer centre.

Alongside these local developments, attempts were being made to improve education about computers on a national and international basis. In 1970 the three-year Chelsea College Science Simulation project[36] started in London with funds provided by Shell. Then, in 1972, the Computer Education Information Service was started to provide information for all British schools; its final newsletter, perhaps predictably no. 13, announced its end in 1975 because of lack of financial support. Meanwhile, the British Government funded the National Development Programme in Computer Assisted Learning (N.D.P.C.A.L.) from 1973 until 1977[37] which contributed to some of the projects which will be described later. Discussion between nations has been facilitated by the International Federation for Information

Processing (I.F.I.P) through 'working group 3.1', established in 1967. I.F.I.P. was responsible for a World Conference in Amsterdam in 1970[1,38] and one in Marseilles in 1975.[2] Educational computing has also been one concern of the Organisation for Economic Co-operation and Development (O.E.C.D.)[39] whose support in 1973 helped to set up, in Edinburgh, the International Information Centre for Computing in Secondary Education.[40] Partly through its news-letter, it provided a valuable dissemination of information until the centre closed in 1976. From these newsletters, together with back copies of *Computer Education* and the weighty I.F.I.P. world conference reports, a reader can compare the development of educational computing in other countries with the British develop-ment outlined here.

Development in the 1980s is already affected by the advent of microcomputers, which can be programmed and operated in schools by teachers and pupils. With these microcomputers, computing across the curriculum is easier. Although mathematics teachers may lose some of their overall control of computing, formal courses will become less necessary as pupils experience more computing in their general life at home and school. Planned leadership at national, L.E.A. and school level is needed. The shortage of suitable teachers must also be eased by means of the in-service training of some present staff and also by encouraging professionally qualified computer people to become teachers.

Research using educational computing

This brief section is not concerned with educational research using computing, for example, the computer analysis of research data, but it is about research using educational computing, for example, the optimization of steps in a computer assisted learning program. The researcher programs one or more sequences of steps which are planned to lead a student to attain an educational objective, perhaps to solve certain specified arithmetical problems. The computer then presents these steps in a determined order to every student and the students' responses are recorded for future analysis. This analysis allows the researcher to amend the steps and thus to improve the learning process.

More exciting research applications are exemplified by the work of Seymour Papert, where he aims to creatively engage pupils in mathe-matical work.[41,42] With Marvin Minsky at the Artificial Intelligence laboratory of the Massachusetts Institute of Technology, he has led research 'to work out and communicate models of the process of education itself'.[43] Similar broad-based approaches, not merely using computers to transmit knowledge and test attainment, have been used in the French 'l' Informatique' scheme[44] and at the University of Leeds Computer Based Learning project.[45]

Developments of computer based learning (described later in this chapter) have necessitated new investigations of the interactions between teacher, pupil and curriculum. A fourth factor, the form of communication with the computer, provides further interactions to be studied and these are especially important if there is to be an increased use of computers in teaching and learning.[46] The development of computer based school timetabling has meant that researchers have studied the traditional techniques used by senior members of staff so that suitable computer based methods can be designed.

Reverting to computing in mathematics teaching, problem solving[14] is a research area which will continue to be used. For such research, most people are satisfied to use a standard programming language but there has been at least one attempt[47] to construct a language which reflects basic mathematical structures and concepts. The introduction of microcomputers in schools has brought new opportunities for research by teachers[48] and for projects by pupils.

Programming languages

A program provides the computer with a sequence of instructions which it has to follow, for example, in order to solve a set of equations. The computer must be able to read each instruction, and act accordingly, and this is achieved by writing the instructions in a programming language before they are put into the computer. As computers can often read instructions input in any of several languages, the teacher or pupil may have a choice of languages when writing programs. The choice, which depends upon the educational reason for the programs being written, can most easily be explained by considering the two main types of programming language, namely, low level and high level.[49]

Low level languages are chosen if the teacher either wishes to show pupils how the computer uses its own simple language, or wishes the pupils to use only a few straightforward instructions, even though a complete program will then be correspondingly long. One of the most common low level languages is the Computer Education in Schools Instructional Language (CESIL).

High level languages are chosen if the teacher either wishes to show pupils that the computer is a powerful machine, for example, to perform a series of calculations while solving a problem, or wishes to use the language which has a structure like the specification of a problem. The most common high level school language is the Beginners All-purpose Symbolic Instruction Code (BASIC).

As well as CESIL and BASIC, there are hundreds of other languages, many of which might seem suitable. In practice, the choice of languages will also be determined by machine limitations associated with the computer, by syllabus requirements, by availability of suitable instruction manuals and by the need to work with other teachers who are involved with the courses. When a teacher is using one of the already prepared educational packages for administration or computer based learning which are described in the next few pages, the computer language already used will affect whether the package program can 'run' on the computer. If it does 'run', then it becomes an educational resource for which the programming language is unimportant in the same way that the width of a film is educationally unimportant if the school has a projector on which the film will run. Many computer based learning packages are, in fact, written in BASIC because this is the programming language with which many teachers and pupils are familiar.

THE DIFFERENT RÔLES OF EDUCATIONAL COMPUTING

So far, this chapter has discussed various aspects of educational computing without analysing its various forms, or rôles. This analysis now follows.

The place of educational computing in schools

It may help to explain the place of educational computing in schools by considering the familiar place of English Language in our schools. English is both a departmental subject, and a language which is used in that subject and in all other subjects. Similarly, though not so essentially, computing can be considered both as a subject, and as a resource which must be used by that subject and may be used by other subjects. The similarity between English and computing can be carried one stage further, because both can be used in the administration of a school. All are therefore included in figure 9.2, which also emphasizes that there is education *about* computing and education *using* computing.

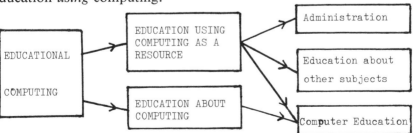

Figure 9.2 The place of educational computing in schools

A classification of the different rôles of educational computing

In the coming pages, the different rôles of educational computing in schools will be explained. These rôles can be classified into groups, as shown in figure 9.3.

R Ô L E	C L A S S I F I C A T I O N	
Timetabling Pupil Records Careers Guidance	Administration	
Assessment Prescription Learning Records	Computer Managed Learning	Computer Based Learning
Exerciser Tutor Laboratory Information Retrieval	Computer Assisted Learning	
Computer Appreciation Computer Studies	Computer Education	

Figure 9.3 A classification of the different rôles of educational computing

Administration

Administration is the management of a school, for the benefit of the teachers and pupils. This management can be assisted by educational computing[50] and teachers often see two advantages for such assistance. The first advantage is that many administrative tasks linked with teaching (e.g. preparing examination mark lists) are completed more quickly and accurately, and these are tasks which may previously have taken up a significant amount of a teacher's time. The second advantage is that teachers and pupils have an on-going course in computer appreciation, because they provide and receive information which is processed by the computer.

Preparation of the timetable is often one task which takes a highly paid and experienced teacher away from the pupils for between one and three weeks. The teacher and pupils should benefit if a computer is used to assist that experienced teacher, allowing him to make the educational decisions while the computer handles the nitty-gritty of class grouping, subject spread, consistency checking, etc. Three major systems have been evaluated by an N.D.P.C.A.L. funded project[51,52] and it should soon be possible for any school to consider using computer assistance in preparing the master timetable.

Whether the master timetable has been prepared by hand or by computer, computer assistance then offers many proved advantages. Once information from the master timetable has been stored in the computer, it can be instructed to accurately select and print time-tables for any teacher, class or room, and many other lists.[53] It can be programmed to select replacements for teachers who are absent, providing an immediate service which ensures a logical and fair choice over any term or year. If pupils have special tuition, for example, in music or remedial mathematics, the computer can also provide a timetable which withdraws the same pupil from different subject periods in successive weeks.

A recurring problem which links timetabling with pupils' records is the selection of options, for example, for activities periods or for general studies. There may be 180 pupils who make first and second choices of three options out of five and, especially if the pupils indicate these choices on 'mark-sensed' cards (described later in this chapter) which can be inserted directly into the computer's card reader, several hours of a teacher's time will be saved. Instead of that teacher compiling and recording the names of pupils for the different option groups, these administrative tasks are done by the computer program. It is possible to keep many of a school's administrative records in a computer and, once the details for each pupil have been added to the stored information, the computer can be instructed to select and print lists or details for pupils and teachers, and even for the yearly returns required by the education authorities.[54]

The regular administrative use of a computer, in ways like those just mentioned, contributes to the second advantage mentioned above; such an on-going course in computer appreciation might be completed when pupils use a careers guidance program, like the one developed by International Business Machines and Cheshire County Council.[55]

Computer Based Learning (C.B.L.)

Computer based learning has its roots in programmed learning, where a pupil progresses through a programmed course by making the correct response at each small step. (See 'Programmed learning and correct responses' in chapter 4.) The original programmed courses were in books or on film strips but the computer was then seen to be an ideal tool to present such programmes to individual pupils. They could work at their individual speeds, possibly following alternative paths which catered for pupils different interests and cognitive styles. A concern for individualization is evident within the following two roles of C.B.L.[8]

Computer Managed Learning (C.M.L.)

In computer managed learning the computer helps the teacher to guide each pupil's learning. The computer will have been programmed to relieve the teacher of some tasks which are repetitive, leaving him more time to spend with groups of pupils or individual pupils. The tasks which are automated are selected parts of pupil assessment, prescription of lessons and recording the learning which the pupils have achieved. The computer can perform these tasks between lessons; during a lesson the teacher and pupils have no direct link with a computer, and in many cases they use quite ordinary types of work cards, books and apparatus.

The Hertfordshire Computer Managed Mathematics Project is a good example of a complete scheme that has been successfully used in fourteen schools. It provides a two-year mathematics course for 11 to 13 year old pupils in mixed ability classes. The major part of the course uses classwork with video-tapes and individual worksheets. Some worksheets with open-ended questions are marked by the class teachers but others with short answers are marked by the computer. The computer then provides a result sheet for the teacher to use in the next lesson, with perhaps a prescription about remedial guidance needed by some pupils. It also provides 'Current' and 'History' learning records, so that the teacher can easily monitor the progress of all the pupils and thereby employ his teaching time most effectively.

Other C.M.L. schemes have been designed so that they are not restricted to one teaching subject and examples are P.L.A.N.,[57,58] I.P.I.,[59] the Havering C.M.L. system[60,61] and C.A.M.O.L.[62] Although complete C.M.L. schemes operate in only a small number of schools, there are many schools which regularly use the computer for assessment or records of learning. Articles by teachers have appeared in nearly all computer education journals and newsletters, and other writers have analysed the problems[63] and future developments[64,65] of

C.M.L. As the value of these data-processing methods can be appreciated by non-computing teachers, and because the methods often need no extra computing equipment, this is probably an expansion area in educational computing.

Computer Assisted Learning (C.A.L)

In computer assisted learning the computer contains learning materials which are presented to the pupil during lessons and these materials are often accompanied by non-computer material such as books and worksheets. The lesson is generally managed by the teacher, although there can be overlap of C.A.L. and C.M.L. and two examples of overlap are:

1. the Hertfordshire Computer Managed Mathematics Project, which also prepares C.A.L. material in the form of an individual graded arithmetic test for each pupil to use in class[56] and
2. the Edinburgh, Falkirk and Paisley MATLAB project, which provides mainly C.A.L. material but which also aims to provide students' and teachers' files for C.M.L.[66]

Many pupils and teachers have written simple programs to place the computer in the role of an exerciser so that a pupil can practise, for example, simple arithmetical skills. After the pupil has sat at a screen and keyboard, the computer screen presents an exercise, perhaps $17 + 3 \times 2$, and the pupil presses the keys which show his answer. When he presses 23, the screen probably shows 'CORRECT' and presents the next exercise. Pocket calculator type exercisers with a similar rôle can be easily obtained now that they are based on a pre-programmed silicon chip. Although these exercisers may offer the pupil different periods of time (e.g. five seconds) in which to press the keys for the answer, their educational use is fairly limited. With a computer, if the pupil presses a wrong answer while using a well written program, the computer may be able to act as a tutor. The screen could show 'HAVE YOU REMEMBERED TO MULTIPLY BEFORE ADDING? ANSWER BY TYPING YES OR NO'. This might be followed by other questions which should finally lead the pupil to the correct answer: 23. If the pupil does not get 23, he must be referred to the teacher who is managing the lesson. The teacher is therefore working with the pupils who most need help, while the other pupils work with the computer system.

The computer's rôle as an exerciser and tutor is often applied to mathematics education in two situations:

1. for remedial instruction, at any stage from number-bond practice by 9 year old pupils to learning supportive math-

ematics which 17 year old pupils need when studying other subjects[67] and

2. for research about learning, as with an investigation at Leeds into effective feedback procedures when learning to multiply numbers.[68]

Tutorial programs can be used almost independently of the teacher and other resources. However, there are several reasons why this method is rarely adopted in schools. A major reason is the expense of providing computing equipment for a whole class, and supporting this with enough different tutorial programs. Another reason is the perceived need for personal relationships by most pupils of school age, and a final reason is that the computer lacks many of the different skills which the teachers possess. The computer can receive and print letters and numbers and can, perhaps, use photographs, drawings and audio tapes from a pre-determined and programmed set, as in the Illinois P.L.A.T.O. system.[69] In addition to all these actions, the teacher can also freely respond by listening, looking and moving around the classroom. However, C.A.L. systems have been developed which try to allow each pupil to develop his own learning sequence, producing a really individualized lesson.[8,65,70] These adaptive systems have capabilities more like those of an experienced teacher.

In the project MATLAB, which has been mentioned, the name is an abbreviation for Mathematics Laboratory. This is an example of one rôle of C.A.L. where the computer is used in a similar way to equipment in school science laboratories. There are two general approaches; firstly, where the pupil uses the computer as a sophisticated calculator, or as a problem solving tool, and writes his own programs; and secondly, where the pupil or teacher uses the computer to simulate or model some situation from which the pupil can learn, and uses programs which are already in the computer.[71]

With the first approach, the pupil must be able to write programs. With high level languages and well designed computer systems, it takes only an hour or two to learn to write simple but useful programs. Subjects for programs may be suggested by the teacher, the topics ranging from simple number patterns to sixth form numerical methods,[72] or the pupil may write a program which relates to some personal problem or project.

With the second approach, the program may have been written to aid the learning of one concept or idea. These programs are very often interactive, so that the computer acts on information provided by the teacher or the pupil. One such program has the aim of increasing the pupils' understanding of the ordered co-ordinate pair (x,y) for all integers between +10 and −10; this program allows pupils to play the game of 'battleships', as shown in figure 9.4. In this game, the computer will secretly decide where to place each line of stationary battleships, say at $(3, -6)$ $(5, -6)$ and $(7, -6)$, and the class have to bomb them by providing these unknown co-ordinate pairs. With such a game, pupils quickly realize the difference between $(3, -6)$ and $(-6, 3)$ and, hence, the significance of the word 'ordered'.

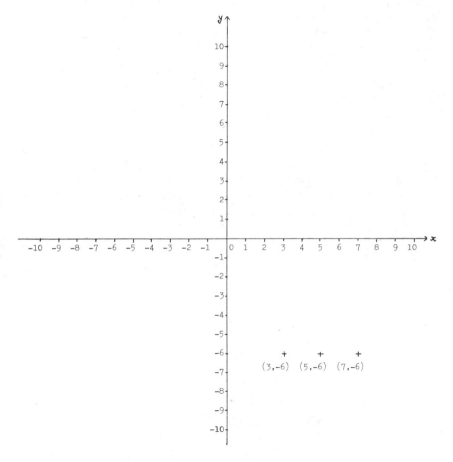

Figure 9.4 The three crosses represent battleships, in a game to learn about the ordered coordinate pair (x, y)

Many laboratory programs exist in educational computer systems and some programs have much broader aims than the example just given. Understanding basic concepts in mathematics[73] or introducing aspects of modelling in mathematics and physics,[74,75] are typical of such broader aims.

Programs which are to be used by many teachers and pupils need to be supported by written material such as pupils' work sheets, teachers' notes and technical program specifications. When put together, this material makes a 'computer software package' or 'teaching package' but, like many other teaching resources which are based on new ideas, these are not necessarily easy to use. Teachers may need a great deal of support from colleagues, as well as from texts such as the *Computing in mathematics* books (published by the Cambridge University Press) of the School Mathematics Project and the materials published by International Computers Limited – Computer Education in Schools (I.C.L.–C.E.S.) (see address list at the end of this book).

I.C.L.–C.E.S. have been one of the leaders in the educational use of information retrieval, and their FIND package was used in an interesting N.D.P.C.A.L. project for local history teaching. Suffolk census data was used and pupils instructed the computer to search the data so that they could then discuss and write history based on the evidence that they discovered.[76] Similar searching of established data has been used elsewhere to retrieve historical and other information, e.g. for geography teaching in Hertfordshire[77,78] and in Essex where children from 9 years old upwards have worked with personal data.[79] A comprehensive data-base takes hours of work to set up, but it is then a resource which can be used by pupils in many individual ways. Pupils could be allowed to retrieve information from parts of the data-base used for school administration, and the results would become increasingly interesting as current data was added during successive years.

Computer education

Computer education is education *about* computing, which nearly always involves education *using* computing (look again at figure 9.2). Computer education has two rôles:

1. computer appreciation which aims to let pupils understand what computing can do, and know the social implications of computing and
2. computer studies which combines computer appreciation with some detailed technical knowledge about computing.

Computer appreciation courses need to be regularly modified because of changing viewpoints, changing needs and changing technology. Thus, details in the original outline of a computer appreciation course from 1969 need significant modification in 1979.[29] Further changes are likely to occur in the next decade, as more adults gain an appreciation of computers and more pupils go to schools where computing is an established resource for teaching and administration. Perhaps because of the transient nature of computer appreciation, teachers tend to base any course on the time available and the apparent need of the pupils. There are probably only two completely developed courses in Britain. The first[80] is a course for 'Computer Awareness' which is defined as 'the possession of sufficient knowledge to enable inferences, social and general, to be made on the basis of what is seen or heard about computers'. The second course,[81] entitled 'Information', aims to 'provide a framework within which insights and intuitions might be gained by children about many things. One... is the place of the computer and its effects on the way in which people live and work.'

Computer appreciation has not been restricted to secondary schools, since primary school pupils ask questions about, and show interest in, computers.[82,83,84] Three suitable approaches at this age are by:

Flowcharts to make pupils think about ordered sequences; for example, a pupil could draw a flowchart to represent the stages used when baking cakes. Each stage contains details such as mixing certain amounts of flour and lard, or placing cakes in an oven at a certain temperature, and the stages have to be arranged in a suitably correct sequence.

Punched cards which enable pupils to classify, record and retrieve information; for each pupil there could be a record divided into sections which will contain information such as how many sisters the pupil has. The information would be recorded on the pupil's card by punching holes in some sections.[82] When all the cards for one class are formed into a pack, it is possible to pass a knitting needle through so as to retrieve the cards of those pupils with, say, just one sister.

Films, videotapes or a microcomputer to allow pupils to appreciate the speed and power of computers.

Computer studies courses usually lead to a C.S.E. examination, or to a G.C.E. O-level or A-level examination (the A-level course may alternatively be called Computer science). In 1977, slightly more than half the schools with computer studies courses had pupils who were following Mode III C.S.E. syllabuses (see chapter 10). However, the balance will change as more Mode I syllabuses are offered by the C.S.E. boards. If a common 16+ examination is finally introduced, there will probably be an even faster change to Mode I because more syllabuses will then be initiated by the boards rather than by the schools as in the early 1970s. G.C.E. syllabuses have been predominantly Mode I at O-level, and completely Mode I at A-level.

Computer studies courses invariably have two parts, theory and practical, with the theory contributing from 50 per cent to 80 per cent of the marks. The theory syllabus normally includes:

1. structure and operation of the computer
2. peripheral devices
3. information and data processing
4. low and high level languages
5. software
6. programming
7. computer applications
8. history of computation.

The practical part requires several short programs, or fewer long programs, which demonstrate applications of parts of the theory. The computer studies syllabuses are now independent of the mathematics syllabuses, and may be taken in combination with any other subjects. Some pupils take computing courses in preparation for employment or further study, but most take courses either for interest or at least in the hope of finding them interesting. Teachers may obtain more details from the syllabuses published by examination boards.

SUPPORT FOR TEACHERS

Teacher support: people and associations

Teachers who feel that they need help with their educational computing activities should usually first seek support from people, and associations of people, at a local level. These people are familiar with the local situation and may be able to arrange personal contact with people doing similar work. Teachers should be ready to discuss both their successes and their problems with fellow professionals and, whether a school staff has one, or more than one, teacher of computing there should be regular contact with other teachers in the Local Education Authority (L.E.A.). As well as there being an L.E.A. adviser or inspector who is responsible for computer education, there may be supporting staff at a computing centre who can easily make the teachers' work more effective. One common method, for example, is by arranging meetings, or working parties, of teachers who are all preparing pupils for the same computer studies examination.

The L.E.A. adviser should also know about regional support which is available. This may come from members of the Computer Education Group, which has Branch Chairmen, or from members of the British Computer Society, which has Education Liaison Officers.[85] These people can be especially helpful in arranging speakers and visits. The I.C.L.-Computer Education in Schools team work through regional panels whose interests go beyond I.C.L.'s commercial involvement. Other support is also available from lecturers in colleges, polytechnics and universities in the region, who may have special knowledge about certain aspects of educational computing.

At national level, information can often be obtained through the published material mentioned at the end of this chapter. Requests for further information should be directed to the most suitable of the following sources – addresses are listed on pages xix–xxi.

1. The education officers of the British Computer Society (B.C.S.) and the National Computing Centre (N.C.C.).
2. The International Business Machines (I.B.M.) information service.
3. The International Computers Limited – Computer Education in Schools (I.C.L.-C.E.S.) officers.
4. The secretaries of examination boards.
5. The directors of special projects.

There is one national gallery, 'Computing Then and Now', at the London Science Museum. This is a well planned display of digital and analogue equipment which is especially suitable for pupils interested in computing.

Teacher support: hardware

Hardware is the term used for computing equipment which, in general, feels hard. For example, there are metal or plastic boxes containing parts of computers, and keyboards by which people control computers. Nearly all school educational computing uses digital computers; these operate on discrete bits of information, such as on an input tape with holes punched in some places but not punched in other places. There are two main ways of using these computers; firstly, in *interactive mode*, usually using a keyboard as on a typewriter, by which the user can provide information and control the program as it runs; and secondly in *batch mode*, where the user often provides all the program and information before the start, the computer processes them, and the user then sees the results. Each mode is more suitable for certain educational applications but in both modes the computer may be in the same room as the user, or it may be miles away. Interactive mode must have some electrical contact, such as a wire or telephone cable, from the keyboard to the central computer. Batch mode can be operated by sending paper tape or cards by post or by courier (for example, a pupil on a bicycle).

Figure 9.5 Computer hardware being used by pupils

For either mode of use, the computer may be one of these three types:

1. a large, or mainframe, computer
2. a minicomputer
3. a microcomputer.

There is no clear dividing line between these three types, but they can be explained in general terms. A *mainframe computer* will serve many users and will probably be situated in a specially staffed computer centre. If it is not wholly dedicated to educational computing, school use must have similar priorities to use for other applications so that regular lessons can be organized. A *minicomputer* will serve one, or a few, users and may belong to a school where staff and pupils have a special interest in education about computers. A *microcomputer* will probably serve one user at a time and, as it is relatively cheap to purchase, many schools are likely to own one or more microcomputers. They often have only a visual display output, which is ideal when the computer is used as a teaching resource but is a draw-back when pupils are working on the practical part of a computer studies course.

When a program has been run on a computer, any resulting information is normally output on either a printing device or a visual display unit (V.D.U.). The printing device produces typing on a roll of paper and many V.D.U.s reproduce similar typing on a television type of screen. Both these forms of output are rather limited and developments using drawings of lines, curves and shaded areas[86] offer many possibilities to mathematics teachers and pupils. Multi-coloured geometrical drawings can be displayed on 'high-resolution graphics' V.D.U.s, which first became generally available in 1980. Within a few years, each school may have one of these V.D.U.s, as part of a de-luxe microcomputer, to provide dynamic displays which illustrate mathematical ideas much more effectively than is done by a blackboard illustration. As well as owning this de-luxe resource, a school is likely to have several cheaper microcomputers for other purposes,[87] such as programming by pupils who are solving mathematics problems.

Although they are not computers, two associated items of digital hardware should be mentioned. The first is the programmable calculator[88] which can function in such a similar way to a micro-computer that people do not know which name to use. (The decision can finally depend on your choice of name or definition.) Because of the more limited range of language which is available, and the smaller memory, writing a calculator program is often more difficult than writing a computer program. However, a few readily available pro-grams could prevent a school computer being wastefully used for pro-cedures which only merit the use of a programmable calculator or even a straightforward pocket calculator. The second associated item is the logic tutor, which is an electronic kit which allows a pupil to build up circuits in order to gain an understanding of Boolean algebra or computer principles.[89] Not many teachers have found logic tutors useful, especially now that school computer education courses em-phasize the practice, rather than the theory, of computing.

This survey of hardware would not be complete without a brief consideration of the analogue computer. This uses continuous electric currents, instead of digital pulses. It has hardly been used in educa-tional computing and, although it can perform mathematical opera-tions, it is more a tool of the engineers.

Teacher support: software

Software is the term used for computing material such as programs, which are written on paper or stored on punched cards or tape. This 'soft' material makes the computer into a useful educational resource. There are three main types of educational software:

1. programs, often provided by the manufacturer, which allow the machine to operate as a computer
2. programs written by pupils, e.g. to gain programming experience
3. teaching packages which aim to provide further, deeper or faster learning by the pupils, or more efficient management or organization by the teachers.

The first type of software is not the concern of most teachers and, therefore, we will only consider aspects of the other two types.

There is usually one stage during a computer course when nearly all the pupils are writing programs and it used to be difficult to prepare the programs for input to the computer, as there was usually only one card punch or tape punch. This problem is now often overcome by giving each pupil some printed 'mark-sensed' cards. With a soft pencil, the pupil marks the cards in the places which represent words, letters or numbers which make up his or her program. With a main frame computer or minicomputer, these cards are placed directly in the computer input, which senses whether a mark has been made on the card instead of testing, as previously, whether a hole had been punched in that place. Cards or paper tape can rarely be used with microcomputers and pupils generally use the keyboard to input their programs which are then stored on ordinary audio tape.

As already explained, educational computing teaching packages have to include more than a program if they are to be useful to anyone other than the originator. The packages produced by the University of London Chelsea College projects, on Science Simulation[90] and Computers in the Curriculum,[91] are examples of good teaching packages. Because a great deal of time has been put into producing such packages, it would be uneconomic if they could not be transferred for use in many schools, and this transfer has to be both from computer to computer and from one educational system to another. Careful consideration of the problems of transferring packages has been made since 1970[92,93] and the knowledge which has been gained is now being applied, especially to packages and programs for the new microcomputers. For example, some L.E.A.s recommend that only one make of microcomputer should be used in their schools so that every program or package may be easily transferred.

Teacher support: published material

Any L.E.A. which has an active educational computing group will publish useful documents and perhaps a regular, or irregular, newsletter. For material which is nationally available, the single most useful publication for any teacher is the booklet *Computer Educational Aids and Resources for Teachers*.[85] This has two major sections which list and describe film materials and books[94] and also includes many shorter sections with details, for example, of wall-charts which are available from several sources. The range of books mentioned is extensive, starting from *How it works – the computer*[95] which is a 'Ladybird' book suitable for primary school pupils, and progressing through many others up to teachers' reference books such as *A glossary of computing terms for introductory courses*.[96]

Teachers can keep up to date with educational computing by reading some of the journals listed on page xxi. Within these, good information is regularly published in *Computer Education, Computers in School* and the *I.C.L.-C.E.S. Newsletter* (which is designed to support the many teachers whose pupils use the I.C.L.-C.E.S. books). Information about all aspects of computing is provided in the newspapers *Computing* and *Computer Weekly* which are distributed free to many places involved with educational computing. There is also an increasing selection of magazines available from bookstalls and publishers; these vary from the serious *Practical Computing* to the amusing *Creative Computing*.

Conclusion

This chapter has shown that educational computing, which is frequently controlled by mathematics teachers in a school, is rather different from many other school subjects. Its development has been closely linked with, and supported by, groups of people who have professional and business interests in computers. However, to make it an acceptable school subject, its development has also had to be linked with the public examination system[97] which is more fully discussed in the next chapter.

Annotated References for Chapter 9

1. Scheepmaker B. & Zinn K.L. eds. (1970) *World conference on computer education, 1970.* Wolters Noordhoff: Groningen; Science Associates International: New York.

   All the papers from the Amsterdam conference and preparatory symposia, which provide a comprehensive picture.

2. Lécarme O. & Lewis R. eds. (1975) *Computers in education: Proceedings of the I.F.I.P. second world conference.* North-Holland: Amsterdam, Oxford; American Elsevier: New York.

   All the papers from the Marseilles conference, which provide valuable information.

3. I.C. (1972) *Computing in schools conference, Book 1, invited papers*. Imperial College Computer Centre: London.

4. I.C. (1972) *Computing in schools conference, Book 2, secondary papers*. Imperial College Computer Centre: London.

5. I.C. (1973) *Third annual computing in schools conference, Book 2*. Imperial College Department of Computing and Control: London.

6. I.C. (1975) *Fifth annual computing in schools conference*. Imperial College Department of Computing and Control: London.

References 3–6 are some reports from the five valuable annual conferences, held during a major growth period of educational computing in schools.

7. Hooper R. & Toye I. eds. (1975) *Computer Assisted Learning in the United Kingdom: Some case studies*. Council for Educational Technology: London.

C.A.L. illustrated by work done in some N.D.P.C.A.L. projects.

8. Howes V.M. ed. (1970) *Individualizing instruction in science and mathematics*. Collier-Macmillan: London, New York, Toronto.

A book containing early articles about aspects of C.B.L.

9. H.M.S.O. (1979) *Aspects of secondary education in England: a survey by H.M. Inspectors of schools*. Her Majesty's Stationery Office: London.

The report of a thorough investigation of the final two years of education in 384 schools (10% sample).

10. Beveridge W.T. (1972) The work of computer education centres. *Mathematics in School*, vol. 1, no. 4, pp. 4–5.

Scottish computer education in the early years.

11. H.M.S.O. (1969) *Curriculum papers 6, Computers and the schools – an interim report*. Scottish Education Department. Her Majesty's Stationery Office: Edinburgh. See p. 6.

The first report of the Bellis committee, followed by Curriculum Papers 11 in 1972.

12. I.F.I.P. (1972) *Computer education for teachers in secondary schools: aims and objectives in teacher training*. International Federation for Information Processing Societies: Geneva. See p. 5.

One of four booklets available from the British Computer Society.

13. Berry P.C. et al. (1970) *Using the computer to compute: a direct but neglected approach to teaching mathematics*. In reference 1, pp. 2/25–2/31.

The use of a computer within the secondary mathematics curriculum.

14. Polya G. (1962–65) *Mathematical discovery: on understanding, learning and teaching problem solving, vols. 1 & 2*. Wiley: London, New York.

Polya has written other books on structuring problem solving.

15. Hart M. (1980) Computer programming in mathematics teaching. *Mathematics in School*, vol. 9, no. 3, pp. 10–11.

A few comments about interest in this link between computers and mathematics.

16. Papert S. (1981) *Mindstorms*. Harvester Press: Brighton. A stimulating book about children's mathematical activity.

17. Papert S. (1972) Teaching children to be mathematicians vs. teaching children mathematics. *International Journal of Mathematical Education in Science and Technology*, vol. 3, pp. 249–62.

    Papert uses a mechanical turtle and a special computer language.

18. O'Shea T. (1978) Artificial intelligence and computer based education. *Computer Education*, no. 30, pp. 25–8.

    A useful summary report which includes thirty-six references.

19. Arsac J.J. (1970) *Informatics and computer education*. In reference 1, pp. 1/69–1/72.

    A definition and consideration of information processing, related to courses in schools and universities.

20. Barker J.G. (1971) Introducing informatics. I.F.I.P. conference report stapled in *Computer Education*, no. 7.

    A summary of contributions to the Amsterdam world conference.

21. Samuelson K. (1975) *An informatics curriculum and its similarity to other international university programs*. In reference 2, pp. 255–61.

    The theory and practice of an informatics course in Sweden.

22. Girardot L-A (1975) *Informatique au lycée de la Celle-St.-Cloud: une expérience en 4ème*. In reference 2, pp. 273–6.

    Computer education led by teachers of English, French, geography, mathematics, music and Spanish.

23. Felton G.E. (1957) *Electronic computers and mathematicians*. In reference 24, p. 12.

    A paper by an employee of Ferranti, whose Pegasus computer took 33 hours to calculate pi to a given value of 10 000 decimal places.

24. Oxford Mathematical Conference for schoolteachers and industrialists (April 8–18, 1957); Abbreviated proceedings. Technology, The Times: London.

    This conference showed the value of school/industry cooperation, which has now greatly developed in computer education.

25. B.C.S. (1974) *The computer in secondary education*. British Computer Society: London.

    A report of achievements and expectations.

26. Coulson A.E. (1972) *Ten or eleven years of school computing, and a glimpse into the future*. In reference 3, pp. 1/1–1/4.

    A personal account by one of the first school teachers in educational computing.

27. Tinsley J.D. (1975) *The Schools Committee of the British Computer Society*. In reference 2, pp. 207–10.

    An account of the work of the Schools Committee since its foundation in 1964.

28. B.C.S. (1969) *Computer education for all*. British Computer Society: London.

    An outline for computer education in schools.

29. B.C.S. (1979) *Syllabuses for the future*. British Computer Society: London. Reprinted in *Mathematics in School*, vol. 8, no. 5, pp. 12–14.

A short report from the B.C.S. Schools Committee working party.

30. Tagg W. (1973) *The development of 'A' level computer science as a subject*. In reference 5, pp. 10.1.–10.3.

An L.E.A. Adviser, and Chief Examiner, describes G.C.E. Advanced-level.

31; B.C.S. (1971) *Computer studies in the Certificate of Secondary Education*. British Computer Society: London.

The aims, and content, of some early C.S.E. courses.

32. I.C.L.–C.E.S. (1980) *Newsletter no. 37*. International Computers Limited – Computer Education in Schools: Reading.

One of their interesting, and regular, newsletters on topical issues.

33. Hampson-Evans C. (1975) *'Computer Education in Schools' project*. In reference 2, pp. 291–4.

A history of co-operation between education and the computer industry.

34. Bellis B.T. (1970) *The formal introduction of computer education into secondary schools in Scotland*. In reference 1, pp. 2/15–2/19.

A report of effective national planning.

35. McDonald P.P. (1972) *Some problems in setting up a computer centre for schools*. In reference 4, pp. 2/1–2/14.

An account of an early development in Northern Ireland.

36. Morris R.M. & Dean P.G. (1974) The use of interactive simulation in biological science teaching. *International Journal of Mathematical Education in Science and Technology*, vol. 5, no. 3, pp. 389–94.

A report of work done at the Open University and Chelsea College.

37. Hooper R. (1977) *National Development Programme in Computer Assisted Learning: Final report of the Director*. Council for Educational Technology: London.

The end of five years' development to assist secondary and tertiary education.

38. Barker J.G. (1971) Introducing informatics. I.F.I.P. conference report stapled in *Computer Education*, no. 7.

A summary of contributions to the Amsterdam world conference.

39. O.E.C.D. (1971) *Seminar on computer sciences in secondary education, Sèvres 1970*. Organisation for Economic Co-operation and Development: Paris.

A report of discussions at this seminar.

40. Tomasso C. (1975) *A dynamic approach to ihe collection and dissemination of information*. In reference 2, pp. 937–44.

Information about the International Information Centre.

41. Papert S. (1972) Teaching children to be mathematicians vs teaching children mathematics. *International Journal of Mathematical Education in Science and Technology* vol. 3, pp. 249–62.

Papert uses a mechanical turtle and a special computer language.

42. Howe J.A.M. (1975) *Artificial intelligence and education.* In reference 7, chapter 9.

An account of creative mathematical development at Edinburgh.

43. Minsky M. (1970) Form and content in computer science. *Journal of the Association for Computing Machinery,* vol. 17, no. 2, pp. 197–215. See p. 205.

A research paper, but of special interest.

44. Hebenstreit J. (1974) Computer science in education. *International Journal of Mathematical Education in Science and Technology,* vol. 5, no. 3, pp. 297–306.

A paper by one of the leaders in French l'informatique.

45. Hartley J.R. (1975) *Some experiences with individualised teaching systems.* In reference 7, chapter 8.

A case study from a leader of the Leeds University C.B.L. Project.

46. Dowsey M.W. & Bloomer J. (1977) *An experiment using computer based educational games and simulations in secondary schools, Report UKSC 0087.* International Business Machines: Peterlee, Durham.

Research using three games in three schools.

47. Schmitt A. (1975) *Simulative transfer of mathematical concepts by interactive programming.* In reference 2, pp. 811–15.

A special language, MATHCALC, is explained which reflects mathematical structures.

48. Investigations on Teaching with Microcomputers as an Aid (I.T.M.A.). This project is studying the classroom use of microcomputers as a 1980s resource for teachers. I.T.M.A., College of St. Mark & St. John, Derriford Road, Plymouth PL6 8BH.

49. B.C.S. (1973) *Programming languages for school use.* British Computer Society: London.

A survey of languages and the reasons for their use.

50. B.C.S. (1976) The use of the computer as a management aid in schools: a report from the British Computer Society Schools Committee. *Computer Education,* no. 23, pp. 13–20.

A discussion of day-to-day applications of the computer.

51. Miles R. (1975) *Computers in school timetabling.* In reference 7, chapter 4.

A case study written during an N.D.P.C.A.L. project.

52. L.A.M.S.A.C. (1978) *Computer assisted school timetabling project report.* Local Authorities Management Services and Computer Committee: London.

The final report of an N.D.P.C.A.L. project, presenting the state of the art or science.

53. Dawkins C.C.H. (1973) *Databanks for school administration.* In reference 5, pp. 13.1–13.6.

A description of work done in one school, which shows various possibilities.

54. Piddock P. (1975) Computers in school administration – D.E.S. form 7. *Computer Education*, no. 21, pp. 19–20.

Some uses of a fairly large computer, based in a South Wales school.

55. Dowsey M.W. & Butler A.M. (1976) Use of a computer in careers education and guidance. *Journal of the Society for Academic Gaming and Simulation in Education and Training*: Loughborough, vol. 6, no. 1, pp. 20–8.

A description of a project using pupils from Cheshire.

56. Leeson C.M. & Jaworski J. (1975) *The Hertfordshire computer managed mathematics project*. In reference 2, pp. 31–6.

A clear description of the project.

57. Dunn J.A. (1972) *The guidance program in the P.L.A.N. system of individualised education*. American Institute for Research: Palo Alto, California.

A description of a C.M.L. project which covers several subjects.

58. See reference 8, pp. 165–8.

59. Cooley W.W. & Glaser R. (1969) The computer and individualised instruction. *Science*, no. 166, pp. 574–82.

An article about I.P.I., an early C.M.L. scheme.

60. Broderick W.R. & Lovatt K.F. (1975) *Acceptability of computer managed instruction in the classroom – three years experience*. In reference 2, pp. 47–51.

A study, by the research leaders, of the acceptability of C.M.L. by teachers.

61. Broderick W.R. (1975) *The Havering computer managed learning system*. In reference 7, chapter 3.

A case study about a system used for mixed ability science teaching.

62. Piddock P. (1979) Travels with C.A.M.O.L.: the continuing tale of a C.M.L. experiment. *Computer Education*, no. 33, pp. 2–6.

An article based on experiences with mainframe (and micro) computers in Birmingham L.E.A.

63. Hawkridge D.G. (1973) *Problems in implementing computer managed learning*. N.D.P.C.A.L., Council for Educational Technology: London.

A wide ranging investigation and consideration of the problems.

64. Allen M.W. (1975) *Computer managed instruction, a definitive design*. In reference 2, pp. 115–22.

A presentation of an advanced, but not proven, design.

65. Rushby N.J. ed. (1977) *Computer managed learning in the 1980s; Technical report no. 16*. Council for Educational Technology: London.

Expectations and needs for the future development of C.M.L.

66. MATLAB (1977) *Matlab – information booklet*. Council for Educational Technology: London.

A description of a C.A.L. mathematics laboratory system.

67. Daly D.W., Dunn W. & Hunter J. (1977) The computer assisted learning project in mathematics at the University of Glasgow. *International Journal of Mathematical Education in Science and Technology*, vol. 8, no. 2, pp. 145–56.

C.A.L. used by students who need further mathematics.

68. Tait K. et al. (1973) Feedback procedures in computer assisted arithmetic instruction. *British Journal of Educational Psychology*, vol. 43, no. 2, pp. 161–71.

A report of one investigation of the C.B.L. project, University of Leeds.

69. Travers K.J. et al. (1977) *Mathematics teaching*. Harper & Row: New York, London. See pp. 290–2.

A book to develop a teacher's competence in planning, teaching and evaluating.

70. Athanassov A. & Popova J. (1975) *Computer-aided application of a method for control and self-control in mathematical instruction*. In reference 2, pp. 817–22.

A paper about a teaching and learning system which adapts to the needs of the student.

71. Lewis R. (1975) *Computers as a resource for learning*. In reference 7, chapter 1.

A case study by the Director of the Chelsea C.A.L. projects.

72. M.A. (1971) *Computers and the teaching of numerical mathematics in the upper secondary school*. Bell: London.

A booklet from the Mathematical Association.

73. Hart M. (1977) Using computers to understand mathematics. *Mathematics Teaching*, no. 80, pp. 40–2.

The relationship between BASIC and some mathematical concepts.

74. Bork A. (1975) Effective computer use in physics education. *American Journal of Physics*, vol. 43, no. 1, pp. 81–8.

An outline of five successful uses, including interactive proofs and mathematical paths.

75. Harris J. (1975) *How can the computer help us teach physics?* In reference 2, pp. 27–9.

The manipulation and testing of models, as distinct from simulations.

76. L.H.C.P. (1977) *The local history classroom project: Final report, October 1977*. Council for Educational Technology: London.

Approaches to the teaching of local history, and the use of historical data-banks for C.A.L.

77. Lewis J.W. (1975) *A case study in the development of an information retrieval package*. In reference 6, pp. 11.1–11.4.

A report of work linked with the Hertfordshire Advisory Unit for C.B.E.

78. A.U.C.B.E. (1978) *Information retrieval*. Advisory Unit for Computer Based Education, Hertfordshire County Council: Hatfield.

A booklet on school use of data files about geography, history, literature, astronomy, food and careers.

79. Jackson B.J. (1975) *Data bases in the classroom*. In reference 2, pp. 567–71.

A system with two simple programs to allow pupils to set up, and interrogate, their own data base.

80. Makkar L. (1976) Computer awareness III: is it real? *Computer Education*, no. 24, pp. 25–9.

A researched appreciation course by a British Petroleum Fellow at the University of Surrey.

81. Longworth N. (1977) Teaching 'information' in the secondary school. *Computer Education*, no. 25, pp. 16–18.

A nine-module non-mathematical course developed in Hampshire.

82. Nuffield (1972) *Computers and young children*. Chambers: Edinburgh, Murray: London, Wiley: New York.

A Nuffield Mathematics Project book which includes copies of work done by children.

83. Taylor R.P. (1975) *Computerless computing for young children*. In reference 2, pp. 847–52.

Activities for primary and middle school children.

84. Leverett S.M. (1978) Computing in primary schools: pilot scheme 1977. *Computer Education*, no. 29, pp. 2–4.

Objectives and methods used in Essex schools.

85. N.C.A.V.A.E. (1977) *Computer educational aids and resources for teachers*. National Committee for Audio-Visual Aids: 33 Queen Anne Street, London W1M OAL.

An invaluable source of information, prepared by the B.C.S.

86. Brissenden T.H.F. & Davies A.J. (1975) Computer graphics in the teaching of science and mathematics. *Mathematics Teaching*, no. 72, pp. 49–54.

A report of schoolteachers' use of university techniques.

87. Blow D. (1980) Microprocessors in schools. *Mathematics in School*, vol. 9, no. 1, pp. 14–15.

Some comments about the use of three machines in one school.

88. Henderson D. (1975) *Trends in the development and evaluation of computer education opportunities in a major public school system*. In reference 2, pp. 277–82.

Effects of changing from computers to programmable calculators.

89. B.C.S. (1974) Logic tutors. British Computer Society: London. Inserted in *Computer Education*, no. 18, pp.13–20.

A schools committee report on use and choice of logic tutors.

90. C.S.S.P. (1975) *Chelsea Science Simulation Project*. Edward Arnold: London.

C.A.L. packages for sixth-form science teaching, which were the first major set produced in Britain.

91. Computers in the Curriculum, Educational Computing Section, Chelsea College, University of London.

92. Turnbull J.J. (1975) *Transferability of computer software for education*. In reference 2, pp. 989–92.

An overview of the problems, and studies of their solution.

93. Williams D.M. (1975) C.A.L. portability and documentation. *Computer Education*, no. 21, pp. 3–5.

Transferring someone else's packages onto your computer system.

94. B.C.S. (1976) *Computer booklist for schools*. British Computer Society: London.

An annotated list of books which have been found useful by teachers and pupils.

95. Ladybird (1971) *How it works – the computer*; Ladybird series 654, no. 11. Wills & Hepworth: Loughborough.

One of a series of books with clear descriptions and many coloured illustrations.

96. B.C.S. (1977) *A glossary of computing terms for introductory courses*. British Computer Society: London.

An attempt to standardize words and meanings for use in courses and examinations.

97. Reeve T. et al. (1979) A response to the N. & F. proposals. *Computer Education*, no. 33, pp. 22–4.

A discussion of computer education examinations for 18 year old pupils.

CHAPTER 10

ASSESSMENT AND EVALUATION

Introduction

Assessment and evaluation are both terms which measure educational effects. However, the terms differ in that assessment measures a pupil's progress whereas evaluation judges the merits of an educational system. Evaluation is therefore a broader term; it measures the achievements of pupils, teachers and curriculum, and is linked with the themes of change and choice which are evident throughout this book. When a pupil learns mathematics, he changes from a state of nonunderstanding, or misunderstanding, a mathematics topic to a state of understanding it. The extent of the change is assessed by the pupil's teacher. From this assessment the teacher can choose further topics or different teaching styles which will be suitable. Consider, for example, the pupils and teacher in a classroom, where the teacher is controlling a continually changing situation. As the lesson progresses, the teacher may discover some pupils who are successfully doing mathematics, some pupils who have misunderstood something and other pupils who are just bored. The teacher must respond to these discoveries in a suitable way. As an identical situation has never before arisen, every teacher plays the rôle of an experimental scientist in a classroom where the three reagents are the teacher, the pupils and the curriculum materials. All three are interacting and the scientist (teacher) must continually:

1. decide which information may be worth collecting
2. collect, sort and interpret that information
3. use the interpretation to decide how the lesson will continue.

This example applies the three stages of educational evaluation to a classroom lesson, but the stages can also be used to evaluate the effectiveness of curriculum materials or other forms of teaching. Evaluation, in the strictest sense of the word, means to represent by a number. We need to modify this strict definition because numbers are seldom useful enough to represent even simple situations. For example, a teacher may know that one pupil scored six marks out of ten when given a simple arithmetic test but that information alone does not help the teacher to diagnose that pupil's learning difficulties. Teachers must also be very cautious about using numerical comparisons to evaluate more complex situations. In a school, for example, the information that pupils in the mathematics department gain more G.C.E. Ordinary-level passes than pupils in the English department does not necessarily mean that the mathematics department is the better. A major aim of the English teachers may be that their pupils gain a broad experience of using the English language, and this experience is not tested by most Ordinary-level examinations. The modified and broadened view of evaluation must include, and often start with, the benefits of education. As these benefits are largely qualitative and only approximately defined, it is not surprising that it is often difficult to evaluate any part of education and that the results are often inconclusive.

Categories of evaluation

The historical record in chapter 2 shows that evaluation has almost always existed as part of education; two specific examples of its use were nineteenth century teachers being paid according to the results of their pupils and the matriculation examination which controlled entry to university. In these two cases evaluation was based on the attainment of individual pupils, in the former case against a predetermined standard and in the latter case against the standard of other examination candidates. As both these measurements were taken at the end of a course, they are in the category of *summative evaluation*.[1] During this present century, another category of evaluation has become increasingly used; this is *formative evaluation* in which information is gained during a course so that it can be used to modify the next stages of that course. The modification is undertaken by the curriculum developer, the teacher or the pupil who receives that information. Within this formative evaluation two subcategories have emerged, namely *comparative evaluation* which investigates the effectiveness of alternative curriculum materials or styles of teaching and *financial evaluation* which investigates the costs of developing and using a new course. The distinction between summative and formative evaluation is whether it takes place after or during a course. Both categories may use either subjective or objective information, but the main benefit of formative evaluation is that it leads to improved teaching and learning.

ASSESSMENT TESTS

The different kinds of tests

Tests used in the assessment of pupils[3] are either norm-referenced tests (see 1 and 1a below) or criterion-referenced tests (see 2, 2a and 2b).

1. *Norm-referenced tests* compare the standards of performance between different pupils or over different times. A familiar example is a test set by a teacher and taken by all the pupils in a class; from the results the pupils can be placed in a rank class order. These tests can provide a measure of the general mathematics performance of pupils.

1a. *Standardized tests* are norm-referenced tests which compare an individual pupil's performance with the performances of a large (often national) sample of pupils of similar age. These tests are standardized by using statistical techniques. Familiar examples are the National Foundation for Educational Research (N.F.E.R.) Mathematics Attainment tests.[4]

2. *Criterion-referenced tests* assess whether an individual pupil can achieve certain stated mathematical objectives.[5] These objectives usually test lower levels of understanding (e.g. knowledge, skills, concepts) of particular parts of the curriculum; for example, whether a pupil can use the memory of a pocket calculator to correctly store and retrieve numbers during certain calculations. The results are expressed simply (e.g. Yes/No) for each item included in the test. There is often no time limit for the test as it does not aim to compare pupils. Examples are the N.F.E.R. tests from the Concepts in Secondary Mathematics and Science project.[4]

2a. *Diagnostic tests* are criterion-referenced tests which locate a pupil's nonunderstanding or misunderstanding (see chapter 3) of parts of a topic, so that remedial action can be taken.[6] Formal diagnostic arithmetic tests were pioneered by Fred and Eleanor Schonell[7] but informal diagnostic tests are continually used by many mathematics teachers.

2b. *Mastery tests* are criterion-referenced tests with objectives limited to the actual content of a course (i.e. without application of course material to unfamiliar problems). A final score of over

80 per cent is often considered as a suitable level for a pupil who has mastered the course. Examples of these tests are the 'check-cards' at the end of each section of some work card schemes, and tests used in the assessment of numeracy.

Objective and essay questions

Norm-referenced and criterion-referenced mathematics tests may contain objective questions or essay questions. An objective question has a unique acceptable answer and is typified by a multiple choice question as in figure 10.1(a).

(a) If I={1,2,3,4} and P={2,3,5}
     then which one of these
     statements is true ?

        $I \subset P$

        $I \cap P = \{2,3\}$

        $I \cup P = \{2,3\}$

        $I \supset P$

        $I \cap P = \{1,2,3,4,5\}$

(b) Yesterday, my watch was 2
     minutes slow at 7am, and
     1 minute fast at 4pm.   On
     that day, when did it show
     the correct time ?

Figure 10.1 An objective question (a) and an essay question (b)

Such questions are easy to mark and, because they are usually quickly answered, a variety of mathematics topics can be tested in a short time. An essay question is a non-objective question. In the example given in figure 10.1(b), the correct result of 1 pm. can be reached in different ways. The marking is therefore more difficult, especially as some pupils will give partially correct answers. An essay question requires a pupil to present a continuous mathematical argument on just one topic. The two types of questions therefore assess the attainment of different goals. If a whole test is composed of objective questions it is often called an objective test.[8]

THE ASSESSMENT OF THE PROGRESS OF PUPILS

The construction of tests

When mathematics teachers construct[9] any kind of cognitive test using either objective or essay questions, the construction generally involves two variables as shown in figure 10.2. The variables are not continuous, as with a number line, but are made up of elements which often tend to form a progressive sequence. For example, the mathematical content of a test on linear algebraic equations might progress[10] from whole number answers (e.g. $x = 5$) through negative answers ($x = -13$) to fractional answers ($x = -\frac{3}{8}$).

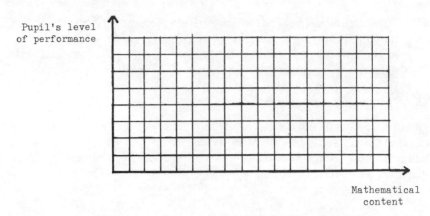

Figure 10.2 The two variables in an assessment test

This progress reflects the structure of mathematics and the sequence which is often used in teaching mathematics. The progressive sequence in the pupils' level of performance[11,12] is usually based on theories of learning and of curriculum development[13] which have been described in chapters 5 and 8 respectively. However, instead of the many levels of performance proposed in some theories, e.g. knowledge, comprehension, applications, etc. of Bloom's taxonomy, a classroom test may have only a few levels or elements.

Three examples of content and performance in tests

The mathematical content and level of performance in a test are often emphasized by the format of the results. In the following three examples, each pupil's attainment would be recorded on a separate diagram, or table, by the teacher putting a tick or other mark in certain squares.

1.   A *numeracy mastery test*[14] may have many basic skills along the mathematical content axis and just two elements along the performance axis, as in figure 10.3. The basic skills need to be defined in more detail than is shown in the figure, before the teacher can assess whether a pupil can or cannot perform those skills. This format (can do/cannot do) also appears in many diagnostic tests.

2.   A *norm-referenced pupil attainment test* may have many concepts and techniques along the mathematical content axis and four levels of performance along the vertical axis, as in figure 10.4. If a pupil is assessed several times during a school year, figure 10.4 can be completed as a record card of that pupil's progress and attainment by placing in certain squares the date of the

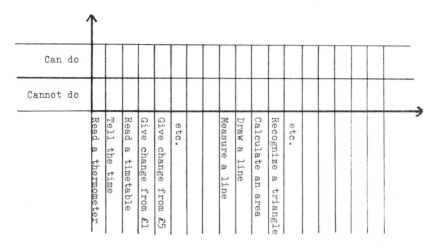

Figure 10.3 Content and performance in a numeracy mastery test

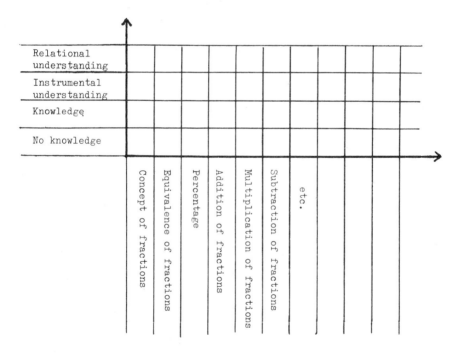

Figure 10.4 Content and performance, to test attainment with simple fractions

assessment. This record gives valuable information to the next teacher when that pupil moves to another class or school.[15,16] Another use of a table, like the one in figure 10.4, is to provide a profile of a pupil's attainment; a prospective employer may use such a table to decide whether a pupil being interviewed for a job has the necessary knowledge. This latter use of a record is being tested by some Mathematical Association members who are developing a *School Leaver's Attainment Profile of Numerical Skills.*[17]

3. A less familiar example of a norm-referenced test is a *standardized test of pupils' projects,* for example as part of the assessment for a C.S.E. or C.E.E. examination. Although pupils may have chosen very different topics for their projects, their work can still be assessed on two variables, i.e. a content axis and a performance axis, as shown in figure 10.5. Because one main aim of a project is to encourage creative mathematical work, the elements along the horizontal axis are rather different from those content elements in previous examples. For each element,

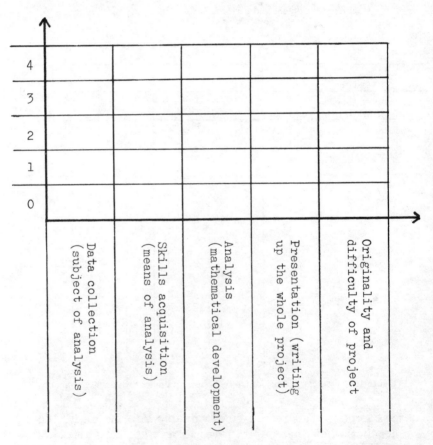

Figure 10.5 Content and performance in assessing projects

the five levels, 0 to 4, of performance obviously need to be specified in detail.[18]

Looking back over figures 10.3 to 10.5, the two variables can be compared for these three examples. Along the horizontal axis, the mathematical content changes from many specific items (e.g. Tell the time) to just five broad elements (e.g. Skills acquisition). Meanwhile, along the vertical axis there is an increasing number of levels of pupil performance. If figures like these are used as record cards the number of entries must be carefully considered; too many entries make it difficult for another teacher to understand the information and too few entries do not give sufficiently explicit information.

The informal and formal assessment of pupils

This chapter has already used examples of formal assessment, where the tests are standardized and the results written down. Although most examples will continue to be from the formal area, readers should realize that most school assessment is informal and of immediate, not lasting, value. Suitable techniques from formal assessment are used by teachers in their classrooms.[4] There, the teachers ask questions, and set written problems, about the mathematical content of the lessons. The pupils respond by answering, perhaps with words or with written symbols or merely by the expressions on their faces. These are the responses which are immediately available to the teachers, who have to use them to continue the lesson.

The language used in assessment

At times, all teachers will have had difficulty in communicating mathematical ideas, or even simple instructions, to pupils.[19] From these experiences, it should be obvious that the language used in informal and formal assessment has to be carefully chosen. If language is chosen which the pupils understand, then we can be fairly certain that it is the pupils' mathematics which is being assessed; if unsuitable language is chosen for part of a test, then the results from that part tell us nothing about the pupils' mathematics. An investigation involving words used in C.S.E. mathematics examinations[20] has indicated that there is a language problem. For example, when the word 'parallelogram' was presented, it was misunderstood by 22 per cent of a sample of pupils and not understood by 41 per cent. Thus only 37 per cent of pupils were likely to fully understand an examination question which included that word.

PUBLIC EXAMINATIONS
Examinations, boards and modes of examination

Public examinations in Britain are summative standardized tests, controlled by examination boards which are independent of the Government, the Local Education Authorities, the universities and the schools. In England and Wales there are eight General Certificate of Education (G.C.E.) boards which control Advanced-level (A-level) and Ordinary-level (O-level) examinations. Most candidates for A-level are aged from 17 to 18 years and most candidates for O-level are aged from 15 to 16 years. There are also thirteen Certificate of Secondary Education (C.S.E.) boards, which control the C.S.E. examinations[21] for 15 to 16 year old pupils and nearly all the Certificate of Extended Education (C.E.E.) examinations for 16 to 17 year old pupils. Each board appoints mathematics lecturers and teachers as part-time examiners, who are responsible for syllabuses and examinations. (Further details about G.C.E. and C.S.E. are included in chapter 2 of this book and C.E.E. is discussed later in this chapter.) Within this already complex public examination system, each of the twenty one boards commonly examines two or more mathematics syllabuses at each level and may use the following three different modes of examination. These are, firstly, the traditional mode I where the examiners control both the syllabus and examinations, secondly, the rarely used mode II, with the syllabus designed by the school staff but the examinations set and marked by the examiners and, thirdly, the increasingly popular mode III[22,23] where school teachers control both the syllabus and examinations but the teachers' marking is moderated by the board's examiners who then award examination grades. (N.B. Educationalists often use phrases like 'mode I examination' to refer to both the syllabus and the examination.) Although the policy for entering pupils for different mathematics examinations varies from school to school, typical figures show that the group of G.C.E. O-level mathematics candidates coincides with the top 30 per cent of the ability range. In a comprehensive school with a good mathematics department, about one-fifth of these candidates will continue to an A-level mathematics course. The group of C.S.E. mathematics candidates coincides with the next 50 per cent of the ability range, making a total of 80 per cent of pupils who are entered for a public mathematics examination[24] before their compulsory schooling ends. Of the C.S.E. candidates, only a few who have passed the examination with high grades will continue to a one-year C.E.E. course or, very occasionally, to an A-level course.

Public examinations: comparison of courses and syllabuses

As public examinations provide summative assessment of pupils within a fairly narrow age range from 15 to 18 years, it is not surprising that the comparable mathematics syllabuses show more similarities than differences. In the school years immediately preceding the examinations, it seems that these similarities lead to generally similar teaching and courses in most schools. It must be realized that these courses are not determined by the syllabuses alone, because teachers often cannot interpret a syllabus until they have studied past examination questions. Reprints of past questions are published, and their common use by teachers and pupils does make it difficult for examiners to materially change the style of examination for any existing mathematics syllabus. The syllabus, course and examination similarities from board to board, from school to school and from year to year[25] can be interpreted in different ways; some people applaud the desirable constancy while others deplore the fact that a summative examination strongly influences the pupils' mathematics for perhaps the two school years prior to the examination.

Many mathematicians would claim that mathematics is an exceptional subject, and this is borne out by its being the only subject in which pupils may take courses for either two separate A-levels, or just one A-level. In these courses most pupils will study some pure mathematics and some applied mathematics, which may be statistics or mechanics. The G.C.E. boards' A-level syllabuses are broadly similar but any proposals for a common core[26] between them may conflict with the diverse needs of different groups of pupils.[27] The other main syllabuses originating from G.C.E. boards are at O-level and, on comparison, these contain a varied amount of 'modern mathematics'. This can produce different emphasis on the mathematical work required from the pupils, even where the mathematical topics seem very alike. Almost all G.C.E. mathematics syllabuses and examinations are mode I, whereas those for C.S.E. commonly use both mode I and mode III. It is in C.E.E. that the use of mode III examinations predominates; this introduces differences between schools which, together with the present developmental structure (which is considered on a following page), means that comparisons between C.E.E. mathematics courses and syllabuses are of only passing interest. During the development of C.S.E. mode I courses, there has been 'an attempt not only to broaden the basis on which assessments are made but also to allow for wider objectives in mathematics teaching.' However, while there are differences between the examinations[28] there is 'considerable conformity over such aspects as the format, questions,...time involved and...conditions' and, comparing O-level and C.S.E, 'the characteristics of written examinations have changed little with the introduction of C.S.E.'[29] What has changed is that course work assessment is included as part of the examination for many mode III C.S.E. schemes. This is a beneficial change for many thorough but slow working pupils; now they can show their understanding of mathematics by good course work which comes from sustained effort over several days or weeks.

Public examinations: comparison of results

Within the British public examination system, the combination of numerous mathematics syllabuses and three different modes of examination means that there cannot always be an exact equivalence between the examination results awarded to pupils. There are four aspects of this equivalence which might concern mathematics teachers and these are illustrated in figure 10.6.[30]

Figure 10.6 Examples of the four aspects of equivalence of public examination results

There is firstly the equivalence between different subjects from one examination board (e.g. between mathematics and English results for all the candidates who entered one board's 1980 C.S.E. examinations); secondly the equivalence between different boards' examinations in the same subject and level (e.g. would the same pupils get higher grades for O-level mathematics from the London G.C.E. board than from the Associated G.C.E. board?); thirdly, the equivalence between the different modes of mathematics examination from the same board[31] (e.g. is a pupil likely to gain a higher grade from a school's mode III examination than from the board's mode I examination?); and fourthly the equivalence between mathematics examination results for the same board over a period of time[32] (e.g. in the 1980 examination, is it easier to obtain a grade A for one O-level syllabus than it was in 1978?). These four aspects of equivalence between examination results illustrate the difficulties involved when making comparisons. At a very fundamental level, syllabuses can be based on different mathematical aims when, for example, a mode III assessment may give credit for a pupil's long-term application to a mathematical problem as well as short-term recall of mathematical knowledge. During lessons, pupils will have teachers who may be inspiring mathematicians and may be very experienced at teaching one syllabus rather than another. Even when the examinations occur, candidates are often given a choice of questions, so that two candidates can be awarded the same mark after showing different mathematical understanding. Differences therefore exist at all stages of a course and it would need a severe restriction of the curricular freedom given to teachers and schools before a precise comparison of results could be made. A few comparisons have been made between mathematics and other subject results from the same examination board.[33,34] These confirm the opinion held by many teachers that mathematics is often more severely graded than other subjects in both C.S.E. and O-level examinations. For example, the average grade for the candidates in the 1976 Metropolitan Region Examination C.S.E. board was 3.84 for mathematics compared with 3.64 for all subjects and 3.47 for English (i.e. the English average was closest to grade 1, the best grade awarded). Another example of different gradings comes from my own experience. After entering a large number of pupils for A-level examinations, I compared their results in Pure Mathematics and in Applied Mathematics. I discovered that, where there was a difference in the grades awarded to a pupil, the difference was consistent instead of being randomly distributed. The result for Pure Mathematics was almost invariably one grade higher than the result for Applied Mathematics, which implied that the latter was more severely marked. This might be explained by some schools not entering their weaker Pure Mathematics candidates for Applied Mathematics examinations; if these weaker pupils could not be awarded the lower grades then other candidates had to receive them.

During the 1970s, a few teachers entered some pupils for the O-level mathematics examinations of two G.C.E. boards, in an attempt to discover whether the two boards' mathematics gradings were comparably awarded.[35] It was sometimes found that individual pupils received different grades from the two boards, but no conclusion can be reached about one board's syllabuses and examinations being easier because the teachers were not equally experienced at preparing pupils for both G.C.E. boards, and because only small samples of pupils were involved.

Comparisons such as those mentioned above can be carried out by teachers, but the purpose should not just be to find fault with the examination boards. The results can be applied usefully in teachers' own schools to improve the effectiveness of the teaching and learning, thereby using external summative evaluation for internal formative purposes. Otherwise, we must acknowledge the boards' assurances[36] that their monitoring and control of comparability is satisfactory, and we must realize that many people are expecting too much comparability between examination results.

For many years, there has been an agreement that C.S.E. grade 1 is equivalent to a simple pass (now grade C) at O-level, and this agreement is generally honoured for C.S.E. pupils who wish to enter employment or higher education. Any further comparability between C.S.E. and O-level mathematics seems almost impossible to specify, despite suggestions that the *Rasch* statistical model[37,38] could achieve this by using a common bank of examination questions from which one group of questions may be selected for the C.S.E. examination and another group for the O-level examination.

Public examinations: developments and proposals

For many school teachers, the comparability of the results of G.C.E. and C.S.E. examinations seems to be less important than the differences between their courses and syllabuses, which mean that G.C.E. and C.S.E. pupils have to be in separate groups. This produces practical problems in timetabling; human problems when one alternative has to be chosen for each pupil; and curricular problems about the common core of mathematics which all pupils should study.[39,40,41] One proposal to overcome these problems by introducing a single common examination, the *General Certificate of Secondary Education (G.C.S.E.)*, was considered by the Waddell committee between 1976 and 1978, and some G.C.E. and C.S.E. boards then worked together to investigate the feasibility of a common examination for pupils of a great range of abilities. Such a common examination in mathematics was found to be especially difficult because of the nature of the subject and the vastly different abilities within the 80 per cent of pupils who follow courses for C.S.E. and G.C.E. O-level examinations.[42] (These examinations are only intended to be used for pupils within the upper sixty per cent of the ability range). However, some boards co-operated and devised a type of G.C.S.E. 'examinations with choice of paper (according to ability) which worked well enough to point towards a satisfactory approach within a common system.'[43] This quotation is in a report which recommends that a common system of examining should be designed, but a full G.C.S.E. seems unlikely to soon be in operation despite the support of many teachers' organizations. Some opposition is based on the need to maintain O-level as both a recognizable public standard and a personal stepping stone towards higher education. Therefore, we have entered the 1980s with a compromise decision by the government, namely to introduce a single consistent system of clearly defined examination grades which will be used by C.S.E. and G.C.E. boards and to establish national criteria for syllabuses.[44]

A number of pupils who enter the sixth forms in schools or colleges do not have O-level grades A, B or C (which are commonly considered as pass grades) and many of these pupils will only remain at school for one year. In some sixth forms they can study for the *Certificate of Extended Education (C.E.E.)*, an examination which began in 1973 but whose development[45,46,47,48] up to 1980 had not led to its acceptance by the Secretary of State for Education as a regular part of the national system. Unluckily for many pupils who would have benefited from the C.E.E., the recommendation for its acceptance[48] came during a general move-ment to simplify the examination system. The recommendation was also in a period of financial stringency and falling rolls, when some sixth forms were being amalgamated into tertiary colleges. The less academic students in these colleges could already study for the more vocationally orientated awards of the *Business Education Council (B.E.C.)* and the *Technician Education Council (T.E.C.)*,[49] which, unlike the C.E.E., are recognised by government, colleges and employers. All B.E.C. award students study mathematics within an integrating core of subjects, and T.E.C. mathematics courses are needed by all student technicians.

In the academic sixth form, mathematics has always been an important subject in its own right, but it is now increasingly important as a support for other subjects. Since the 1959 Crowther report[50] which expressed concern about early subject specialization by grammar school pupils, there have been various proposals to encourage the study of mathematics as part of a broader academic sixth form curriculum.[51] Almost every possible pattern of broadening must have been proposed as an attempt to replace the three specialized A-levels, and several terminologies have been used and then rejected. The main proposals have been 'two Minor and two Major subjects';[52] 'two Qualifying and three Further subjects';[53] and 'three Normal (N) and two Further (F) subjects'.[54] These last N and F proposals were extensively developed and supported by seven group studies of the feasibility of teaching and examining[55] various mathematics syllabuses.[57,58,59] This work by, and on behalf of, the Schools Council has left us with many ideas about the mathematics which might be taught and examined in a broad sixth form curriculum. However, the N and F proposals were finally rejected in 1979 because they were not widely acceptable and there was a fear that they might lower the existing A-level standards. Research showed that the N and F proposals might also have reduced the percentage of pupils who studied mathematics as a major sixth form subject, although N-level mathematics would probably have been chosen by many pupils as the fourth or fifth subject[60] which A-level does not at present allow. It would have been a dis-service to future mathematics education if fewer mathematics pupils (at F-level) had led to less people studying mathematics at university and college, thus reducing the supply of mathematics teachers from 1990. At present, there are almost certainly not enough mathematics teachers available in Britain to teach mathematics as a compulsory subject to all pupils during the whole of their time at school. Such compulsory mathematics, which has been proposed for British schools (e.g. in the 1968 Dainton report[61]), already exists in other European countries and is a requirement of the *International Baccalaureate (I.B.)*.[62,64] For the I.B. Diploma, by which a few British pupils enter British universities each year, the pupils follow a broad curriculum of three subjects at Subsidiary level and three subjects at Higher level, which has many similarities to the proposed N and F curriculum.

The purpose of public examinations

One of the early uses of public examinations was to differentiate between pupils so that they could be placed in order of attainment; the pupils highest in the order qualified for higher education or for entry to their chosen profession. This use still exists, although in a much less competitive form because now, for example, any pupil who gains O-levels and then A-levels at grades C, or above, can begin a degree course. Many pupils, teachers, parents and employers still consider that it is important for pupils to pass public examinations, and therefore there are teachers who narrowly concentrate on examination-type study for their pupils, thereby teaching a complete but uninspiring mathematics course. Although in some ways undesirable, this is not disastrous; some of those teachers are the weaker members of the profession who might not teach a complete course without the guidance of a public examination mathematics syllabus. Satisfactory teaching with such a syllabus can be made the starting point for in-service teacher training, which will lead to better mathematics courses in schools.

Many people in Britain feel that two purposes of public examinations are to provide evidence that personal standards are being achieved and that national standards are being maintained. This has been clear from public comment, both a few years after the general disappearance of the 11 + examination and in the late 1970s when there was discussion about the replacement of existing examinations. Years earlier, when a public examination did not exist for pupils in secondary modern schools, it was also public pressure which brought the introduction of the C.S.E. examinations. The parents wanted their children to be able to gain generally acceptable qualifications, and pupils and teachers saw that the examinations would provide an incentive for worthwhile teaching and learning.

The above two paragraphs show that public examinations which assess the standards reached by pupils also evaluate each school's curriculum.[65,66] Only about three-quarters of British pupils are candidates for public mathematics examinations but all pupils are assessed in other ways during their school careers. These assessments also help to evaluate schools' curricula, as the following quotation shows:

... the main purposes of the assessment of individual pupils are:

(i) to provide teachers with information about the progress and needs of pupils for whom they are responsible, and to enable them to assess the effectiveness of their own planning and teaching;

(ii) to enable the pupils to know how they are progressing and to provide incentives to better performance;

(iii) to enable parents to be informed about their children's educational progress;

(iv) to provide information about pupils at points of transition within the education system and when they leave school to start work or to go on to further or higher education.[67]

THE EVALUATION OF CURRICULUM MATERIALS AND TEACHING

The evaluation of school mathematics curricula

As the International Baccalaureate was mentioned a few pages earlier, it is fitting to now use the 'International Project for the Evaluation of Educational Achievement (I.E.A.) in Mathematics' to start considering evaluation in Britain. The I.E.A. studied mathematics achievement in secondary schools in twelve countries,[68] by giving pupils and teachers a set of tests and questionnaires which thus provided a wealth of information about the pupils, teachers and curriculum. The data about Britain was collected in 1964 and has, since then, been reanalysed and published under the title *Achievement in Mathematics*.[69] This book can be used in two ways, firstly as an analysis of British secondary education in 1964, and secondly as a guide for using more modern information in a similar way. Fairly recent national information is available in the yearly *Statistics of Education*[70] published by Her Majesty's Stationery Office and in the yearly statistics published by some examination boards. Local information available for L.E.A.s and schools can be used for formative evaluation of any school's curriculum materials and teaching. (N.B. The comparative evaluation of teaching mixed ability or similar ability groups of pupils is included in chapter 6 of this book.)

Although many school courses and text books are never evaluated objectively, there are other teaching and learning materials which have had formative or summative evaluation. These latter materials have often been produced by nationally funded projects such as 'Mathematics for the Majority' (i.e. for average and below average ability pupils) where the use of formative evaluation[71] was a part of the work plan submitted to gain funding by the Schools Council. It is also common for sets of mathematics work sheets or work cards to have had preliminary testing by groups of pupils and teachers in several schools. It should not be imagined that formative evaluation can only come from written information. Educational researchers sometimes use interviews with teachers and pupils, and classroom observation, as sources of information. Teachers can similarly discover a great deal about the curriculum and teaching in a school by talking to pupils and to other teachers. As it is the pupils who learn mathematics and the teachers who teach mathematics, then their views should be discovered and considered.

The Assessment of Performance Unit (A.P.U.)

If formative evaluation were commonly used to improve the teaching and learning of mathematics in many schools, then we could probably expect a steady increase in the national standards monitored by the Government's *Assessment of Performance Unit (A.P.U.)*. The A.P.U. was set up in 1975 'to promote the development of methods of assessing the achievement of children at school, and to seek to identify the incidence of under-achievement.'[72] Since 1977, the A.P.U.'s work has been extended to provide a national picture of pupils' performance over a broad range of the curriculum. For example, the A.P.U. mathematics tests are not narrowly limited to any one syllabus and they try to assess pupils' ability to use mathematical skills and concepts in both pure mathematics and everyday applications of mathematics. Other A.P.U. assessments are of English language, a foreign language and science; future assessments may include pupils' personal, social, aesthetic and physical development. This national picture of the English and Welsh education system is being built up by testing about two per cent of school pupils every year so that, over the years, the results are expected to show[37] whether national standards are increasing, steady or decreasing. The A.P.U. tests will not indicate standards in individual schools, but the unit intends to make equivalent tests available for purchase by people who wish to monitor standards in schools and L.E.A.s. It is to be hoped that these equivalent tests will not be used to make invidious, and sometimes false, comparisons between different schools and teachers. This could be an unintended consequence of the A.P.U.'s national testing.

The monitoring of mathematics[73,74] is being done by assessing pupils of two ages, 11 and 15 years. The first assessment was based on the already existing *Tests of Attainment in Mathematics in Schools (T.A.M.S).*[75] These tests deal with mathematics content and mathematics processes, and the A.P.U. is supplementing them with the first national tests of pupils' attitudes to mathematics. Results are not yet available for any 15 year old pupils but the first assessment of 11 year old pupils was in 1978 and the published report[76] provides the base line with which future years' results can be compared. It is, however, also interesting to use that report in another way, by looking for facts about 1978 school mathematics. Some of these facts are already known by teachers of mathematics, for example that pupils are more likely to find the right answers when questions involve situations which pupils have personally experienced, and that 11 year old boys are worse than girls at simple arithmetical computation. Other evidence from the report shows regional differences (e.g. higher mean scores from Wales), and suggests that better mathematics education is provided by smaller primary schools, especially outside the metropolitan areas. This last evidence supports the feeling (subjective assessment) of some parents and teachers that such schools can give better educational value, even if the annual cost per pupil is higher than in larger primary schools.

The financial cost of mathematics education

Although the benefits of mathematics education cannot be measured in pounds sterling, teachers cannot efficiently promote learning unless they consider the financial climate in which they work. This climate involves two main costs, namely the cost of materials and the cost of people, and each can be illustrated by a simple example from school mathematics. A teacher may plan for some less able pupils to develop their numeracy by a scheme which uses battery operated pocket calculators but the scheme cannot be used if there is no money with which to buy batteries. Another teacher may run a very successful optional course which the school would like to offer to more pupils, but it cannot be offered if the members of staff are already fully committed to other courses. This second example involves an educational evaluation (i.e. that the course is considered to be very successful) and a financial evaluation (i.e. about the cost in teachers' time, which is easily converted into a cost in money). It may be that the senior mathematics teacher could find a way of offering the optional course to more pupils, perhaps by cancelling another option or by rearranging a chosen year-group of pupils (into say four sets averaging thirty pupils instead of five sets averaging twenty-four pupils). It is easy for the senior mathematics teacher to evaluate such suggestions in quantitative cost but it is only possible to evaluate their educational value in the largely qualitative terms already mentioned in this chapter. Although this educational evaluation is approximate it should still be attempted alongside the more precise financial cost, when considering any educational change. An example of fairly straightforward financial evaluation, which mainly investigates whether a change is possible, can be taken from a hypothetical school which is introducing a new series of text books but is not altering the way in which it groups pupils into classes. The senior mathematics teacher will calculate the cost of buying each set of books from the series, perhaps allowing for the purchase of one set a year as the new books are progressively introduced into the different year classes. If pupil numbers are not increasing and the books do not fall to pieces too soon, then the total cost calculated can be considered alongside the educational benefit which the books are expected to bring.

Recently a more detailed financial cost scheme was devised as part of the National Development Programme in Computer Assisted Learning (see chapter 9). For any course, the scheme makes a separate costing for the total development phase (£D) and the yearly running (£R) so that an annual cost for the expected life (N years) of the course is £(D ÷ N + R). This scheme has been applied[77] to the Kent Mathematics Project (already mentioned in chapter 2) to give an annual cost of around £2 per pupil, when the course is estimated to have a life of ten years, by which time a major revision may be necessary. Once such a figure has been calculated, teachers can try to decide whether this is an acceptable extra cost to be paid for the benefits of a certain mathematics course. The same financial scheme can also be applied to cut-backs in education, which may involve an extra initial reorganization cost followed by a yearly saving.[78]

Conclusion

This final chapter has considered many details of assessment and evaluation, and has frequently referred to public examinations because they provide the greatest amount of verified information. Often, however, any conclusions also refer to school teachers' numerous everyday uses of assessment and evaluation. A pupil's profile of attainment has been mentioned and some teachers feel that a complete profile report of each pupil who leaves school[79] would be of more use than a public examination certificate. The latter has the advantage that it is nationally accepted but the former might allow secondary school teaching to become less restricted. Teachers have always feared, with some justification, that the summative evaluation of any course is a major factor in determining its mathematics content and teaching style. However, if a teacher's attention is focussed less on summative evaluation and more on formative evaluation, the evaluation becomes an ally for that teacher, who can then foster good mathematics education.

Annotated References for Chapter 10

1. Wynne-Willson W.S. (1978) *Examinations and assessment*. In reference 2, chapter 10.

   An interesting chapter about examinations and their use.

2. Wain G.T. ed. (1978) *Mathematical education*. Van Nostrand Reinhold: Wokingham.

   A collection of chapters on mathematics and mathematics education, by respected contributors.

3. Creswell M. (1977) Testing and diagnostic testing in mathematics. *Mathematics in School*, vol. 6, no. 4, pp. 25-7.

The distinction should be between tests that sample the curriculum and tests that cover it.

4. M.A. (1979) *Tests*. Mathematical Association: Leicester.

Information about available tests and their uses.

5. Nichols E.D. (1972) Are behavioural objectives the answer? *The Arithmetic Teacher*, vol. 19, no. 6, pp. 419, 474-6.

Walbesser H.H. (1972) Behavioural objectives, a cause célèbre. *The Arithmetic Teacher*, vol. 19, no. 6, pp. 418, 436-40.

Two articles from a proponent and an opponent of behavioural objectives.

6. Bailey T.J. (1979) Arithmetical difficulties of less able pupils in secondary school – some thoughts on assessment and remediation. *Remedial Education*, vol. 14, no. 4, pp. 204-10.

Advice on diagnosis and teaching, with examples of pupils' incorrect work.

7. Schonell F.J. & Schonell F.E. (1957) *Diagnosis and remedial teaching in arithmetic*. Oliver & Boyd: Edinburgh.

A teachers' book which includes the background and use of the well-tried Schonell diagnostic tests.

8. Wilson N. (1970) *Objective tests and mathematical learning*. Australian Council for Educational Research: Victoria.

An explanation, for teachers, of the functions and construction of tests.

9. See reference 8, chapter 9.

10. Ekenstam A.A. & Nilsson M. (1979) A new approach to the assessment of children's mathematical competence. *Educational Studies in Mathematics*. vol. 10, no. 1, pp. 41-66.

The expected sequential difficulty in mathematical content was not evident in practice.

11. Wood R. (1968) Objectives in the teaching of mathematics. *Educational Research*, vol. 10, no. 2, pp. 83-98.

Behavioural psychology has led to objective testing, with examples of its use in projects.

12. Glenn J.A. ed. (1977) *Teaching primary mathematics: strategy and evaluation*. Harper and Row: London, New York. See chapter 6.

Recommendations for producing successful teaching and learning.

13. Lawton D. (1973) *Social change, educational theory and curriculum planning*. University of London Press: London. See chapter 4.

Curriculum principles, traditions and practice.

14. Kenny R. (1978) Basic competencies in Vermont. *The Mathematics Teacher*, vol. 71, no. 8, pp. 702-5.

Paul F. (1978) New York basic competency examinations. *The Mathematics Teacher*, vol. 71, no. 9, pp. 767-8.

Two short articles about the content and application of competency testing.

15. Sumner R. & Bradley K. (1977) *Assessment for transition: a study of new procedures.* National Foundation for Educational Research: Slough.

The report of a project in the London Borough of Hillingdon, which developed materials in mathematics and English.

16. Stephens J. (1979) Monitoring mathematics – the microscope end. *Mathematics in School,* vol. 8, no. 2, p. 12.

Pupils' records; an introduction to I.L.E.A. Checkpoints.

17. The current booklet, *School Leaver's Attainment Profile of Numerical Skills,* can be purchased from Mr. R.L. Lindsay, S.L.A.P.O.N.S., Shell Centre for Mathematical Education, The University, Nottingham NG7 2RD.

18. M.A. (1980) *The use of pupil's projects in secondary school mathematics.* Mathematical Association: Leicester.

A booklet about the content, supervision and assessment of projects.

19. Love E. & Tahta D. (1977) Language across the curriculum: mathematics. *Mathematics Teaching,* no. 79, pp. 48–9.

A viewpoint on the place of language.

20. Otterburn M.K. & Nicholson A.R. (1976) The language of (C.S.E.) mathematics. *Mathematics in School,* vol.5, no. 5, pp. 18–20.

Nicholson A.R. (1977) Mathematics and language. *Mathematics in School,* vol. 6, no. 5, pp. 32–4.

Nicholson A.R. (1980) Mathematical literacy. *Mathematics in School,* vol. 9, no. 2, pp. 32–4.

Three articles about the language difficulties of pupils.

21. Schools Council (1979) *G.C.E. and C.S.E.: A guide to secondary school examinations for teachers, pupils, parents and employers*: 2nd. edition. Evans/Methuen: London.

This booklet provides a very good summary.

22. Schools Council (1976) Smith C.H. *Mode III examinations in the C.S.E. and G.C.E.*; Examinations Bulletin no. 34. Evans/Methuen: London.

A survey of the use of mode III by schools and boards.

23. Limb M.E. (1978) First impressions of a mode III scheme for mathematics. *Mathematics in School,* vol. 7, no. 1, pp. 32–4.

A teacher's view of the advantages and disadvantages.

24. H.M.S.O. (1979) *Aspects of secondary education in England: a survey by H.M. Inspectors of Schools.* Her Majesty's Stationery Office: London. See chapter 10.

The report of a thorough investigation of the final two years of education in 384 schools (10% sample).

25. Watson F.R. (1976) *Developments in mathematics teaching.* Open Books: London. See pp. 42,44.

A discussion of recent changes in school mathematics, with five chapters of case studies.

26. S.C.U.E. & C.N.A.A. (1978) *A minimal core syllabus for A-level mathematics*. Standing Conference on University Entrance & Council for National Academic Awards: London.

Suggestions for a syllabus of core and options, compiled by considering present syllabuses and the needs of university departments.

27. Knowles F. (1980) Core syllabuses and A-level mathematics. *Mathematics Teaching*, no. 90, pp. 40-3.

The disadvantages, advantages and possible content of syllabuses.

28. Graham J.D. (1977) Maths and C.S.E.: part 1 & part 2. *Mathematics in School*, vol. 6, no. 3, pp. 30-32 & no. 4, pp. 14-16.

Two articles about mode I syllabuses and examinations.

29. Schools Council (1972) *C.S.E.: Mode I examinations in mathematics*; Examinations bulletin no. 25. Evans/Methuen: London. See p. 7.

A study of current practice in fourteen examination boards.

30. Schools Council (1979) *Standards in public examinations: problems and possibilities*; Occasional paper no. 1. Schools Council: London.

This consideration of C.S.E. and G.C.E. examinations shows only broad and imprecise comparability.

31. Schools Council (1977) *Mode comparability in the C.S.E.*; Examinations bulletin no. 36. Evans/Methuen: London.

A description of procedures used by two boards, applied to biology and geography.

32. Schools Council (1977) Willmott A.S. *C.S.E. and G.C.E. grading standards: the 1973 comparability study*. Macmillan: London.

A careful research study. The conclusion that grading standards appeared to fall between 1968 and 1973 may be because: (1) they fell, (2) teaching improved or (3) pupil motivation fell.

33. Schools Council (1974) *Comparability of standards between subjects*; Examinations bulletin no. 29. Evans/Methuen: London.

A look at standards across years and across boards.

34. Phipson G. (1977) Exam results – a comparison. *Mathematics in School,* vol. 6, no. 4, pp. 11-12.

A consideration of one school's M.R.E.B. and London O-level results.

35. Schools Council (1975) *Comparability of grade standards in mathematics at G.C.E. A-level*; Examinations bulletin no. 30. Evans/Methuen: London.

This shows that problems exist, even for one subject at one level from three boards.

36. G.C.E. (1978) *Comparability in G.C.E.* Joint G.C.E. board publication.

A summary of thirteen years work on comparative standards.

37. Goldstein H. & Blinkhorn S. (1977) Monitoring standards: an inappropriate model. *Bulletin of the British Psychological Society*, vol. 30, pp. 309-11.

Doubts about the statistical methodology and pedagogic implications of the A.P.U. surveys.

38. Tall G. (1979) The possible dangers of applying Rasch to school examinations and objective testing. *Mathematics in School*, vol. 8, no. 3, pp. 19–22.

A proposed comparability model for C.S.E., G.C.E., A.P.U., etc.

39. Schools Council (1971) *A common system of examining at 16+*; Examinations bulletin no. 23. Evans/Methuen: London.

An early report, only six years after C.S.E. began.

40. Schools Council (1975) *Examinations at 16+; proposals for the future*. Evans/Methuen: London.

This paper describes the work of six mathematics groups, as well as describing the general position.

41. H.M.S.O. (1978) *Curriculum 11–16*. Her Majesty's Stationery Office: London. See pp. 24–6.

How a curriculum which is tied to examinations can meet the needs of pupils and society.

42. See reference 24, section 7.3.24.

43. H.M.S.O. (1978) *School examinations: Part I, main report; Part II, educational & cost reports*. Her Majesty's Stationery Office: London. See Part I, p. 11.

A report about the G.C.S.E. which includes a feasibility report for each subject.

44. Hansard (1980) Mr. M. Carlisle's reply to a parliamentary question by Mr. F. Silvester; 19 February. Her Majesty's Stationery Office: London.

45. Schools Council (1972) *16–19 Growth and response*; Working paper no. 45. Evans/Methuen: London.

A consideration of the new sixth form and discussion about C.E.E.

46. Schools Council (1975) *C.E.E.: proposals for a new examination*. Evans/Methuen: London.

A discussion document, with reports and recommendations.

47. M.A. (1978) *Mathematics in the proposed Certificate of Extended Education*. Mathematical Association: Leicester.

A suggested syllabus and assessment to meet the needs of technical education.

48. H.M.S.O. (1979) *Proposals for a Certificate of Extended Education*. Her Majesty's Stationery Office: London.

The Keohane committee's report which recommends a C.E.E.

49. Easingwood T. (1979) The technician and business education councils. *Mathematics in School*, vol. 8, no. 3, pp. 12–17.

A description of T.E.C. and B.E.C. courses.

50. H.M.S.O. (1959) *15 to 18: a report of the Central Advisory Council for Education (England)*. Her Majesty's Stationery Office: London.

The Crowther report, covering many aspects of concern about school leavers.

51. Dean J. & Choppin B. (1977) *Educational provision 16-19*. National Foundation for Educational Research: Slough. See chapter 7.

    A study of different forms of sixth form education.

52. Schools Council (1966) *Sixth form curriculum and examinations*; Working paper no. 5. Schools Council: London.

    A proposal for two major subjects (8 periods) and two minor subjects (4 periods).

53. Schools Council (1969) *Proposals for the curriculum and examinations in the sixth form*. Schools Council & Standing Council on University Entrance: London.

    A joint proposal, which would introduce three subsequent annual examinations for pupils.

54. Schools Council (1973) *16-19 Growth and response*; Working paper no. 46. Evans/Methuen: London.

    N & F examination proposals for the new sixth form.

55. Warwick N. (1979) *Implications for assessment and grading*. In reference 56, pp. 24-47.

    Informed comments about N & F assessment.

56. I.M.A. (1979) *The N and F proposals in relation to mathematics*; Symposium proceedings no. 20. Institute of Mathematics and its Applications: Southend.

    A reprint of the six papers given at this symposium.

57. Schools Council (1977) *Schools Council 18+ research programme studies based on the N and F proposals*. Report of the mathematics syllabus steering group. Schools Council: London.

    Notes and syllabuses from the seven commissioned groups, bound into a duplicated booklet.

58. Schools Council (1978) *Examinations at 18+; the N and F studies*: Working paper no. 60. Evans/Methuen: London.

    Detailed studies on the N & F proposals.

59. Schools Council (1980) *Examinations at 18+; report on the N and F debate*; Working paper no. 66. Evans/Methuen: London.

    Some conclusions about the proposals.

60. Schools Council (1978) *Examinations at 18+; resource implications of an N and F curriculum and examinations structure*: Examinations bulletin no. 38. Evans/Methuen: London.

    A survey of the probable effect in different schools.

61. H.M.S.O. (1968) *Inquiry into the flow of candidates in science and technology into higher education*: Council for Scientific Policy. Her Majesty's Stationery Office: London.

    A report about the decreasing proportion of science pupils in the sixth form.

62. Morgan J.B. (1973) *The International Baccalaureate*. In reference 63, pp. 254-61.

    An account of the I.B. and its mathematics courses.

63. Howson A.G. ed. (1973) *Developments in mathematical education*. Cambridge University Press: Cambridge.

A survey of, and papers from, the 1972 International Congress at Exeter.

64. Peterson A.D.C. (1972) *The International Baccalaureate*. Harrap: London.

A full description by the director of the I.B.O.

65. Pidgeon D.A. (1970) *Expectation and pupil performance*. National Foundation for Educational Research: Slough. See chapter 4.

Some studies of the influence of environmental factors on motivation and performance.

66. Schools Council (1976) *Examinations; their use in curriculum evaluation and development*: Examinations bulletin no. 33. Evans/Methuen: London.

The Nuffield A-level chemistry course was used in this research.

67. H.M.S.O. (1977). *Education in schools, a consultative document*. Her Majesty's Stationery Office: London. See paragraph 3.8.

The Green Paper linked with the Great Debate.

68. Husen T. ed. (1967) *International study of achievement in mathematics*, vols. I & II. Wiley: New York, London.

A comparison of secondary mathematics education in twelve countries.

69. Pidgeon D.A. ed. (1967) *Achievement in mathematics*. National Foundation for Educational Research: Slough.

A national study of secondary schools.

70. e.g. H.M.S.O. (1979) *Education statistics for the United Kingdom: 1976 and 1977*. Her Majesty's Stationery Office: London.

A comprehensive volume from the annual statistics of education surveys.

71. Schools Council (1973) *Evaluation in curriculum development: twelve case studies*. Macmillan: London.

This book includes two studies of mathematics projects.

72. D.E.S. (1978) *Assessing the performance of pupils*: Report on education no. 93. Department of Education and Science: London. See p. 1.

A report on the current programme of the A.P.U.

73. Bell A.W. (1977) The A.P.U. and the 1978 mathematics survey. *Mathematics Teaching*, no. 80, pp. 24–7.

A detailed explanation by a member of the A.P.U. Mathematics Steering Group.

74. D.E.S. (1978) *Monitoring mathematics: A.P.U.* Department of Education and Science: London.

A discussion document about the ideas and framework.

75. Sumner R. (1975) *Tests of attainment in mathematics in schools – monitoring feasibility study*. National Foundation for Educational Research: Slough.

    Kyles I. & Sumner R. (1977) *Tests of attainment in mathematics in schools – continuation of monitoring feasibility study*. National Foundation for Educational Research: Slough.

    Details of a D.E.S. project, later used by the A.P.U.

76. D.E.S. (1980) *Mathematical development; primary survey report no. 1: A.P.U.* Department of Education and Science: London.

    The results of the 1978 assessment of 11 year old pupils.

77. Fielden J. & Pearson P.K. (1978) *Costing educational practice*. Council for Educational Technology: London. See case study E.

    A guide, with case studies, to weighing value against costs.

78. See reference 77, pp. 44-5.

79. S.C.R.E. (1977) *S.C.R.E. profile assessment system: manual*. Scottish Council for Research in Education: Edinburgh.

    A handbook about profiles, used as an assessment when leaving school or during school.

INDEX